Excellence
in **Coaching**

More praise for *Excellence in Coaching*

"What a wonderful offering that covers an impressive range of material from practical issues to applicable theories to ethical and supervisory issues in coaching! Individuals looking for the 'how-tos' and 'whys' of coaching will find this book a vital resource to their development."

Dianne Stober, faculty, Organizational and Management Development, Fielding Graduate University, co-editor of *Evidence Based Coaching Handbook: Putting best practices to work for your clients*

"Top managers are increasingly turning to specialist coaches to help them think, learn and redirect – challenging advisors with whom they can test, reflect and share in confidence. This very helpful book is for those in the growing profession of coaching, the facilitative partners who are helping today's executives maximize their own performance. It provides important guidance, methodologies and insights to help coaches coach better."

Greg Parston, Director, Institute for Public Service Value, Accenture

"The variety of chapter contributions is commendable and the cumulative effect is both affirming and edifying."

Dr Elaine Cox, Director of Postgraduate Coaching and Mentoring Programmes, Westminster Institute of Education, Oxford Brookes University

Excellence in **Coaching**

The Industry Guide

Edited by
Jonathan Passmore

London and Philadelphia

First published in Great Britain and the United States in 2006 by Kogan Page Limited
Reprinted 2007

120 Pentonville Road	525 South Street, #241
London N1 9JN	Philadelphia PA 19147
United Kingdom	USA
www.kogan-page.co.uk	

Association for Coaching – formed in the United Kingdom in 2002, the Association for Coaching is a non-profit and independent professional body whose aim is to promote best practice and to raise awareness and standards of coaching while providing value-added benefits to its members – whether they are professional coaches or organizations involved in coaching.
www.associationforcoaching.com 'promoting excellence and ethics in coaching'

ISBN-10: 0 7494 4637 4
ISBN-13: 978 0 7494 4637 6

British Library Cataloguing in Publication Data

A CIP record for this book is available from the British Library.

Library of Congress Cataloging-in-Publication Data

Excellence in coaching : the industry guide / [edited by] Jonathan Passmore.
   p. cm.
  ISBN 0-7494-4637-4
1. Employees--Coaching of. I. Passmore, Jonathan. II. Title.
HF5549.5.C53E93 2006
658.3'124--dc22
                       2006008960

Typeset by Datamatics Technologies Ltd, Mumbai, India
Printed and bound in Great Britain by MPG Books Ltd, Bodmin, Cornwall

Contents

About the editor

Jonathan Passmore is one of the UK's leading executive coaches. He is a chartered occupational psychologist, accredited coach and coaching supervisor. He works with senior executives on coaching, organization change and leadership programmes. Jonathan has worked at board level in the private, public and not for profit sectors and currently works for OPM; a leading coaching and training consultancy in London, where he leads on coaching training.

Excellence in coaching is Jonathan's seventh book, and he is currently working on a new title for Kogan Page, *Creative conversation for change: Using appreciative inquiry,* which is due out in Autumn 2007.

Contributors

Geoffrey Abbott is an executive coach and researcher currently based in El Salvador where he has been completing his doctoral studies on coaching with the Australian National University. Geoff was previously an executive with the Special Broadcasting Service in Sydney, Australia, where he managed strategic planning processes and cross-cultural research. He is an Associate of ESEN (the School of Economics and Business) in San Salvador. Geoff works mainly in Central America with clients from the commercial and development sectors. He has a particular interest in cross-cultural coaching as a strategy for enhancing global competitiveness. He can be contacted at geoffabbott@yahoo.com

Graham Alexander is often described as a 'super coach' and has been attributed with introducing business coaching to the UK. He is one of the few people coaching at the top level of UK/international business, specifically CEOs, Boards and Senior Executives, and has coached more UK CEOs than anyone. Graham developed the GROW model which has become the world's best-known business coaching framework. He has published two books and is Senior Vice President, Europe, of the Hudson Highland Center for High Performance. Graham can be contacted at graham@grahamalexander.com

Frank Bresser is an international coach working with top executives, a consulter, project manager and author in the field of coaching. He holds an MBA with Distinction (London), wrote his Master Dissertation on coaching and is the initiator and head of the *Coaching Research Project 2005* on best implementation of coaching in business. Frank can be contacted at mail@frank-bresser.com

Professor Cary L Cooper is Professor of Organizational Psychology and Health, Lancaster University Management School and Pro Vice Chancellor (External Relations) at Lancaster University. He is the author of over 100 books (on occupational stress, women at work and industrial and organizational psychology), has written over 400 scholarly articles for academic journals, and is a frequent contributor to national newspapers, TV and radio. Professor Cooper is the immediate past President of the British Academy of Management. He is a Fellow of the Academy of Management (having also won the 1998 Distinguished Service Award) and in 2001 he was awarded a CBE in the Queen's Birthday Honours List for his contribution to organizational health.

Hetty Einzig is a Performance Consultants partner and executive coach working in the areas of business coaching, transpersonal coaching, organizational and team development, transformational leadership, organizational synthesis and emotional literacy. Her coaching style is holistic, spanning work, life and strategic development issues. She is a UKCP registered psychotherapist and a Fellow of the Royal Society of Arts. Hetty can be contacted at hetty@performanceconsultants.co.uk

Dr Anthony M Grant is a Coaching Psychologist. He holds a BA (Hons) in Psychology, a Masters of Arts in Behavioural Science and PhD. Anthony left school at the age of 15 with no qualifications, completed his training as a carpenter and ran his own contracting business. He embarked on a second career in direct sales and marketing, before beginning tertiary studies in 1993 as a mature-age student and commencing a third career in his 30s as a coaching psychologist. In January 2000 Anthony established the world's first Coaching Psychology Unit at the School of Psychology at Sydney University where he is the director. He has co-written and/or co-edited five books on evidence-based coaching and has over 30 coaching-related publications. He can be contacted at anthonyg@psych.usyd.edu.au

Dr Peter Hawkins Peter is Chairman of Bath Consultancy Group, a leading international consultancy in the field of organizational transformation, culture for performance and leadership, which he co-founded in 1986 and which runs leading training courses in coaching supervision. He also co-founded Centre for Staff Team Development in 1979, one of the leading organizations in the field of supervision development across all the professional fields. He is author of *The Wise Fool's Guide to Leadership* and co-author of the best-selling *Supervision in the Helping Professions* and *Coaching, Mentoring and Organizational Consultancy*. Peter can be contacted at peter.hawkins@bathconsultancygroup.com

Allard de Jong Allard is a personal and professional development specialist, performing team coaching, process facilitation and leadership coaching. He is currently Director of Training at CoachVille, Lead Coach for Penna PLC in Europe, as well as a frequent lecturer on the subjects of change, teams, coaching and leadership at MBA programmes throughout Spain where he resides. He holds a Masters Degree in Communication Studies and Bachelor Degree in International Business Administration. Allard can be contacted at allard@changeandchallenge.com

Ian McDermott is founder and Director of Training for International Teaching Seminars (ITS). For nearly 20 years ITS has been committed to training the next generation of NLP trainers, practitioners and coaches. Named one of Britain's Top 10 Coaches and described as 'the Coaches' Coach' (*Independent on Sunday*), Ian has pioneered the integration of NLP and Coaching. He continues to work personally with key senior executives focusing on strategic issues. His work is featured in the Open University MBA course 'Creativity, Innovation and Change'. His numerous books include the bestsellers *The Art of Systems Thinking, Way of NLP, The NLP Coach, Your Inner Coach* and *The Coaching Bible* and have been translated into 15 languages. Ian can be reached on +44 (0) 1268 777125 or at www.itsnlp.com

Michael Neenan is an honorary vice-president of the Association for Coaching, co-director of the coaching training programme at the Centre for Coaching, Blackheath, an accredited cognitive-behavioural therapist and a visiting tutor at Goldsmiths College, University of London. He has co-written (with Professor Windy Drained) over 20 books on cognitive behaviour therapy including the best-selling *Life Coaching: A Cognitive Behavioural Approach*. His coaching practice focuses on both personal and professional development. Michael can be contacted at neenanmikel@aol.com

Jonathan Passmore is a chartered occupational psychologist, accredited coach and coaching supervisor. He works with senior executives on coaching, organization change and leadership programmes. He holds four degrees and is an active contributor through articles, books and conference speeches. Jonathan has worked at board level in the private, public and not-for-profit sectors and has worked for a range of firms including PricewaterhouseCoopers, IBM and OPM where he delivers AC and ICM accredited courses in coaching and undertakes executive coaching. In his spare time he keeps bees. Jonathan can be contacted at jonathancpassmore@yahoo.co.uk

María Alicia Peña is a Chartered Counselling Psychologist and Occupational Psychologist. She has worked both in the NHS and in the private sector, and is now Assistant Head of Counselling Service, Reading University. For her doctorate she is researching the factors that lead to an effective return to work after being off with stress, anxiety or depression. Her clinical work focuses on both individuals and couples across a wide range of mental and health issues. She is qualified to use EMDR, an effective method to help people overcome the effects of trauma. Alicia can be contacted at apena@tiscali.co.uk

Philippe Rosinski is an expert in executive coaching, team coaching, and global leadership development, sought after by leading international corporations. He is principal of Rosinski & Company (www.philrosinski.com). He is the author of *Coaching Across Cultures* and his pioneering work in bringing the crucial intercultural dimension into the practice of coaching has won him worldwide acclaim. Philippe is the first European to have been designated Master Certified Coach by the International Coach Federation.

Alex Szabo is a qualified and accredited personal and professional coach. She is a business professional with extensive experience in strategic management and operations. Her background of psychology, training, merchant banking, and entrepreneurial experience led her to found Tailored Coaching which provides results orientated personal, business, executive and group coaching. Alex was a nominee for the Honorary AC Awards Influencing coaching category; and is co-founder of the Association for Coaching, the UK's leading professional body. She can be contacted at www.tailoredcoaching.com

Katherine Tulpa is Chair and founder of the Association for Coaching and Director of Urban Calm®. As an executive coach, leadership consultant and coach supervisor, she has an extensive background working with large international firms across the UK, US and Europe. Katherine is passionate about creating change on a global scale and awakening performance with leaders at all levels. She is the recipient of the AC Honorary Awards for Influencing and Impacting the Coaching Profession (2004 and 2006), a Fellow of the RSA, and a frequent speaker on creating a coaching culture and corporate well-being. Katherine can be contacted at ktulpa@urbancoaching.com

Sir John Whitmore was a successful professional racing driver before moving into business. He then moved to California to study and promote the emerging psychologies, before returning to the UK to set up a tennis and ski school based on a new learning method called The Inner Game, which redefined coaching. He then teamed up with former Olympians to found Performance Consultants, bringing coaching into business. In 2004, he was made recipient of the *AC Honorary Award for Impacting the Coaching Profession* and his book *Coaching for Performance* is a business best-seller and has been translated into 14 languages. www.performanceconsultants.co.uk

Carol Wilson is Honorary Vice President and Head of Accreditation at the Association for Coaching. She experienced the value of a coaching culture first-hand while working at board level with Richard Branson during the early years of Virgin and now runs a management consultancy focusing on creating a coaching culture at work, as well as a coach training school. She has trained over 400 individuals from the public and private sectors in coaching skills and co-founded Clean Coaching with Clean Language creator David Grove. In addition, Carol is a keynote speaker, broadcaster and writer, a nominee for the AC 'Influence in Coaching' award and the author of a comprehensive guide to coaching called 'All about Performance Coaching'. Carol Wilson can be contacted at carolwilson@cultureatwork.net

Foreword

Books about coaching generally offer the perspective of a single coach drawing on their experiences from the field. My book *Coaching for Performance* is one of those. They serve to contribute to the body of coaching knowledge and to the income and the reputation of the author.

This one is different. It brings together a range of the best writings on the subject without judgement or favour. As such, it gives the reader an opportunity to sample the field and take responsibility for their own choice of which path or paths to follow or combine, or whether to carve out a new path of their own. Any coach, or would-be coach, is bound to gain from the richness that is offered from practical experience and advice of running a coaching practice to important issues such as standards, ethics and supervision; this book embraces many different methodologies.

A recently emerging theme in the coaching industry is the recognition of the need to collaborate for the benefit and the reputation of the industry as a whole and its clients, rather than maintaining the protective self-interest that has characterized much of business in the past. This book reflects this view, for example the editor and contributors have not received any payment for their efforts, and have thereby made a genuine contribution to the industry as a whole, one that transcends personal gain.

Coaching has now been established for more than two decades, and it is now coming into maturity and revealing more of its depth. At a superficial level, coaching helps people to clarify their goals, to schedule their actions, and to succeed more readily at work and in life. It helps people to learn and perform better by enhancing their awareness, responsibility, self-confidence and self-reliance. At a deeper level, when undertaken well and responsibly, it helps people along their evolutionary journey towards higher or deeper levels of themselves – to discover who they really are. It is a psycho-spiritual journey that is both universal and as pre-programmed as is the Darwinian one of biological evolution.

The principal and practice of coaching is a choice of making kit on a micro scale, and let us hope, that these principles will spread to the macro in time. We are a fledgling industry but as Margaret Mead said, 'Never believe that a small group of dedicated individuals can not change the world – indeed it is the only thing that ever has'. Is the Association for Coaching such a group? Let us cast aside our self-limiting beliefs and cooperate towards a higher goal, higher version. This end is something to which this book contributes and of which it is an example.

John Whitmore
Author of Coaching for Performance

Preface

This book came about during a conversation at an Association for Coaching event in London. Katherine Tulpa and I reflected on the need for a single guide to coaching practice that would bring current issues together.

With the help of the back of an envelope and a delayed train from Kings Cross station this book moved from a vague conversation over coffee to a book proposal. The simple idea was to bring together the top English-speaking coaching writers to contribute to a single book. This book assembles a dozen of the world's top coaches all of whom have written and published elsewhere and are experts in their individual fields. It covers issues which have not been written about previously such as coaching supervision and coaching ethics, but which are of importance if coaching is to develop as a profession. It also aims to offer the reader a selection of the most popular coaching models, written by the leaders in each of these areas, along with guidance on getting started in coaching.

The book is divided into three sections. The first is what we have called 'Coaching basics', and covers the themes of 'What is coaching?', 'Coaching within organizations' and 'Running your coaching practice'. If you are new to coaching, studying coaching or are setting up your coaching practice this section will be of interest to you. The second section contains a selection of the most popular coaching approaches with chapters by the leading writers in each of these areas. Most coaches use a single model in their coaching practice; by offering an accessible description of a range of models we hope coaches will be able to develop their practice further, first by reading and then securing further training in some of the specialist areas such as conginitive, transpersonal and motivational interviewing. The third section explores current issues within coaching from supervision to ethics and diversity. Much of the material in this section is new thinking and seeks to take forward the debate in these areas.

As always with editions like this, as editor I end up frustrating authors who wanted to bring a creative touch to their writing while I attempted to create some consistency in look and feel throughout the book. On the other side is the frustrated publisher keen to move forward while I attempt to herd authors towards the finish post of the publication deadline. The result is never the perfect book, but I hope it will be a useful addition to every coach's book shelf.

Throughout the book we have tried to use the term coachee for the person who sits in the session with the coach, and the term client for the person who commissions the coaching and pays the bill. Sometimes theses are the same person, however often in organizational settings they are different people.

The ideas and views expressed in each chapters are those of the individual authors, and do not necessarily represent my own views as editor or those of the Association for Coaching.

As the editor, a chartered occupational pshychologist, coaching practitioner and a researcher into coaching practice, I am interested to hear your views. You can enter the debate and also find out more about the themes in the book on the website: www.excellence-in-coaching.co.uk

Jonathan Passmore

Acknowledgements

I would like to express my thanks to Katherine Tulpa and Alex Szabo who supported the idea of the book and for their encouragement during the process. Thanks are also due to the authors who gave of their time, without payment, to contribute to this collaborative piece and for putting up with my desire for redraft after redraft.

I would like to pay tribute to my wife, Katherine, who has allowed me to spend many hours at the keyboard typing and engaged in discussions about the book during the past year. Her help was invaluable. This book is dedicated to her.

Introduction

Jonathan Passmore

COACHING: THE EMERGING FUTURE

In the past decade coaching as a development tool has emerged from the world of sport to become an important tool in personal development at work, and an option alongside counselling for those seeking to review life choices.

This growth in the demand for coaching has been matched by a growth in demand for coaching resources. A review of any bookshop will reveal that the coaching book market can be divided roughly into three. The most popular are the wide range of self-help guides, which provide advice and techniques to help readers through their current dilemma. The second type of book is aimed at professional coaches. These typically offer a single model, and draw upon the author's experience through a series of stories and case studies. This book falls into the third category: books that offer the reader a number of alternative perspectives and a wide range of evidence-based materials to help the skilled coach widen and deepen his or her professional practice, and to support those new to coaching to reflect on the key issues within the newly emerging coaching profession.

The book is divided into three sections. The first deals with issues facing coaches. These chapters cover how coaches can establish and best manage their business and how to work in parallel with clients and coachees. The second section of the book is concerned with coaching models and techniques. Rather than concentrate on a single model we have offered a number of models: behavioural, cognitive behavioural, NLP, transpersonal, solution-focused and integrative. Our aim is to help coaches to extend their professional practice. Most people are taught a single coaching model, but as experience grows they begin to develop their own personal model. We hope the range of models here will help that process. The third section deals with professional issues that coaches face.

Coaching at work

The research evidence from CIPD and others demonstrates that coaching has become a popular organizational intervention that now ranks alongside leadership development and management skills programmes. Further, there is a belief in organizations that coaching delivers results (Anderson and Anderson, 2003; Olivero *et al*, 1997; Smith *et al*, 2003).

It has been suggested that coaching is the most powerful method for developing managers (Lee, 2003). However, the ability to harness this gain takes self-awareness, self-belief, personal motivation and tools to enable the coachee to put new ideas into new ways of behaving. The role of the executive coach in the relationship is to facilitate and coordinate these elements, working in harmony with his or her coachee. Some have suggested that the harmonic relationship in coaching should be like conducting a band, waving the baton of the question and focusing attention on each element in turn. I would prefer to see this more like playing jazz, with the coach and coachee working together to weave the journey that emerges from the process.

In organizations there is the added complexity of working with a second 'client': organization sponsors. They have their own views about what needs to be delivered from coaching. Experience to date is that organization sponsors are still relatively naïve about how they can direct coaching, possibly fearing that they may cross the confidentiality boundary. As the market develops and HR professionals become more confident in managing coaching contracts, it is likely that all coaching relationships will start with tri-partite meetings to set the scene and agree the objectives, and will close with a similar review.

Life coaching

In the arena of life coaching the market too has been growing. The market itself is even more diverse, ranging from coaches working in health areas such as smoking cessation, stress and diet management, to more traditional lifestyle work. For these health interventions coaches are typically trained with backgrounds in health services or psychology. The emergence of this work may develop further as the health sector recognizes the potential of coaching as an alternative to counselling, with its associated negative images. At the lifestyle end of the spectrum coaches and coachees are working on relationships, faith and work-life balance.

Coaching training standards

What is clear from the developments in the sector is a need for robust training and the maintenance of ethical practice. At present becoming a coach is as easy as saying the word. There are no standards or licensing arrangements in the USA, UK or Australia. While national or state-managed licensing adds to the bureaucratic burden, accreditation and training through professional bodies is becoming a voluntary minimum standard. The challenge, however, with such voluntary schemes is ensuring that coaches participate and the public understand the scheme.

The issue is still not settled and there is ongoing debate about the benefits and value of accreditation, training and licensing. Such debate mirrors much of what has gone before in other professions, such as counselling and psychotherapy as they moved towards standards in the 1980s (Mowbray, 1995).

While the debate continues, the professional bodies have responded. The Association for Coaching (AC), based in the UK, with members across the world, has established an accreditation scheme for coaches and course recognition, and there is work to develop a similar accreditation model for coaching supervisors. The International Coaching Federation (ICF), which has a strong membership in the USA, has established its standards for accreditation with certified coaches. The European Mentoring and Coaching Council (EMCC) has also contributed to the debate on standards through the publication of a set of coaching competencies. At the same time, universities are starting to offer specialist coaching courses in the USA, UK and Australia. This can only be a good thing.

Coaching competences

The issue of what skills a coach needs to be effective is beginning to emerge (Grant, 2006). In an environment where few coaches were trained, it was of limited importance. The development of coaching and its journey towards becoming a profession brings with it the question of standards and training.

What does a coach need to learn to be effective? A small number of writers have sought to answer this question. Alexander (2005) suggests that a number of key competences are important. He felt that coaching competences should be divided into three clusters: relationship, being and doing. In the first of these, relationship, coaches need to demonstrate that they are open and honest and that they value others. In the second cluster, being, coaches need to have self-confidence to be able to work with their coachee through difficult challenges. They need to maintain an enabling style, and avoid slipping into a directive approach with their coachees. They also need to be self-aware. In the third cluster, doing, coaches need to hold a clear methodology, be skilful in applying the method and its associated tools and techniques, and be fully present. Few of these competences easily lend themselves to formal training.

Research in the UK of senior executives' coaching experiences (Passmore, unpublished) suggests that coachees have a very clear view of what they value within a coaching relationship. They expect their coaches to have strong communication skills to be able to listen, recall information accurately, challenge while maintaining support for them as an individual and direct attention through questions. The senior executives in the study also expressed the view that relationship skills were important. In this respect credibility and previous experience helped to establish and maintain the relationship, alongside empathy and affirming the coachee. There was also a view that knowledge about human behaviour and knowledge of the sector were also valued (Passmore, in press). The second of these, sector knowledge, is often contested but this may reflect a desire to divide coaching and mentoring into neat boxes. My experience suggests that the two areas are intertwined and mixed; see Table 0.1.

The table suggests pure forms, while in reality coaching and mentoring run between the polarities illustrated.

What this means for training is that we need to review the coaching training that is being offered to ensure it meets the needs of the sector. First, training should have a strong skills component. Coaches should be encouraged to use learning logs as a minimum, and where possible to record their coaching practice for discussion at a later date with their supervisor. Second, coaching and mentoring should be viewed in parallel, as the skills between these two areas overlap. Third, coaches should

Table 0.1 Contrasting coaching and mentoring

	Coaching	Mentoring
1. Level of formality	**More formal:** contract or ground rules set, often involving a third-party client	**Less formal:** agreement, most typically between two parties
2. Length of contract	**Shorter term:** typically between 4 and 12 meetings agreed over 2 to 12 months	**Longer term:** typically unspecified number of meetings with relationships often running over 3 to 5 years
3. Focus	**More performance-focused:** typically a greater focus on short-term skills and job performance	**More career-focused:** typically a concern with longer-term career issues, obtaining the right experience and longer-term thinking
4. Level of sector knowledge	**More generalist:** typically coaches have limited sector knowledge	**More sector knowledge:** typically mentors have knowledge of organization or business sector
5. Training	**More relationship training:** typically coaches have a background in psychology, psychotherapy or HR	**More management training:** typically mentors have a background in senior management
6. Focus	**Dual focus:** more typically a dual focus on the needs of the individual and the needs of the organization	**Single focus:** more typically a single focus on the needs of the individual

add to their own sub-qualifications in specialist areas. This may include training with executive coaching, health coaching, stress coaching and lifestyle coaching. A coach skilled in one area may not necessarily have the skills to successfully operate in another.

A fourth implication is the need for coaches to develop an understanding of a range of models. We should expect trained coaches to be able to move from basic intervention using behavioural models, through intermediate stages of using cognitive, to more advanced skills in specialist trained areas such as motivational interviewing or eye movement desensitization and reprocessing (EMDR).

The final area is that training needs to be evidence-based. Coaching students need to understand which interventions will offer the best results in different cases. As yet the research is still developing, but experience from the counselling world leads us to believe that certain intervention models are better suited to specific challenges. There is no reason to assume coaching is any different, and that cognitive behavioural may be the best intervention to address low self-esteem and poor performance, while transpersonal may offer a more effective model to work on issues of life purpose.

Conclusions

This book, we hope, will provide readers with an enjoyable, stimulating read across the current debate within coaching. We have created a website that goes along with the book at www.excellence-in-coaching.co.uk, and we would welcome you using this and the materials we have added. These include free downloads of interviews with the world's top coaches, and additional readings.

References

Alexander, G and Renshaw, B (2005) *Supercoaching*, Random House, London

Anderson, D and Anderson, M (2003) *Coaching that Counts*, Elsevier, Burlington, MA

Lee, G (2003) *Leadership Coaching: From personal insight to organisational performance*, CIPD, London

Mowbray, R (1995) *The Case Against Psychotherapy Registration*, Trans Marginal Press, London

Olivero, G, Bane, KD and Kopelman, RE (1997) Executive coaching as a transfer of training tool, *Public Personnel Management*, **26**, pp 461–69

Passmore, J (unpublished) What do executive coachees value? Part of a doctoral research project at University of East London

Passmore, J (in press) Executive coaching and leadership mentoring – the role of experience and sector knowledge, *International Journal of Mentoring and Coaching*

Smither, JW, London, M, Flautt, R, Vargas, E and Kucine, I (2003) Can working with an executive coach improve multi-source feedback ratings over time? *Personal Pshychology*, **56**(1), pp 23–44

Part 1

The business of coaching

1

What is coaching?

Frank Bresser and Carol Wilson

COACHING: THE NEW PROFESSION

This chapter sets out to describe the nature of coaching: its boundaries with other helping interventions, the skills required to make an effective coach and the evidence of the impact of coaching on individuals and organizations.

Coaching is one of the fastest growing professions. Having emerged from the area of sports in the 1960s, coaching transferred to business throughout the 1970s and 1980s, underwent a high degree of diversification and popularization in the 1990s, and is today accepted as a respected and widely used resource for personal development. Accordingly various forms of coaching (life coaching, executive coaching, career coaching, sports coaching, etc) now exist. This chapter addresses the question of what is the essence of coaching, what qualities, skills and competencies a coach actually needs, what are the relevant differences between coaching and other disciplines, and what benefits coaching offers.

DEFINING COACHING

Leaving aside the hyperbole that currently surrounds the term 'coaching', there exists a common understanding of what it actually means. Although different definitions abound, they mostly describe the same phenomenon.

COACHING IS . . .

▌ 'unlocking a person's potential to maximize their own performance. It is helping them to learn rather than teaching them' (Whitmore, 2003)

▌ 'a collaborative, solution-focused, results-orientated and systematic process in which the coach facilitates the enhancement of work performance, life experience, self-directed learning and personal growth of the coachee' (Grant, 1999; basic definition also referred to by the Association for Coaching, 2005)

▌ 'a professional partnership between a qualified coach and an individual or team that supports the achievement of extraordinary results, based on goals set by the individual or team' (ICF, 2005)

▌ 'the art of facilitating the performance, learning and development of another' (Downey, 2003)

At the heart of coaching lies the idea of empowering people by facilitating self-directed learning, personal growth and improved performance.

Beyond this shared understanding, a host of issues are still under discussion within the profession. We have summarized 12 dimensions (Bresser, 2004, 2005) that are part of this wider debate; see Figure 1.1.

1. Terminology

The term 'coaching', is used to describe a wide range of interventions, which is in part a result of the absence of a legally binding definition. So, any one is free to call anything 'coaching'. The slow movement to professionalization of the sector will help both coachees and clients better understand what coaching is, how it can help and when to use it.

2. History

A number of writers argue that coaching, as a one-to-one learning conversation, has existed since the dawn of civilization. A contrary approach presents this discipline as a new invention of the second half of the 20th century. Most writers recognize that although single coaching elements may always have existed, the development of models and their use in

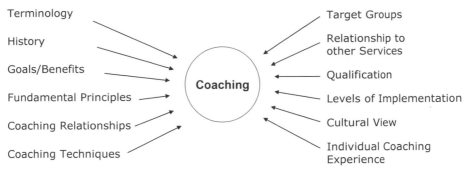

Figure 1.1   The 12 dimensions of coaching

workplace environments are more recent. Questions still remain however about what models, methods and techniques are most effective.

3. Goals/Benefits

Commonly mentioned benefits of coaching include enhanced personal and organizational performance, better work-life balance, higher motivation, better self-reflection, optimized decision making and improved change management.

One question remains the subject of ongoing debate: whose goals — those of the coachee or the sponsor organization – should be primarily served by coaching? Some argue that above all it is in the very nature of coaching to serve the coachee's goals, others emphasize the sponsor's payment and organizational context as dominant elements and prioritize the interests of the sponsor organization. The effective coach needs to balance these competing priorities.

4. Fundamental principles

Commonly agreed fundamental principles of coaching are willingness, self-responsibility, respect, acceptance, confidentiality, integrity, transparency, flexibility and neutrality. However, debate continues about the interpretation and practice of the principles. How should the coach handle possible conflicts of interest? How can the coach be resilient towards external pressures? How does the coach most effectively deal with his or her own blind spots?

5. Coaching relationships

There is a broad consensus that the coachee retains responsibility and ownership of the outcomes and is the leader of the whole coaching process, while the coach tailors the coaching around the coachee's needs and remains detached. Coaching requires a coaching contract as the fundamental basis for a good coaching relationship. This relationship is commonly described as an equal one, neither participant being superior or subordinate to the other. This assumes the coach is external and independent. What happens in more complex relationships where coaching is used within organizations? Can a manager coach a direct report? What impact does delivery by human resources within the organization have on the coachee's willingness to share fully his or her story?

6. Coaching techniques

The techniques of listening, questioning, clarifying and giving feedback are essential. How these are applied, however, is subject to debate. The pros and cons of alternatives to face-to-face communication, such as the telephone, e-mail or videoconferencing, are open to dispute. What effect do these have on the coaching process and outcomes?

7. Target groups

Coaches vary in who they offer services too. Some coaches are willing to work across issues and sectors, others are more specialist. A debate persists over whether and to what extent coaching is equally applicable to all these target groups, what approaches work best with different issues and whether coaches are effective when they attempt to work across all domains.

8. Relationship to other services

A clear distinction between coaching and other services (eg mentoring, therapy, counselling) is crucial and is dealt with below. Where coaching and another service are mixed, some argue that this is not coaching; others argue that the term 'coaching' encompasses every service that includes any element of coaching.

9. Qualification

Listening, questioning and clarifying skills are indispensable for any coach. Depending on each coaching approach, additional coaching skills may also be required. But how far should the coach understand the issues faced by the coachee? Should they have management or sector knowledge? The main source of coaching proficiency (talent/natural ability, learning/training, experience or a combination of these) is also a topic for controversy, and contributes to the debate about training and development of coaches.

10. Levels of implementation

The importance of each level is assessed differently depending on the school of thought. However, that coaching is a professional service provided by professional coaches, is commonly accepted. Whether it is preferable that such coaches are external (from outside the organization) or internal (own staff) is again a matter of debate.

One distinction that is useful to be aware of is between managers who coach their direct reports and managers who demonstrate a coaching leadership style. While the first category are acting like professional coaches and giving formal sessions, the latter maintain their role as managers and integrate coaching elements, such as listening, skilful questioning and empowerment, into their everyday methods of management.

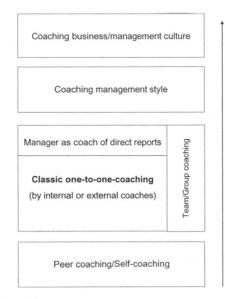

Figure 1.2 Levels of implementation

11. Cultural view

Coaching extends across various cultures at the global, regional, national, organizational and individual level. There is some debate over how far coaching can be applicable to all cultures and to what extent different cultures require different coaching definitions.

COACHING IN JAPAN

About 10–20 per cent of Japanese executives are aware of coaching. In contrast to many Americans who, for example, may simply 'jump right in and tell you what they want', the typical attitude in a Japanese coaching session is more likely to be, 'You tell me! I'm here to learn from you!' (Foster, 2004: 31). Coaching in a Japanese organization might therefore tend to be slightly directive, which may not be the practice in other countries.

---

12. Individual coaching experience

Each person's unique coaching experience inimitably shapes their individual understanding of coaching. People may see and define coaching in a certain way simply because of how they came across it for the first time. Reflection on and acknowledgement of one's own subjectivity regarding coaching is key to maintaining sound detachment and the right context.

Coaching is still work in progress. The 12 themes illustrate the issues that are part of the ongoing debate as the coaching profession develops. It is this diversity of approaches that provides the rich source of inspiration required for the beneficial advancement of today's coaching profession.

COACHING QUALITIES, SKILLS AND COMPETENCES

Core elements

Good coaching encompasses the qualities of empathy, perspective, clear focus, intuition, objectivity and strength to challenge a coachee; see Figure 1.3. The fundamental skills the coach will use in exercising these qualities are listening, questioning and clarifying within a framework of goals, strategies and actions.

Coaches are often drawn to their work by a desire to make a difference to other people. There is nothing more satisfying to coaches than witnessing their coachees move forward. However, coaches are not simply 'do-gooders' or sponges who absorb their coachee's woes.

Figure 1.3 Core elements of good coaching

Role of the coach and coachee

There are two components to the coaching session: the process and the content (see Figure 1.4). The coach is in charge of the processes, such as:

█ timekeeping;

█ ensuring that the client sets clear goals, strategies and actions;

█ holding the client accountable;

█ keeping the coachee's focus on track.

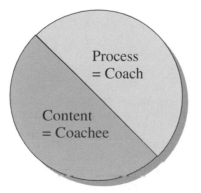

Figure 1.4 Two components to a coaching session

The coachee is in charge of the content, such as:

- choosing the area of the coaching;
- creating the specific goals, strategies and actions to be worked on;
- deciding upon the time frame.

If coaches allow themselves to be sucked across the line into 'content', for instance by giving advice or asking questions out of curiosity, they are no longer of any use to the coachee. Paradoxically, there are times when the coach has some specific advice or insight to offer and, when this is the case, he or she may mark this as separate from the coaching by asking permission: 'Can I offer you some advice from my own experience?' or, 'Can I share with you my insight about this?'

The coach acts as a mirror, reflecting back the coachee's thoughts, words and ideas to enable the coachee to see things more clearly and, in doing so, work out how to move forward. Coaches believe that coachees have all the knowledge they need; the coach is there to help them tap into it.

There are countries where it is customary nod to mean no, and to shake the head to mean yes. This is a result of their culture and customs. However, big misunderstandings can result if we visit such a country without knowing about this custom. People have different customs across the world, arising from their cultural background, their upbringing or experiences in life. It would literally take a lifetime for a coach to map all these experiences in enough detail to understand where the coachee has come from and where they need to go next. However, in the space of a session, an effective coach is able to reveal significant points on this map to the coachee and uncover whatever self-knowledge the coachee needs to see and master the way forward.

Coaching skills

Listening

Clearly, the coach will expect to spend a large part of each session listening to their coachee. We would suggest it's more than just listening: the coach needs to be active in the listening process through using the skills of questioning and clarifying.

In human communication, five levels of listening can be identified, with effective coaching taking place at Levels 4 and 5.

Level 1

Planning what to say instead of listening to what the speaker is saying. This is the most irritating level of listening because the speaker can tell that the listener is not listening:

Speaker: 'I think we should arrange a staff meeting about that.'
Listener: 'Yes, but the answer is to hire some consultants.'

Level 2

Giving a reply that is about the listener not the speaker. This is probably how the majority of conventional conversations are conducted:

Speaker: 'I don't know what to do about getting a promotion.'
Listener: 'I've put in an application to move up a grade.'

Level 3

Giving advice. This is still more about the listener than the speaker, and can be close to Level 1 in the irritation stakes if the speaker is looking for a sympathetic ear rather than direction:

Speaker: 'I don't know what to do about getting a promotion.'
Listener: 'If I were you, I would. . .'.

Level 4

Listening and inviting more. People often work things out while they are talking and a prompt from the coach may help the flow:

Speaker: 'I don't know what to do about getting a promotion.'
Listener: 'What are you not sure about?'

Level 5

Listening behind and between the words; listening to the silences; using one's intuition:

Speaker: 'I don't know what to do about getting a promotion.'
Listener: 'What are you not sure about?'
Speaker: 'I have to arrange a meeting with the boss and I never seem to find the time to do it.'
Listener: 'What's getting in the way?'
Speaker: 'Oh, I don't know. I'm busy, or she's busy. I don't seem to be able to stop long enough to work out how to do it.'
Listener: 'Is there anything else that's stopping you?'
Speaker: 'Actually, I keep putting it off because I hate asking.'
Listener: 'And what do you hate about asking?'
Speaker: 'I'm afraid she will say no.'

In the example the speaker in the final exchange at Level 5 has gained an important new insight – that fear of rejection is the block, not lack of time.

At best, a coach listens at Level 5 throughout every session. This may sound like hard work, but is in fact stimulating and energizing, rather like being in a game and calculating how and when to return the ball.

Questioning

Questions are the precision tools in the coach's toolkit. The coach will skilfully intertwine open and closed questions in order to expand the coachee's learning and channel new insights into actions. Some examples of questions have already been included in the previous section, because questioning is a helpful element of active listening. Here are some further examples of how questions support the coaching process:

Coachee:	'My staff tell me I'm diversifying too much. They think we should just focus on one thing and do it well.'
Coach:	'Your staff tell you you're diversifying too much?'
Coachee:	'Most of the books I read by business gurus say you should focus on the one thing you do best and make it a success before diversifying. We're at the building stage of the business, so perhaps they are right.'
Coach:	'What is your own sense about this?'
Coachee:	'All the areas are related to our core business, so they aren't different as such.'
Coach:	'What is your overall vision for the business?'
Coachee:	'It involves several different dimensions. All my businesses have had several threads. I seem to be quite good at knitting different elements together simultaneously to make one strong business.'
Coach:	'What is your insight about that?'
Coachee:	You know, I never saw it before, but I think my core business is diversification.'
Coach:	'Your core business is diversification?'
Coachee:	'Yes! It's not a lack of focus. I realize that now. Diversification is the right thing for me to focus on.'
Coach:	'And how can that work for you in this situation?'
Coachee:	'The way it always works. I have the ideas, test them out, follow them through, and when the framework is there I put someone in charge to look after the details.'
Coach:	'And is there any action you would like to take about that?'
Coachee:	'Yes. I'll set up a staff meeting and see if I can get them to understand it too.'

Notice how a sense of energy came into the conversation as the coachee reached the new insight that diversification was his core business. Notice also that the coach asked the coachee to move forward ('how can that work for you in this situation') only after the coachee had gained this insight through the exploration of his current reality.

Clarifying

Clarifying encompasses the skills of:

∎ repeating back in different words;

∎ summarizing;

∎ reflecting back the exact words.

REPEATING BACK IN DIFFERENT WORDS

Repeating back in different words enables both coach and coachee to understand what has been said. This is a useful tool in helping the coachee to gain new insights:

Coachee:	'I don't like going to the marketing meetings because everyone talks at once.'
Coach:	'They won't let you have your say?'
Coachee:	'It's more that I have trouble asserting myself.'

Summarizing

Sometimes coachees get bogged down in story telling and detail. Shortening what they have said is a polite way of interrupting and may also provide clarity in the same way as the previous example:

Coachee:	'I've had the most awful day. I got stuck on the telephone, then the train was late so I missed my connection. And I'd forgotten to charge the mobile so . . .'.
Coach:	'Sounds like you had a calamitous start to the day. How are you feeling now?'

Reflecting

Reflecting back the coachee's exact words is one of the most powerful tools in coaching. It affirms to coachees that they have been heard, that what they have said is worth hearing, and that they can now move on:

Coachee:	'I want to start my own business, find a good partner to work with and get some clients.'
Coach:	'You want to start your own business, find a good partner and get some clients?'
Coachee:	'Exactly!'

It may sound trite or awkward to a third-party listener, but coachees receive a boost when they hear their own words coming from someone else.

Another reason for reflecting back is to ensure that both coach and coachee are on the same cultural map, as we discussed earlier in this section.

Goals, strategies and actions

Goals

To be effective, a goal must be inspiring, challenging, measurable and have a deadline. It must also resonate and be congruent with the coachee's values and personal culture. A goal with such qualities emanates a magnetism that pulls the coachee towards it. One of the ways in which this works is through the brain's reticular activation system (RAS). This is the part of the brain that screens out 99 per cent of life's daily bombardment to the senses, allowing us to notice only what is immediately useful. A goal featuring the qualities specified above will embed itself into the subconscious and, through the RAS, we will start to notice pointers along the way that we might have otherwise missed.

People frequently find that once they know what they want (and to find out is often the reason they hire a coach in the first place), extraordinary coincidences seem to occur that bring their goal closer. Coaches have been heard to say that once you have set the right goal, 'the universe brings it to you'. This may well be the case and it may also be true that the universe relies heavily on the RAS in doing so.

Strategies

One of the areas where a coach can be of greatest help is in strategic planning. An effective coach ensures that all the essential groundwork is in place to achieve the goal, always remembering that it is the coachee who must decide what that groundwork will consist of. Strategies act like a ladder to take the coachee up to the goals.

Actions

If strategies are a ladder, then actions are the rungs upon it. Setting actions in coaching is quite different from setting them in ordinary life. Actions in the real world are often regarded as chores that we tend to put off. A good coach will not ask the coachee to set an action until that coachee has reached a new level of insight. Once this is reached, the insight acts as a springboard catapulting the coachee into action; indeed it would be hard to stop someone from taking action at this point. The coach's job here is simply to channel the coachee's energy into suitable, challenging and productive actions, with deadlines for carrying them out.

A coach who can bring both structure and the principles of self-directed learning to coaching is most likely to achieve great results. It also pays to remember that there is an underlying journey for the coachee: uncovering new awareness and new insights, and changing deep-seated habits. At the end of the coaching series, it is often the case that whatever coachees have achieved in terms of their goals, the result that they prize most highly is the new knowledge they have gained about themselves along the way.

COACHING, COUNSELLING, PSYCHOTHERAPY AND MENTORING

Coaching draws its influences from and stands on the shoulders of a wide range of disciplines, including counselling, management consultancy, personal development and psychology. However, there are a number of core differences that distinguish coaching from its related fields and these are most easily highlighted through the metaphor of driving a car:

- A therapist will explore what is stopping you driving your car.
- A counsellor will listen to your anxieties about the car.
- A mentor will share tips from his or her own experience of driving cars.
- A consultant will advise you on how to drive the car.
- A coach will encourage and support you in driving the car.

1. Coaching is forward focused

Coaching always focuses on moving the coachee forward. Counselling may be more appropriate than coaching for, say, the newly bereaved who need to explore their grief over a period of time before moving on. Psychotherapy is a broad field and is usually sought in order to fix a particular problem arising from past trauma. Although the overall effect of both of these disciplines is sometimes to move the client forward, it is not therapy or counselling's primary focus as is the case with coaching. While therapy may be about damage and counselling about distress, coaching is about desire.

2. Coaching is coachee led

Psychotherapists sometimes use techniques that lead and influence the patient and which could cause damage to the psyche if applied by an insufficiently experienced practitioner. However, coaches should be trained not to lead, judge, advise or influence their coachees. Their role is to respond to the desires and expressed needs of their coachees, and to operate with the belief that the coachee has all the required knowledge to solve his or her own problem. The role of the coach is thus limited to one of a facilitator, unleashing the coachee's potential.

3. Coaching is about improving performance

The focus of coaching is about enhancing performance. In this sense, executive and life coaching are similar to sports coaching. As a result, a key feature of coaching is behaviour, supported by exploring cognition and motivation.

4. Coaching is not mentoring

Mentoring, while having similarities to coaching, is fundamentally different. A mentor has experience in a particular field and imparts specific knowledge, acting as adviser, counsellor, guide, tutor, or teacher. In contrast, the coach's role is not to advise but to assist coachees in uncovering their own knowledge and skills and to facilitate coachees in becoming their own advisers.

THE BENEFITS OF COACHING

Coaching, when properly applied, can create win-win situations to the benefit of all stakeholders. Potential outcomes of coaching – both short and long term – can be identified at an individual, team and organizational level. The key benefits for each level are specified below:

Individual level:

▌ better self-awareness and self-reflection;
▌ increased individual performance;
▌ higher motivation and commitment;
▌ better leadership skills;
▌ personal growth;

- higher quality of life/work-life balance;
- clarity in purpose and meaning;
- better management of change processes;
- improved communication and relationships;
- efficient implementation of acquired skills;
- sustainable form of personal development.

Team level:

- improved team efficiency/performance;
- clearer vision development and objectives;
- improved team spirit and conflict management;
- better communication and relationships;
- creating synergies;
- higher motivation;
- unleashing group potential.

Organizational level:

- improved organizational performance;
- higher profitability/return on investment/productivity/sales;
- better staff motivation and retention;
- less absenteeism;
- buy-in to organizational values and behaviours;
- better flexibility/ability to change;
- more effective communication;
- open and productive organizational culture;
- realizing the learning organization;
- sustainable form of learning and development.

The actual impact of a coaching intervention varies, of course, from case to case and is influenced by a number of factors, for example organizational receptiveness or the coaching approach taken.

A key decision affecting the outcome of coaching is choosing the appropriate level of implementation (see dimension 10, above), which can dictate the different degrees of organizational penetration by coaching (see Bresser, 2005/2006).

Research evidence

While there is limited research, the evidence that is available confirms the benefits of coaching (Fillery-Travis and Lane, 2006; Jarvis, Lane and Fillery-Travis, 2006).

On the level of quantitative evaluation/ROI

The return on investment of coaching was measured at 529 per cent (and at an astonishing 788 per cent when including the financial benefits from employee retention) for a coaching programme integral to a leadership programme implemented at Nortel Networks (Anderson *et al*, 2002; MetrixGlobal, 2005). The Manchester study in 2001 (see Johnson, 2004) measured a return of 5.7 times the initial investment for executive coaching, and one-to-one career coaching produced an ROI of 100 per cent with enhanced staff retention (Skiffington and Zeus, 2003). According to Dembkowski (2005) US studies go so far as to indicate a possible ROI of up to 22:1.

Qualitative, perceptual evaluation of outcomes

According to the CIPD (Jarvis, 2004) study in the UK, 99 per cent of the organizations using coaching say that it can deliver tangible benefits to both individuals and organizations. In Germany, 89 per cent of executives being coached and 93 per cent of HR managers see coaching as a successful tool (Böning and Fritschle, 2005; Heidrick and Struggles, 2004), and 99 per cent have a positive attitude towards coaching according to another study (PEF, 2005). In Switzerland, 92 per cent confirm the bene-ficial impact of coaching (Mindmove, 2005).

Four out of five executives think they would benefit from coaching at work and 93 per cent of managers believe coaching should be available to all employees regardless of seniority (*Industrial and Commercial Training*, 2002). Moreover, more than 70 per cent of HR professionals believe that coaching is actually more effective than training courses as a means of changing behaviour and improving the performance of senior executives and high-flyers (*Training Strategies for Tomorrow*, 2003).

These and other findings unambiguously make a strong case for coaching as a worthwhile investment leading to potentially tremendous benefits. At the same time we need to continue to develop our understanding of which coaching elements specifically support these outcomes and to use this knowledge in refining coaching practice and training.

References

Anderson, M C, Dauss, C and Mitsch, B F (2002) The return-on-investment of executive coaching. In J Phillips and D Mitsch, *Coaching for Extraordinary Results*, ASTD, pp 9–22

Association for Coaching (2005) Coaching definitions. www.associationfor-coaching.com/about/coachdef.htm

Böning, U and Fritschle, B (2005) Coaching fürs Business, managerSeminare, Bonn

Bresser, F (2004) What is the core of coaching – statements, theses, debates, in Association for Coaching International Conference 2004, CR4, October

Bresser, F (2005) The 12 dimensions of coaching, *Coach the Coach*, **15** and **16**

Bresser, F (2005 and 2006) Best implementation of coaching in business, *Coach the Coach*, Dec and Jan

Dembkowski, S (2005) *Executive coaching* – die 7 größten Vorurteile. www.coaching-magazin.de, pp 1–5

Downey, M (2003) *Effective Coaching*, 2nd edn, Thomson Texere, New York

Fillery-Travis, A and Lane, D (2006) Does coaching work or are we asking the wrong question? *International Coaching Psychology Review*, **1**(1), 23–36

Foster, M (2004) Enter the coach: Executives learn to learn from the experts as change sweeps across corporate Japan, *ACCJ Journal*, May, pp 28–33

Grant, A M (1999) *Enhancing Performance through Coaching: The promise of CBT*, Paper presented at the First State Conference of the Australian Association of Cognitive Behaviour Therapy (NSW), Sydney

Heidrick and Struggles (2004) Führungskräfte. Manager mit Coaching. Wirtschaftswoche, **18**, 04/2004, p 140

ICF (2005) FAQs about coaching, www.coach-federation.org

Industrial and Commercial Training (2002) Managers urge wider use of coaching, **34**, (6/7), p 294

Jarvis, J (2004) *Coaching and Buying Coaching Services*, Chartered Institute of Personnel and Development, London (www.cipd.co.uk)

Jarvis, J, Lane, D and Fillery-Travis, A (2006) *Does Coaching Work?* Chartered Institute of Personnel and Development, London

Johnson, H (2004) The ins and outs of executive coaching, *Training*, **41**, 5, pp 36–41

MetrixGlobal (2005) Executive briefing: Case study on the return on investment of executive coaching, www.metrix-global.net/images/pdfs/metrixglobal_coaching_roi_briefing.pdf

Mindmove (2005) MindMove Coachingmarktstudie, www.mindmove.ch/images/stories/mgtsummary05.pdf

PEF (2005) Forschungsbericht – Bedeutung und Einsatz von Coaching in der Personalentwicklung, www.pef.at/news.aspx

Skiffington, S and Zeus, P (2003) *Behavioural Coaching: How to build sustainable personal and organizational strength*, McGraw-Hill, Sydney

Training Strategies for Tomorrow (2003) When executive coaching fails to deliver, **17**, (2), pp 17–20

Whitmore, J (2003) *Coaching for Performance*, 3rd edn, Nicholas Brealey, London

2

Coaching within organizations

Katherine Tulpa (illustrations by Phillip Cornwall)

THE NEED FOR THE HUMAN TOUCH

This chapter sets out to explore current methods, new thinking and success factors for coaching within organizations. Written primarily for the executive/group coach or companies providing coaching services, it is not intended to serve as an extensive 'how to' guide, but one which will hopefully challenge, encourage learning and promote coaching best practice.

Inspired by futurist John Naisbitt's book *Megatrends* while I was in business school during the 1980s, there is a theme that has stayed in my consciousness since: an opinion that could be a key factor behind the remarkable growth and attraction of coaching, which is, 'The more high technology around us, the more the need for human touch' (Naisbitt, 1982).

Naisbitt hypothesized that in order for human beings to evolve, we will need to find greater ways to connect and find balance as society and technology accelerate. In other words, become more high touch in a high tech world.

Today, we find ourselves in an even quicker, more complex society, where technology expands globally. Organizations need to take notice of how they lead, develop and engage their stakeholders in a climate where e-mails and remote ways of working can hamper effective communication.

It is a society where many of the baby-boomers in white-collar jobs are feeling tired, unfulfilled, or are looking for deeper meaning and purpose. A society where the younger generation Y, or 'millennial' (born after 1979), are expected to have higher, more demanding expectations of their employer than their predecessors (Raines, 2002).

Added to this is an emerging need for employees to find more meaning at work. This is highlighted in recent research by Penna (2005), indicating that employers who create an environment that promotes a greater sense of 'self', community and challenge that is 'more than just a job' will help to increase motivation, loyalty and staff productivity.

So what do these trends have to do with coaching? If you accept that professionals and leaders in our high tech world will need to further connect with themselves and others in their quest for deeper meaning, balance and success, then this is an opportunity and a role for coaches or providers working within organizations.

Additionally, this creates a responsibility. As the coaching profession is still in its infancy, those within it now are pioneers. Our actions and ways of working will help to shape and harness the uptake of our services in decades to come. Our profession will hopefully be one that is not only sustainable and models excellence, but also continues to provide a human touch to help our clients evolve and achieve significant change.

ORGANIZATIONAL COACHING FRAMEWORK

Successful coaching within organizations goes far beyond the quality of the delivery. When coaching was in the early adapter stage, there may have been latitude where the coach and the executive (eg coachee) could go off into a private room somewhere, enjoy six months of one-to-one professional development, then conclude the sessions with little or no reporting back to the client (sponsor, line manager).

However, these times are changing. Based on market indicators and research initiatives such as the Association for Coaching's corporate think-thank forums, the coaching industry is rapidly evolving, with the UK moving into early growth stage (Tulpa, 2005a). Many peers within the profession are pleased we are in this dynamic period, for this is where alliances form to benefit clients and coachees, while also starting to weed out suppliers who don't offer a high level of service.

As demand and usage increases, this will also result in organizations, in particular those driving leadership, talent or learning and development programmes, to bring in more formal coaching processes and measurements. Certainly there are examples of companies, for instance global, multicultural brands, that are more established users of coaching and have set up more consistent ways of working. These organizations are further up the curve.

However, for the most part, at least in the UK, sponsors are currently pressured to investigate how they buy in their coaching services, how they manage them, and how they measure them. According to the CIPD (Jarvis, 2004) the key challenges facing HR practitioners are:

▌ Integrating coaching with the bigger picture.

▌ Opening 'closed doors'.

▌ Meeting the needs of both the organization and the individual.

▌ Information flow and confidentiality.

▌ Scoping and controlling costs.

Discussions with other coaching professionals and buyers of coaching within organizations suggest that other challenges occur when the coaching programme or group intervention is unfocused. The right chemistry or 'fit' isn't there between the coach, coachee and company culture; or there is unclear communication as to the purpose of the programme, the way it is 'sold in', or what the outcomes are.

These are issues that will not go away immediately, but over time we, as providers of these services, can adapt our approach to be more systemic and this will help close the gap and meet our coachees' needs. My personal view is that if we want to make a real difference and stay within the organizational coaching arena, we will need to master our game and stretch ourselves to have greater discipline. This includes aligning with the needs of not just the coachee, but also his or her manager, the sponsor and organization as a whole.

There is one more dimension, which is to choose and align our services with coachees that are appropriate to our own personal and business requirements. When the fit is right, this is highly energizing and one where we add the most value. When it's not, this can deplete not only our energy and focus, but those of others, too. Having the courage to say 'no' at times is not only acceptable, but good practice.

Taken into account these points, I have illustrated an organizational coaching framework (OCF) that looks to address some of these issues, as well as other areas for successful coaching within organizations (see Figure 2.1).

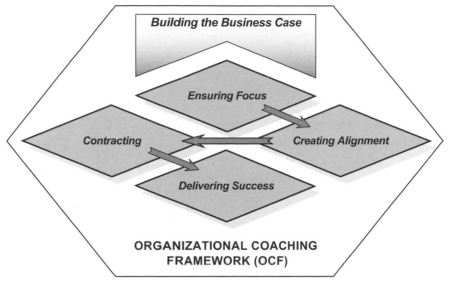

Figure 2.1 Organizational Coaching Framework (OCF)

The content of the framework will be explained in further detail in the rest of the chapter; however as an overview, the main sub-headings are:

1. Building the business case
   - systemic profiling;
   - key challenges;
   - gain commitment.
2. Ensuring focus
   - maintain drive;
   - identify stakeholders;
   - clarify business drivers.
3. Creating alignment
   - establish aims;
   - matching criteria;
   - best fit teams.
4. Contracting
   - goals and outcomes;
   - agreements;
   - commitments.

5. Delivering success
    – build confidence;
    – solicit feedback;
    – measure value.

1. Building the business case

In Chapter 1, the role of the coach, along with coaching definitions, the business return on investment, and the potential outcomes at the individual, team and organizational levels were defined. These are useful as a baseline of knowledge when meeting with clients.

To expand upon this, this section looks at helping organizations understand and buy in to the real value of coaching. As there are still a number of organizations that are not clear on what coaching is all about, helping the sponsor appreciate the business case will increase the likelihood of using coaching as a leadership and cultural change tool. This extends beyond benefit statements, suggesting we resist the hard sell, model a coaching approach, and ensure our needs, as coaches or providers, are met, too. Figure 2.2 looks at the stages involved in building the business case.

Systemic profiling

Two of the fundamental principles of attracting and working with the right kind of clients for your business are: 1) knowing where to target, and

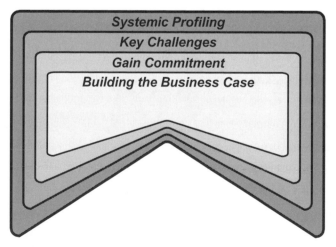

Figure 2.2   Building the business case

2) taking a systemic perspective. I call the two combined, 'systemic profiling'. One way of defining systemic is 'complete' or looking at a situation in its entirety. Like an investigative reporter, it involves discovering information from all angles, with a number of radars, and not accepting the first lead as truth.

On a practical level, the first step to building the business case is starting off with justifying to your own business why you're choosing to work with an organization. In other words, challenge yourself to come up with a systemic rationale that this prospect or client is aligned with your vision, service offerings, capabilities and passions.

As we're currently in a market where there is more supply than demand, it's easy for coaches to adopt the 'I'll take what I can get' approach. However, this can be very stressful and, from a marketing perspective, not very strategic.

In what areas of your business can you carry out systemic profiling?

Once you have satisfied your own criteria, this will not only give you further clarity, but help you know where to target and give you further choice. Like good coaching, it all starts with self-awareness – my suggestion here is that you also need self-awareness for your business.

Key challenges

When identifying 'best fit' clients, it may be useful to investigate the company's vision, size, budgets, reporting lines and offerings, as well as its culture, attitudes and past experiences with coaching. A company website will give a snapshot view; the rest can come from taking a coaching approach in your meetings with them.

Through the art of developing rapport, listening, asking power questions and giving feedback, a client will normally readily give you this information. I've found that by taking the coaching approach, the sponsor will begin to share with you their goals and challenges, and embrace any support you can give them in building the business case for coaching.

For others who are less receptive, it's useful to enter into discussions about their key challenges. These can be further drawn out by asking SPIN™ (situational, problem, implication, needs payoff) questions (Huthwaite, Inc). Typical challenges are listed in Figure 2.3.

Once the organizational challenges are unravelled, the client's level of awareness is raised and they form a basis for entering into discussions on how coaching may help.

1.	*Keeping employees motivated during change*
2.	*Giving our leaders and managers further skills to support the strategy*
3.	*Moving from a transactional (or task based) culture to transformational*
4.	*Having our people stay focused during a sluggish market/low performance*
5.	*Finding ways to build leadership capabilities, innovation and strategic thinking*
6.	*Retaining our best people in a competitive market*
7.	*Discovering ways to reduce stress and increase team morale*
8.	*Identifying ways to engage our people with the company's vision and values*

Figure 2.3 Key challenges

Gain commitment

After you have established that coaching is an appropriate tool for the client's needs, they understand some of the benefits and what it can help them achieve, the last stage is gaining commitment. Note, the goal here is to establish an appropriate 'next step', not necessarily to hire you as their coach or provider.

Again, this is where your natural coaching skills will be useful, as working with a sponsor to commit to a goal or course of action is not that different from working with a coachee. Commitment is defined as follows: 'the act of binding yourself (intellectually or emotionally) to a course of action' (Princeton University, 2003).

A prospective client will be making either emotional decisions, rational decisions, or a combination of both. As a qualified practitioner of the Myers-Briggs Type Indicator (MBTI®), I find these skills along with appreciative inquiry (building on strengths, 'what works') useful when trying to gain greater understand or influence a client. You will have your own approaches, too.

What's important is to draw out options and possibilities from the client, the, 'What could building a coaching culture at X lead to?' so they can witness and experience first hand what coaching is about. From here it is useful to guide them into action, which can result in a commitment to an outcome and, if relevant, having you involved to support their next step.

2. Ensuring focus

This section explains ways to keep up the momentum gained from your initial client meetings, identify key stakeholders and, most important, clarify the organization's aims and objectives.

In the previous section, the focus was on getting to understand your and the client's needs (at this point the sponsor or your first point of contact within the organization). You may also notice that I didn't put the emphasis on trying to promote or sell your 'offerings', as this will evolve naturally as you go through the rest of the process.

Maintain the drive

By this stage, you will hopefully have engaged in some encouraging conversations with the sponsor and they have committed to a next step. So how do you maintain the drive?

One perspective is to continue with normal coaching delivery (the comfort zone), and if the sponsor 'likes' you, they will call – after all, 'one wouldn't want to appear too pushy!' Another perspective is take a proactive view, staying close, and exploring ways to support them – an approach that models behaviours you would have with any coachee.

Many coaches love the delivery part of the business, but dread the 'selling' aspects. To overcome this block, if you can reframe your thinking and continue to focus your energy on the three key activities illustrated in the building the business case section and in Figure 2.4, this will help maintain the drive with the client.

There is a fourth activity too, which is important to our profession: being abundant. By taking an approach to serve, the universe has a wonderful way of giving back to you.

From here, it's a matter of taking responsibility and staying focused on how you can help the sponsor achieve their aims. Become their partner, even before they sign you up. Allow them to invite you into their world and issues, as many organizations are on a steep coaching

1.	Know your company's requirements, challenges and strengths
2.	Understand your client's requirements, challenges and strengths
3.	Take a coach approach eg developing rapport, effective listening, powerful questioning, giving honest feedback

Figure 2.4 Key guidelines

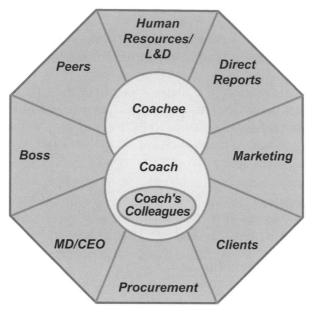

Figure 2.5 Key stakeholder groups

learning curve. Being abundant and sharing your knowledge at the front-end of the process can help set your service apart from the others.

Identify stakeholders

To help ensure focus and support your sponsor in bringing in a successful coaching programme, it's useful to identify key stakeholders as part of an overall delivery plan. Taking a systemic view and looking at all those affected by the initiative will help you and the client adopt strategies for greater buy-in, understanding and communication throughout the process. Figure 2.5 indicates key stakeholder groups.

For smaller programmes, this is a simpler exercise, as there are fewer implications and risks. For larger initiatives, which can be timely and costly, the needs of the key influencers and decision makers need to be considered. Getting the boss and/or most senior leader involved at the onset is vital, to gain top-down support.

At this time, it may be useful to discuss budgets, timelines, other talent, leadership or change initiatives planned, and any other agendas or priorities that could have an impact on the programme's success. At this stage, if the sponsor asks for a proposal, you may wish to defer this until there is further understanding of the drivers, purpose and aims.

Figure 2.6 Creating alignment

Clarify business drivers

There is widespread agreement that successful coaching within organizations needs to be strongly linked to the overall strategy and business drivers. This can be a challenge where the strategy is not always clear amongst the leadership teams, let alone those beneath them.

With that said, I don't believe we will be able to show a quantifiable ROI (return on investment) that we can hold our hand up to as a profession, until we resolve this. While we wouldn't want to lose the magic of the human touch we offer, which is invaluable, we are indeed getting a tremendous amount of pressure to measure how our services impact the organization's bottom line.

Some executive coaches, who also work in the leadership and organizational development domain, can help their clients shape and articulate their strategies. For others, whose expertise is pure coaching, it may be useful to start asking questions to clarify what the company's business drivers are and, equally, the priorities. Someone in the identified stakeholder groups should have the answers.

This quote from the *Thin Book of Appreciative Inquiry*, may inspire you to ask the wider questions: 'The act of asking questions of an organization or group influences the group in some way' (Hammond, 1996).

3. Creating alignment

This section focuses on the third dimension of the OCF – creating alignment – which helps to align the coaching programme and matching process with the needs of the coachee (individual or team), the coach and the business. Figure 2.6 represents this alignment of needs.

There is no doubt that coaching, when done well, can make a difference to an individual's leadership, management and communication skills (CompassPoint Non Profit Services, 2003) as well as increase confidence and job motivation (Association for Coaching, 2004). The CIPD (2004) training and development survey also states, 'when coaching is managed effectively, it can have a positive impact on the organization's bottom line'.

Establish aims

To make a difference to the organization involves creating alignment, which begins by establishing the aims and objectives, key messages, positioning, who the coaching is for, and internal selection criteria. It's also a good opportunity to reinforce the benefits, discuss potential pitfalls and success factors, and how a coaching approach can manifest cultural change.

To do this successfully, it's useful to facilitate a design meeting with the identified stakeholders, linking in the key challenges, business strategy, and other talent and leadership initiatives. If the group doesn't have all the answers, that's ok, as this is where you can bring in your knowledge, where required. The purpose is to gain clarity and buy-in from all those who can be ambassadors of the programme, to ensure it gets a first-class start. 'The most valuable coaching fosters cultural change for the benefit of the organization' (Sherman and Freas, 2004).

Matching criteria

Once the overall programme has been approved (usually a client will request a proposal to confirm the aims, content and fees) and you have helped your client set up a clear and upbeat communications plan (see 'build confidence'), the next stage is making sure that your skills and experience are aligned with the needs of the individuals or teams participating.

A number of organizations and clients that are large users of coaching recognize the value of developing a diverse and rich talent pool of coaches and providers who can accommodate the individual needs and preferences of their executive and managers. In other words, a consistent message is that one size doesn't fit all, with the matching process being one of the biggest challenges and an area it's possible to 'get wrong'.

As coaches or providers, the more we can do to help our clients with this concern, the better aligned we will be with their requirements. Figure 2.7 shows a model that can be used by both organizations and providers when trying to create a match.

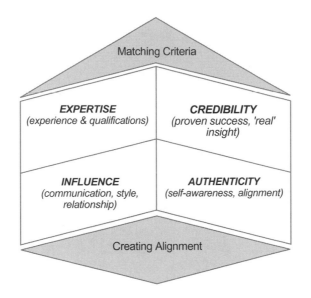

Figure 2.7 Matching criteria

The model recognizes that a good coach, in addition to tangible expertise and credibility, also needs to possess the intangible skills of influence and authenticity.

For selecting tangible skills, some organizations have set up coach matching systems which help managers select a company-approved coach or provider based on their expertise, preferences (eg face-to-face, location) and other search criteria (eg development need). Figure 2.8 displays components for selecting a coach based on expertise.

However, as with most technologies and hard data, this does not replace the need for the human perspective. Usually this means a face-to-face meeting with the manager, where the right fit is also based on instinct, the quality of the relationship and other intangibles.

Best fit teams

The concept of best fit teams is one where you meet with your prospective coachee/s for the first time to determine their needs, with the outcome being to establish whether the two (or more) of you are a best fit. Many organizations call this a 'chemistry' or briefing meeting.

Because coaching is both a relationship and a partnership, an initial briefing is extremely valuable, for it needs to work from all ends. The main point during this process is to be honest about your experience and capabilities. Coaching as a formal discipline is still quite young, so it is unrealistic for clients to expect years of qualifications and experience from a provider. They are buying into 'you', not just your profile and knowledge base.

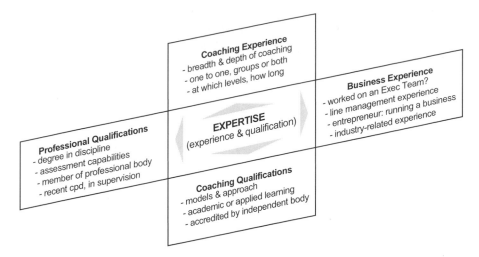

Figure 2.8 Selecting a coach

Taking a coaching approach in the meeting will help you seek understanding. It's also useful to be clear on your ways of working, models used and types of clients that best suit your style. Additionally, it gives you an opportunity to define coaching in your own words and allows them to capture the energy of your passions, strengths and authenticity!

If you identify a client who may not be a good match for your skills and preferences, it's best to hold up your hand – it's not a personal thing. An 'even better' is to provide them with recommendations to source a best fit team (be abundant).

4. Contracting

Once there is agreement of fit with those being coached on the programme, and the needs are aligned with the business, the individual (or team), and you as the coach or provider, the next stage is contracting. Sherman and Freas (2004) define contracting in the context of effective coaching as follows:

> By 'contracting' we mean not just documenting the legal and financial aspects of coaching, but also defining the goals, roles, and accountability of each party. It works when each term gains the uncoerced agreement of all concerned: client, coach, and coachee.

Furthermore, successful contracting sets the psychological contract, while helping to define the outcomes, set realistic expectations and discuss 'what if' scenarios. The ultimate aim is to pave the way for a rich, highly rewarding learning experience, where all parties see the end results – one where communication and openness is a common thread throughout.

Goals and outcomes

To manage expectations, prior to the contracting session it's useful to contact your coachee to explain the purpose of the contracting session, who will be attending, and what to expect. So that they have a chance to reflect on their programme goals, it's also useful to send them a draft 'learning agreement' prior to the session, to include:

▌ company aims;

▌ business goals (eg team, career);

▌ development areas;

▌ desired outcomes;

▌ any previous assessments/feedback.

At the session, these are discussed with all parties, which typically include the coach, the coachee (executive or manager), and their boss and/or sponsor (HR, L&D).

Your role as the coach is to facilitate the process. Encourage candid feedback as the goals, outcomes and priorities of the coachee's development programme are discussed and agreed. The group will also need to conclude that these goals are congruent and integrate with the company strategy, key drivers and aims.

Although the group shares the responsibility – often referred to as a 'triangular relationship' – your role as the facilitator is to check to make sure the goals and desired outcomes are realistic, and there is mutual clarity and understanding. Listen intently, as terminology and the team's 'interference' (Gallwey, 2000) can sometimes get in the way.

Agreements

After the goals and outcomes are clearly defined, the next step in the contracting stage is to discuss and agree the terms. Acknowledging the programme is an investment in the executive or manager's development, fully backed by the company, helps set the tone for the level of responsibility required by all parties. It's also useful to have a one-page overview of the draft terms at hand, to be finalized at the session.

Figure 2.9, adapted from *Coaching in Organizations* (Association for Coaching, 2004), provides some guidelines.

1. **Terms of relationships** – coaching involves the coach, coachee and the sponsor paying for the coaching and/or the line manager
2. **Organization of sessions** – location, length and frequency, along with what basis contact is made between sessions
3. **Commitment to sessions** – is the assignment based on a flexible or open-ended programme, or a fixed number of sessions
4. **Review dates** – agreed measurements and timescales, along with specifying the stakeholders involved in the review
5. **Other participants and roles** – roles to be specified and agreed
6. **Boundaries** – this links with confidentiality and should identify the purpose of the coach's role and therefore boundaries of the relationship
7. **Cancellation and payment terms** – understanding of fees, policies and agreements (NB If this is a part of an overall programme, it may be appropriate to discuss separately)
8. **Confidentiality** – basics include:
   - existing organization confidentiality agreements will be adhered to by the coach
   - the coach should be part of a professional association and abide by a code of ethics, not revealing any personal information
   - the sponsor recognizes the right to confidentiality but may ask for some success measures

Figure 2.9 Guidelines for agreeing contracting terms

One area worth highlighting is confidentiality. There are different views on this. Some professionals feel that any feedback being reported back to the manager or sponsor needs to come directly from the coachee so that it doesn't jeopardize the amount of self-disclosure and trust required for effective coaching. Other views are that, while issues of confidentiality still need to maintained, the client or organization is part of the coaching relationship, so a degree of reporting back is essential. This is to help support the coachee's progress and learning objectives, as well as the overall programme success. It's also a view of the Association for Coaching (2004).

So how does this work in reality? A way to handle this is to discuss in the contracting session the types of information that will be disclosed, at which levels, by whom, and how often. What's important is that all parties are transparent and very comfortable with what's agreed, paying close attention to the views of the coachee.

Commitments

After the goals and agreements are in place, the last step is to confirm the levels of commitment to the programme. This is where it is helpful to allow time for questions and discuss 'what if' scenarios, the promises of each party member, and programme success factors. Here are some typical 'what if' questions, and ones to raise as possible discussion points:

▍ What happens if there is a change of goals?

▍ What happens if, after all this coaching, 'x' decides to leave us?

▍ What happens if I require a different style of coach half-way through the programme?

- What happens if I want additional coaching for my team outside the programme parameters?
- What happens if I find it hard to make the time in my diary?
- What will a successful coaching programme look like?
- What do each of us in this room need to commit to?

There are other questions that may arise, but the important thing is for the group (of which you are part) to discuss and agree how to respond to these, rather than feeling a need to provide the solutions. Like good coaching, this helps to gain commitment.

5. Delivering success

By this time, you're finally at a stage to do some delivery of coaching – whether it's at the executive, manager or individual level, or working with teams. You have also built a strong foundation based on achieving clarity, focus and alignment. This last section looks at how to sustain and deliver success by working with all stakeholders within the programme to build confidence, solicit feedback and measure value.

Build confidence

At the very heart of coaching is a core quality that permeates the entire coaching process – building confidence. Whether we are coaching an individual at a remedial level, a leader at a transformational level, or a group at an organizational level, when people or teams are looking to reach into the horizon, we need confidence in ample supply.

To fuel confidence, our inner power, requires a total belief, trust and respect in not only self, but the client. In 'Coaching for influence and impact' (Tulpa, 2005b), I refer to this Centre of Power™ as one that 'inspires, engages, ignites and creates change':

> If we take a systemic view, in that coaching is what goes on in the space between the coach, coachee and organization, then what can happen if not only we, as coaches, are able to connect with our inner power, but also the manager/leader and the organization?

Building confidence starts off by giving ourselves and our clients permission to not shy away from success stories. For every manager or leader you coach, ask him or her to tell a story of his or her experience. Communication and confidence are partners – to create larger ripples across the organization, a coaching or leadership initiative needs to be communicated widely, and often.

The real impact will come when it has top-down support. When the CEO or leader going through coaching with their team can endorse the programme, there is a greater likelihood of success. Although this type of development is not for everyone, when it's seen as a reward for high performers, helping them become even more successful, it helps to build the case for coaching and create a pull rather than a push.

Solicit feedback

Exchanging success stories isn't the only aspect of communication. To be able to deliver a successful coaching programme, adapt it appropriately, and increase the coachee's learning, soliciting feedback is a key activity.

Beyond using individual assessment and 360-degree tools (multi-rater feedback), there are additional methods you can apply, including:

▮ shadow coaching;
▮ face-to-face feedback;
▮ group feedback sessions;
▮ organizational surveys;
▮ learning surveys (for the coach);
▮ co-coaching forums;
▮ informal feedback forums;
▮ client roundtables;
▮ coaching evaluation forms.

Treating the programme as one that touches and impacts various stakeholders across the organization (see Figure 2.5) will help you select the type required. The main points to consider are ethics: 1) adhering to confidentialities, 2) soliciting feedback on a volunteer basis only, and 3) following up with all those it pertains to in a specific and timely manner.

Finally, as the coach or provider, another important type of feedback is our own. The Association for Coaching (2004) provides a sample coaching evaluation form. It may be useful, when designing your coaching programme with the client, to put together a feedback checklist, as there are a number of items to remember.

Measure value

In the introduction, I spoke about how coaching helps to add a human touch. I've also been using the word 'value', one that goes beyond coaching delivery and delights all people you touch within the organization – the impact can be far and wide.

In Chapter 1, reference is made to ROI studies on organizational coaching. While the results for organizations are evident, it appears that it is the people who have gone through the coaching experience who are the ones measuring the value. They see first hand the effects that coaching has on their skills and performance, which leaves an imprint at a deeper level.

Also, based on usage figures and commitment to spend from organizations that have seen first hand the impression it can make on their people at all levels, coaching is here to stay. Coaching expenditure in the USA is estimated as being around $1 billion per annum (Sherman and Freas, 2004) and there are indicators that other countries will follow suit.

That's not to say that we don't have our work cut out for us. Delivering value to an often complex organization is not an easy task. Green and Grant (2003) give a broader view of today's modern organization: 'An organization is a dynamic system. It is a growing, changing group of people and connections. Patterns emerge, the shape changes, only one thing is certain, it cannot remain the same.'

While we can never control a system's response to a change, we can be mindful of the currents and help to inspire and support our clients' development journeys as they 'ride the wave of change' (Tulpa, 2004).

References

Association for Coaching (2004) Coaching Evaluation Form, Coaching in Organizations, Summary Report: ROI from Corporate Coaching, http://www.associationforcoaching.com

CIPD (2004) *Training Survey*, CIPD, London

CompassPoint Non Profit Services (2003) Executive coaching project: evaluation of findings (based on a study by Harder + Company Community Research), http://www.compasspoint.org

Gallwey, T W (2000) *The Inner Game of Work*, Orion Business, London

Green, J and Grant, A (2003) *Solution-focused Coaching*, Pearson, London

Hammond, S A (1996) *The Thin Book of Appreciative Inquiry*, Thin Book Publishing Company, Bend, OR

Jarvis, J (2004) *Coaching and Buying Coaching Services*, Chartered Institute of Personnel and Development, London

Naisbitt, J (1982) *Megatrends*, Warner Books, New York

Penna plc (2005) Meaning at work (based on Research by Roffey Park), http://www.e-penna.com

Princeton University (2003)WorldNet 2.0, 'commitment', http://dictionary.reference.com

Raines, C (2002) Managing millennials, generations at work, www.generationsatwork.com

Sherman, S and Freas, A (2004) The wild west of executive coaching, *Harvard Business Review*

Tulpa, K (2004) 'Ride the wave of change', welcoming address, Association for Coaching International Conference, London

Tulpa, K (2005a) Forging Ahead in 2005, *AC Bulletin*, **4**, http://www.associationforcoaching.com

Tulpa, K (2005b) Coaching for influence and impact, *Coach the Coach*, **17**

3

Setting up and running your coaching practice

Alex Szabo

PLANNING FOR SUCCESS

The aim of this chapter is to help the self-employed and those thinking of setting up a coaching business to plan their next steps. The chapter focuses on the key elements of running a business, looking at what the individual already has in place, what areas need to be developed, and how to move forward.

A large percentage of businesses fail within their first three years of trading. The reasons for this are usually related to at least one or more aspects of the business that are not being run effectively on a consistent basis. There may be enough clients to generate sufficient turnover, yet the financial control is lacking or the systems and administration processes are not in place. Alternatively, clients may not know who you are or what you do.

The starting point in this process is to ask yourself, what do I want? For most of us this is a difficult question to answer. What would you do if you had a coachee like you? Ask yourself the same questions you would ask them – write down your questions and reflect on your answers.

In planning ahead you might also need to give some thought to a series of questions about the nature of your business:

▌ What do I want my business to look like?

▌ At what stages are the different parts of my business?

▌ What do I need to do to take my business to the next level?

▌ Why do I want my business to grow?

▌ Which areas of my business need to develop?

▌ Who needs to do that?

▌ When does it need to be done by?

▌ How is it going to happen?

SETTING UP A COACHING PRACTICE

Assessing the business

In assessing where you are before starting out, think about your skills under four headings:

1. Your operations/coaching skills.
2. Your financial management skills.
3. Your sales and marketing skills.
4. Yourself.

When you run your own coaching practice you need to be multi-skilled. Talk to others who have run their own businesses, and in particular talk to other coaches who run their own coaching practices. In gathering views, aim to answer five questions for yourself:

1. What should I have in each of the above categories?
2. What do I currently have?
3. What is missing in each area (skill/service/process/technology)?
4. What resources do I need to close the gap?
5. What support do I need?

All of us have gaps in our strengths when we start out: the key to success is having a plan to manage them.

RESOURCING

Charlie is a successful coach. While she is intelligent and probably could have found the time to learn and develop an appropriate financial system for herself, financial management does not excite her. She recognized that this was something she needed to get on top of in order to manage her business successfully.

During her coaching supervision she explored her options. She decided that she did not want to take time to develop herself in this area but rather use the expertise of others to take on these roles. In this way she was able to use her time more effectively to coach others and spend time following her other interests. The actions for her included deciding what she was able to do, clarifying specifically what she wanted another individual to do, deciding what format she wanted the information in, researching a good bookkeeper who lived locally, getting quotes and meeting bookkeepers, deciding on who she was going to use, and making the necessary arrangements to collect her receipts and invoices in a file to be passed over to a bookkeeper to sort and log in the format she needed.

She bought in the necessary resources so that she could focus on what she needed and wanted to do:

▌ What: to manage the financial side of the business.
▌ Why: to be aware of the financial position and be freed up to do what she wanted to do.
▌ Who: someone who has expertise in this area.
▌ When: on a weekly basis.
▌ How: carry out the identified actions and follow a process whereby receipts and invoices would be passed over and presented back in the agreed format.

Planning

Follow the process for yourself, gain clarity about why you need to do this by planning effectively, setting your goals/strategies for each area and take the relevant action. Hold yourself accountable or ask someone you know to do this for you, or work with someone who is going through the same process.

Success arrives much quicker if you plan things first. There may need to have several goals running concurrently, so work in a way that suits you. As a coach, outline the drivers for yourself, your values, the benefits to you and your business, and be clear about the outcomes you want.

YOUR OPERATIONS

This section is about the key day-to-day functions of the business. For the purposes of this chapter it is assumed that you know how to prepare and run a coaching session.

Operations

The systems and administration process that covers initial client contact through to the end of client contracts are known as your 'management information systems'. This consistent service should meet and suit your own and your customers' requirements. Essential elements include:

▌ Preparation
  - details of initial contact with client including payment terms;
  - session preparation
  - first trial session/presentation: setting expectations; coaching; contracting; confidentiality.
▌ Session
  - preparation;
  - delivery;
  - coachee notes;
  - payment record;
  - setting future sessions.
▌ Follow up
  - record keeping;
  - filing;
  - logging feedback;
  - session tracking;
  - financial tracking;
  - continuous evaluation and improvement.

Client and coachee files

Create a checklist and file for each client so the relevant information can be logged. This can include: a record of their details; contracts; client notes; dates of client meetings; recording of the payments made; and an overall summary of the number of sessions. For coachees you may also want to keep brief details of each session.

What supporting processes do you need? As well as having checklists, know what the next steps are within the client engagement process. Consider developing a process that outlines what you need to do and by when. You may need to use a customer relation management (CRM) software package to record and achieve better customer relations.

Coachee notes need to be kept securely and recorded accurately. In particular, your notes need to be legible and laid out in an understandable format. As these are personal data, the coachee can request them, so ensure that what you write is appropriate to share. A second issue is the potential claim on these records by the courts. While coachees would not generally share notes with a client (such as the head of HR in an organization) if legal action is taken the courts may request access to your papers.

Remember in your coaching work you are not giving advice, so your notes need to be simple and useful for you to help guide your journey. One mnemonic that you could use is ACT:

A: Actual or factual information that the coachee shares and is relevant to record.

C: Coaching considerations, which may be further research you need to undertake, or ideas you have during the coaching session that are inappropriate to share at that time.

T: Tasks you agree with the coachees that they will take after the coaching session.

The length of time records are kept for varies and in coaching there are no definitive guidelines. The Association for Coaching recommends a period of at least five years.

Feedback

It is useful to obtain feedback from coachees. Such feedback can help:

▌ monitor the effectiveness of coaching;

▌ draw attention to areas of development for the coach;

▌ emphasize areas that still need to be addressed within the coaching engagement.

Questionnaires are a good way to collect this information.

Technology

Do you have appropriate technology? Invest in a computer that is going to meet your needs with suitable hardware and software. Keep it backed up and up to date. Organize your files methodically so that you can save time retrieving the information or a project that you are working on. You can improve performance by automating routine procedures and free your time to do more creative and productive work.

SALES AND MARKETING

According to one marketing author, the strategic objective of marketing is 'to have your clients, customers, prospects, referral sources and other stakeholders think of you first, often and well'. What would that look like in your coaching practice? If your clients think of you first, often and well, they will happily frequent your business, buy more of your services, do this over a period of time – aka loyalty – and be your best advocate to new business. Prospects will give you first chance at their business and referral sources will talk about you often and with conviction. All of this adds up to a profitable practice with the best return on your marketing investment.

Most businesses fail because they are not properly marketed. Superior products and services poorly marketed are no match for an average product marketed with superiority. Virgin Records started with a handful of unknown brands by an unknown entrepreneur. What makes Richard Branson an exceptional entrepreneur is not the products in and of themselves but his brilliant and innovative marketing skills.

The marketing plan

All plans must start with an objective. Without clear objectives there is no direction, without a clear direction there is little focus and you will end up wasting time, energy and money going in directions that are unrewarding and unprofitable. Clear goals and objectives for your coaching practice are the foundation for marketing yourself. They define success so you recognize it when you arrive! Your marketing plan is really a series of questions to ask yourself.

Positioning

Coaches are competing with other coaches and as the market grows there is competition for the attention of clients and prospects. The noise in the marketplace is overwhelming. Ten years ago the average person was subject to over 2,000 marketing messages per day; this number has swelled to over 30,000! Consequently, not only must your message cut through the clutter, it has to be relevant, compelling and memorable, so that they think of you first, often and well.

TEN QUESTIONS TO BUILD YOUR MARKETING PLAN

1. *Your goals and objectives.* Where are you going?
2. *Your target audience.* Who are you going after?
3. *Your offering.* What are the benefits of your offering that meet the needs of your target audience?
4. *Your positioning.* What makes your offering different from the competition?
5. *Your competition.* Who are you up against and what are they saying in the marketplace?
6. *Marketing message.* What is the core message of everything you do and say?
7. *Branding.* What is your identity/personality?
8. *Marketing instruments.* What marketing instruments are you going to use to reach your target audience?
9. *Marketing calendar.* When are you going to launch the prioritized marketing instruments?
10. *Marketing budget.* How much are you going to invest to attract and retain your clients?

Too many coaches try to be all things to all people, which is impossible to market with credibility and ends up being irrelevant to most. Experience suggests coaches who are tightly focused enjoy greater success and profitability by targeting a niche and becoming the expert in that arena. In other words, make yourself 100 per cent relevant to your ideal client and you will attract more clients that resemble your principal current clients, and those who are unprofitable will disqualify themselves. Finally, your positioning must be:

▮ unique – different from everyone else;

▮ credible – easy to prove;

▮ defendable – no one else can easily lay claim to your positioning;

▮ sustainable – it will work today, next month and next year.

Your marketing message

Imagine walking into an arena where every seat is filled with your ideal prospects. Could you walk out on that stage and present to them effectively? Now let's raise the stakes. The audience is told: 'You had to come, but you don't have to stay. If this person (you) fails to keep your interest, you can simply get up and leave.' What do you think would happen? Are you really ready?

Here's what's probably going on with your audience. At any given time, 3 per cent of your prospects are currently in the market to buy your product or service and looking right now to get it. Another 6 to 7 per cent are open to it, but not currently looking. The other 90 per cent are divided into three nearly equal categories:

1. Not really thinking about it right now.
2. Think they're not interested (but might be, if you did a good job at presenting to them).
3. They know they're not interested.

So here's the real challenge. Let's imagine you have an extraordinary value proposition for your coaching, but at this time, 90 per cent of the audience isn't in the market for your coaching. At least they think they're not interested. That means if you walk out into the arena and begin telling them how great your coaching is, 90 per cent of your audience is going to get up and leave.

What are you going to do?

So you need to 'wow' them by beginning your presentation with information that makes your prospects say: 'I didn't know that.' The focus must be on them and the things of interest to them, not you. So rule number one of your 'killer presentation' is that it must be focused on the prospect and not on you or your coaching (at least not initially).

We have seen presentations that increase closing ratios from one out of ten to eight out of ten. Also, a compelling presentation can significantly increase your ability to just get in front of your prospects in the first place. How?

Offer prospects something of value outside your product or service, something important to them. For example, a marketing coach we know never talks about his coaching, or his marketing experience and skills before telling his clients about 'The four marketing traps and how to avoid them'. Remember, 97 per cent of his prospects think they are happy with their current marketing, but he finds they almost all can relate to the pitfalls and find themselves in one or more of the 'traps', so they begin to listen and relate. Why? Because the information is of value to the prospects even if they have never heard about your offering or do not perceive a current need.

Marketing instruments

There is no shortage of things you can do to market your practice. In fact there are over 125 ways to market your business. The point is to be selective. Pick the right 15 to 20 instruments that will best market your practice and provide the best return on your marketing investment. In fact, you need to assess marketing on a continuous basis, much like managing a financial portfolio. Inevitably you will find marketing instruments that perform well; continue to invest in these, perhaps even invest more. Then there will be those that need some tweaking. Finally, there's the bottom 20 per cent of your marketing activities that perform poorly . . . throw them out and replace them with other marketing activities that could provide better yields on your investment.

Many marketing books have lists of marketing instruments, or a quick web search on 'marketing instruments' will help you.

MARKETING

Luke is an accredited coach with extensive business experience. He knew he had to take the next steps to market himself and his coaching practice. He had little practical marketing experience and decided to employ a marketing coach/consultant. His coach enabled him to achieve his goal of 'To be generating 20 prospects per week and acquiring 12 coachees in the first three months of 2005 through the development of a successful marketing plan supported by a website and a targeted marketing campaign.'

The coach identified with him the elements that would take him to the next level, from the name of his business, the method he would use to deliver his service, the branding, the website content, the stationery, the marketing message, instruments and calendar, public relations, the sales training and sales presentation, through to the growth plan. Today he is a very successful coach with a thriving coaching practice.

Luke became successful because he developed a plan and then took focused and consistent action by implementing the plan according to the agreed timescales. Luke was able to monitor his progress as he could see that everything he was doing was achieving a result. He distinguished himself from the competition and communicated a compelling and relevant message to his target audience using appropriate marketing instruments. His client base exceeded the targets that he had originally set himself.

Execution starts with a plan and is maintained by regular action and reviewing.

Sales

Why all the emphasis on marketing? Sales without marketing means you must constantly beat a path to your prospects' door. But a tenacious marketing strategy properly executed will result in prospects beating a path to your door. As long as you can develop positive relationships and you are priced fairly, you will win over many profitable clients.

Remember to nurture your clients and develop the relationships on an ongoing basis. They will buy more and more from you and also become your referral source through selling on your behalf. Don't be afraid to leverage existing clients or past contacts from another business for more business. This is your most efficient and effective marketing instrument – an active and intentional referral plan.

YOURSELF

To run and manage your coaching practice effectively on a regular basis you need to identify what other areas you need to balance this with. Decide what is important to you, have a look at what is essential to keep, and identify areas you might need to let go of.

Be professional, authentic and true to yourself and your values. This includes your mindset and the brand identity you are presenting, both in appearance and your written and verbal communications. It pays to know your limitations and to take a stand for what you believe in, even if it doesn't suit others.

Balance

You can raise your commitment to a project by identifying the personal and professional benefits that will come out of achieving it.

Time management

Coachees often tell us they want more balance in their lives. What questions would you ask your coachees? It is very easy to let things slip, or feel under pressure to be organized. How do you prefer to work? What works best for you: scheduling or having flexibility? Having set days or putting things in your diary as and when? Do you need to build in 'me' time? What is the first thing that slips when you are busy? Develop an intentional plan that takes these factors into account.

Seek help either through reading, further training, or getting coaching in the areas you need to develop such as procrastination, meeting deadlines, planning, meeting targets and working under pressure. These can be overcome and enable you to move forward and realize your and your company's potential.

TEN KEY QUESTIONS

1. What are my other roles and commitments (parent, partner, work commitments, hobbies and interests, projects, spiritual needs, health, social, etc)?
2. What are the benefits of being involved in these areas?
3. How does being involved contribute towards my vision?
4. What gives me the highest return?
5. Why do I need all of these areas in my life?
6. Which areas aren't aligned to my personal and professional values and are ones that I can let go of?
7. Who needs to do that?/Who do I need to tell?
8. When will I do that?
9. How do I balance the running of my practice with everything else?
10. What process do I need to set up to ensure that I am doing everything that I want and need to be doing?

Working environment

Managing the environment you work in helps you achieve your best. If your office is in part of your home you will need to ensure the following:

▐ separate defined working space;

▐ technology available (computer/fax/telephone/headset);

▐ desk/chair;

▐ filing and storage facilities;

▐ adequate lighting/heating/ventilation;

▐ bookshelf;

▐ set working hours.

If you are seeing coachees from home you will also need an extra chair, to have the office clean and tidy, and ensure your insurance covers you seeing clients from your home office. Adapt your environment to maximize your potential.

Support

Tele-coaching from your home office can be quite isolating. Assess what sort of support you need – see Table 3.1.

There is a vibrant coaching community, so there is no need to work in isolation if you don't want to. Most professional bodies should be able to put you in contact with the type of support that you need, want and will benefit from.

Working with others

If you find that working for yourself is too isolating or you find it difficult to motivate yourself, you may decide that you would like to work with others for a coaching associate company. If so, it's worth considering the following:

▊ the solvency of the company;

▊ the type of work they would be offering;

▊ style of coaching;

▊ frequency of work;

▊ sales commitment;

Table 3.1 Support

Type of support	Support available
Meeting other coaches face-to-face for networking	Coach networking groups
E-mail contact with other coaches	E-mail coach forums
Learning from other coaches. Continuous Professional Development (CPD)	Seminars, professional forums, co-coaching events
Working with other coaches	Professional bodies
Working for other coaches	Coaching associate companies
	Training companies/schools
	Internal coaching programmes
Business networking	Business networking forums
	Professional bodies

- payment (percentage to the coach and percentage to the company);
- payment terms;
- time commitment;
- contractual terms;
- client confidentiality;
- travel/other expenses;
- supervision;
- group meetings;
- structure;
- trust;
- copyright ownership;
- administration processes;
- format of contact.

Personal strengths

Use your personal strengths, skills and experience to adopt a professional attitude and maintain a proactive approach in developing yourself and your coaching practice.

There is no right or wrong way to organize yourself, just more effective ways of working. Most coaches I know work differently and have various strengths. Not all of us get it right all of the time, but the good thing about coaches is that we like to learn. We use techniques and interventions that will help our clients and us.

Appropriate training and skills are a requirement to be an excellent coach. I would encourage everyone to undertake continuous professional development (CPD), which is particularly important if you want to become accredited. Attendance at seminars, events, conferences and reading books all count as hours towards CPD.

Professional body

Membership of a professional body such as the AC can help and support coaches. It can guide your professional practice through its code of ethics and help you to develop your practice through training and personal development opportunities. Bodies like the AC also provide coaches with access to a wider network of like-minded people.

CONCLUSIONS

The aim of this chapter was to see how you and your practice work together and to ensure that key elements of running a business were covered. The focus was on growth coming from what the individual already has in place, what areas they need to develop, and how to move forward, emphasizing understanding the reasons for and the benefits of taking relevant action through a series of questions.

As you have progressed through the chapter, a number of essential elements of running your business have been highlighted. The information that you have gathered and reflecting on the contents can form a base upon which your coaching practice will develop.

Only you have the answers to your questions and it will be your responsibility to decide on the appropriate next step. When you are in the early stages of running a business it can be useful to focus on the day-to-day aspects. However, once you are operational it can pay dividends to think about the long term and to identify objectives and implement some strategic planning around essential best practice.

Part 2

Coaching models and approaches

4

Behavioural coaching – the GROW model

Graham Alexander

THE GROW COACHING MODEL EXPLAINED

The GROW model developed in the 1980s (Alexander and Renshaw, 2005) from my work with senior executives. Over the past 20 years the model has become the industry standard. A Google search conducted in October 2005 identified over a million internet mentions.

In the early days of coaching, although my coachees gave me positive feedback, I wasn't clear why. I questioned whether there was an implicit structure in my interactions, or whether I just made it up as I went along. When I started training coaches, including HR practitioners and middle-level managers, I was forced to clarify my methodology.

I reflected on my countless coaching sessions to understand what was going on. Gradually I saw that there was an inherent structure to what I was doing. It was not always possible to predict how it happened, but it was clear that certain milestones were reached in each effective session. My challenge was to capture them in a simple and memorable format that could be used by other coaches. GROW, a simple and effective

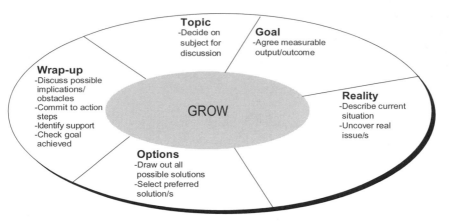

Figure 4.1 The GROW model

model that can be applied to all coaching interactions, stands for Goal, Reality, Options and Wrap-up; see Figure 4.1.

THE GROW MODEL

Effective coaches have GROW or similar models internalized so that it becomes an unconscious competence act (Howell and Fleishman, 1982). Within this framework the coaching is fluid, natural and artistic. The coachee is not subjected to a mechanistic and linear approach. While our language requires us to describe the GROW model as linear, in fact most coaching sessions are cyclical in nature. A coach recaps earlier phases of the GROW model throughout a coaching interaction, helping the coachee to see clearly and move forward.

Step 1. Coaching topic

After establishing rapport and connection, the coach asks his coachee or proposes what he would like to look at during the coaching session.

It is often the case that a coachee does not have full clarity about what she wants to talk about, hence topics are presented vaguely. It's important to unravel a generalized topic and gain clarity about what a coachee really wants to focus on. In some cases gaining this insight plays a large part in resolving the topic.

Step 2. Coaching goal

Perhaps one of the most significant steps in my own coaching work was the recognition of the critical need to differentiate between the topic of a coaching session and a specific outcome. Unless the agreed topic can be distilled into a bite-sized chunk that is achievable during the agreed time frame, it can lead to a frustrating, purposeless and sometimes meandering conversation. Therefore the intention in the goal stage of the GROW model is to set a goal for the session so that the coachee can walk away with a result.

The coach should attempt to establish a goal after agreeing the topic, but the coachee may not be able initially to express it clearly and specifically. The use of further questioning and probing enables the coach to drill down into the topic until a realistic goal becomes clear.

All coaching has a defined outcome and in most cases this takes the form of an action step or steps. Coaching has a defined point to it and it is the coach's responsibility to ensure that the outcome is made crystal clear for his or her coachee.

Step 3. Reality

In my experience the bulk of time in coaching is spent at the reality phase. This is the time when a coach can help shine the light of awareness onto the reality of a coachee. As it is brought into sharp focus the coachee may gain new insights, raise his or her awareness and see an issue or need with more clarity. The use of open-ended questions is the primary tool that enables reality to be understood.

In the majority of cases the options for finding a solution become clearer as a direct consequence of having invested in the reality phase. The intention is to help a coachee probe into things, peel away the layers of the onion, see things specifically, clarify meaning, strip away assumptions and judgements, use precise language and provide real-world examples of assertions.

Step 4. Options

Once the coachee has described his or her reality in rich detail, the coach's role is to help the coachee generate some options to explore how to move forward.

In the vast majority of my sessions I have been astonished at the inherent capability of our coachees to see their way through issues, problems and development needs. In most cases it is not necessary for me to intrude too overtly into this natural process of self-discovery.

In the option phase the most effective strategy is to start by asking open-ended questions. Coaching sessions don't always have to draw out new or particularly novel ideas. Often they bring previous thoughts into sharper focus and confront the coachee with whether certain choices are desirable.

After these base-line questions, coaches can become more creative with their questioning style. The coach's aim is flush out a variety of options to be pinned down or discarded in the wrap-up phase.

At this stage it may be that a coachee would like the coach's perspective. This can happen if the coachee feels blocked, if the solutions he or she has generated are inadequate, or if he or she is covering old ground.

The coachee now has a comprehensive list of options available, which have predominantly come from his or her own wisdom, experience or creativity, with some possible additions from the coach.

Step 5. Wrap-up/way forward

The coaching session now arrives at the action phase. If the coach was rigorous with the previous stages, appropriate actions may have become obvious.

Having established the coachee's immediate preferences it is important to have him or her describe the reason for his or her choices. This tests the coachee's thinking and provides greater clarity about the level of certainty and confidence he or she has in taking particular options forward.

The coachee may still have several options on the table, therefore the crucial thing is to narrow them down. Through this process the coachee arrives at one final option that he or she is ready to break down into specific action steps. This is the moment when the coach needs the coachee to be rigorous about evaluating the implications of the action, its practicality, any obstacles that could arise and any support that he or she may need.

The coachee is now ready to drill down to his or her final action plan, including the specific action steps he or she will take, when he or she will take them, who is involved and when they will be reviewed.

This is one of the key times that taking a challenging approach can be supportive. Using a variety of closed questions or feedback can ensure that a coachee has fully checked his or her position.

Taking this approach will increase commitment and ensure that a coachee feels accountable for any outcome. It is the job of a coach to ensure that his or her coachees have made a full and complete assessment of their potential action steps and what benefit they might derive as a result.

Thus, a coachee can finally get up from his or her coaching session with one or more tangible steps that he or she has contracted to take and that will be reviewed in the next meeting.

WHEN DOES THE GROW MODEL WORK BEST?

A comprehensive report in the UK (Jarvis, 2004) highlights the widespread use of coaching in organizations. Almost four-fifths of

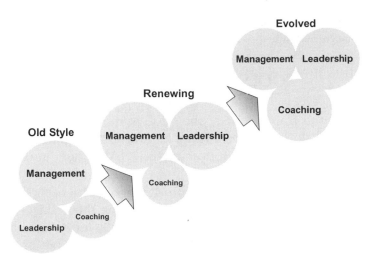

Figure 4.2 The changing mix in leadership

respondents now use coaching in their organization (79 per cent). Use of coaching as a development tool has seen rapid growth in recent years, with 77 per cent of respondents reporting that their organization's use of coaching had increased in the last few years.

Coaching underpins the responsibilities of a manager. It is the glue that binds leadership activities with the achievement of objectives. Thus coaching has to be a large part of what the effective manager does each day (Goleman, 2002). This role of leading using coaching as a key management style has changed over the past 20 years.

For most managers, GROW offers an excellent, accessible and comprehensible approach that allows them to respond to this new agenda. It builds on managers' existing knowledge and offers a perfect tool for a management coaching style in the workplace, alongside other management styles (Goleman, 2002). Unlike many of the other coaching approaches it does not require a psychologist's training or a background in psychotherapy. It assumes that the coachee is functional rather than dysfunctional and that personal development is about working with others as equals.

A second reason to select GROW above the range of alternatives – cognitive behavioural, psychodynamic or solution-focused – is that behaviourist approaches play to the organizational view of the world. GROW, as a behavioural model, is strongly suited to the world of work. One example is the growing use of leadership competencies. GROW's behavioural focus allows the coach to work explicitly with competencies and recognizes their validity as a component to develop improved performance.

Clearly, there is value in working with cognition and with the unconscious. But for many managers who are highly functional and often self-aware individuals, the desire is to reflect on their behaviours and to develop behaviours through goal setting and challenge that will enable them to be even more successful.

TOOLS AND TECHNIQUES

Within the overall framework of the GROW model and continuing to employ the core skills of questioning, listening, summarizing, offering feedback and suggestions, the following tools (Alexander and Renshaw, 2005) are very valuable.

The precision model, shown in Figure 4.3, is a useful tool that enables coaches to become highly attentive when helping their coachee decode what they are saying. I have found that coachees often use imprecise and generalized language and that each coachee has his or her own meaning, so coaches need to avoid making assumptions based on their own frame of reference.

If coachees use a noun such as 'the team' a coach can help them clarify who and what is meant. By asking, 'Who specifically do you mean?', 'Is that all the team or some of the team?', or 'What do you mean by the team?' a coach ensures that coachees see clearly what lies behind the statement.

When coachees use a verb, 'To communicate', to ask what is meant forces the coachee to give detailed thought to a broad statement, for example: 'Be briefer and clearer in what I say', 'To build understanding', or 'To say what I think'.

If coachees use terms such as 'More than', 'Better than', or 'Less than', the coach can clarify what they mean by asking, 'More than who?', 'More than what?', 'Less than who?', 'Better than what?'

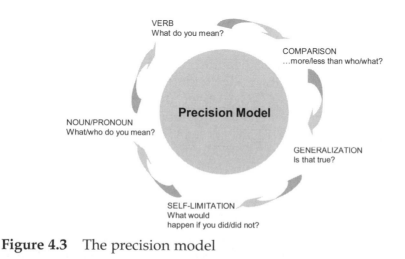

Figure 4.3 The precision model

When a coachee generalizes, saying 'I never have enough time', 'Nobody ever listens to me', or 'Everybody thinks the CEO is too remote' the precision model challenges him or her to think specifically what he or she means. 'Do you really mean that you never have time?' 'Do you really mean nobody ever listens to you?' 'Do you really mean everybody thinks the CEO is too remote?'

In the area of self-limiting statements it can be revealing to challenge the coachee. If the coachee makes comments such as, 'I must finish this report by 6 o'clock', 'I should have one-to-one's with my direct reports every week', or 'I have to be present at every meeting I'm asked to attend', asking, 'According to who?' 'How do you know this?' 'What measure are you using?' 'What would happen if you didn't?' encourages him or her to test the constraint.

In summary, the precision model enables a coachee to move from making general statements to articulating exactly what is meant. This can help to re-evaluate the coachee's thinking, shed new light on an issue and ensure that before taking any action he or she has rigorously tested his or her hypothesis, saving both time and effort.

The 'Structure of a problem'

A problem is a state in which a coachee is 'stuck' in a situation and unclear about how to proceed. It usually involves a topic that plays on his or her mind, causing distraction and internal conflict. Using 'Structure of a problem' helps to address the coachee's mindset and enables him or her to move from a 'problem state of mind' to a 'project state of mind'. The goal is not necessarily to generate a complete

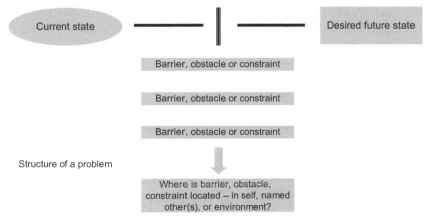

Figure 4.4 The 'Structure of a problem'

Figure 4.5 Issue resolution

solution but to tap into the coachee's internal motivation and help him or her feel empowered, become unstuck and see a way forward.

The process involves using index cards or Post-it notes to jot down various aspects, giving coachees a visual illustration of their situation. First the coach gets the coachees to identify the topic and captures the essence of the problem in a word or short phrase on a card. Next he or she asks the coachee to describe the current reality and summarize it into a few words. It's useful to put pace into this exercise so that the coachee doesn't get bogged down with too much detail. Then move on to the desired future state. The coach asks the coachee to describe it using sense-based language (what he or she wants to see, feel and hear). Again, the coach captures it on a card.

Next the coach asks the coachee to identify any barriers, obstacles or constraints that he or she perceives exist between the current state and the desired future state, and jots them down one per card. Simple questions such as, 'What barriers exist between where you are now and where you want to be?', 'What obstacles do you face?', and 'What constraint do you experience?' flush out the main interferences.

Having identified the obstacles, the coach asks where the coachee locates them in one of three places; in themselves, in another named person or persons, or in his or her environment. It enables the coachee to see clearly where barriers exist and thus helps him or her to take action where possible, and to recognize whether there are other possible barriers outside his or her sphere of control. Generally speaking, the coachee finds that the majority of the barriers exist within themself and so he or she is able to act. Once the coachee has clarified which of the obstacles to tackle it is possible to generate options and wrap-up as per a normal GROW model coaching session. The coachee has moved from stuck to unstuck.

Issue resolution

Index cards can also be used to clarify large or complex coaching topics such as organizational structural issues, managing teams or evaluating job options. Helping a coachee disaggregate the different facets of a topic onto a set of cards enables him or her to see the various aspects of the issue in new ways.

The coach should encourage his or her coachee to jot down in shorthand the various aspects of the issue or problem. The key is to get the coachee's inner world onto cards and laid out in front of him or her as quickly as possible. This act taps into the power of insight and new possibilities come into play once the coachee gains a new perspective.

'Areas of life' cards

A further use of cards is to create a pack at the outset of a coaching programme to help formulate a coaching agenda based on each aspect of the coachee's work and life. This presents an opportunity to externalize his or her internal reality and begin to prioritize what's most important. A coachee could have the cards shown in Figure 4.6.

This tool can then be used for the coachee to describe his or her current reality and aspirations. It also acts as a diagnostic aid to evaluate issues such as work-life balance, time management and personal fulfilment,

Figure 4.6 'Areas of life' cards

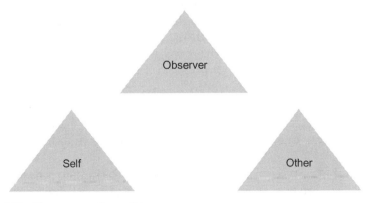

Figure 4.7 Perceptual positions

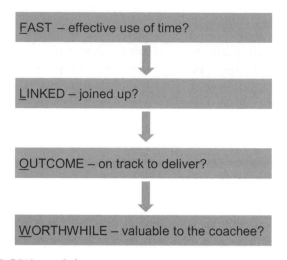

Figure 4.8 FLOW model

providing information to assess where the most valuable focus can be applied. Over time a coachee may want to add to or refine the way he or she has compartmentalized the different areas of his or her work and life.

Many coaching issues have their roots in relationship dilemmas. Perceptual positions (see Figure 4.7) illustrate three standpoints in a relationship: first position, self (how you see the world); second position, other (his or her perspective) and third position, observer (a neutral, objective viewpoint). By taking the position of other and observer, a coachee is able to heighten his or her awareness of a situation and bring valuable insight back into his or her own reality, which may alter his or her perception and behaviour.

A coach can keep moving the coachee around the three positions until he or she has clarity about what the real issue is and what might constitute a way forward. In the third position it can also be helpful for the coachee to imagine a mentor, boss, respected colleague or partner giving advice to add another dimension to the reflective process.

It is important for the coach to assess the quality of the coaching session as it proceeds. With this in mind I developed the FLOW model (see Figure 4.8). This plays on the idea of 'being in flow' within a conversation and as an acronym it stands for 'Fast, Linked, Outcome and Worthwhile'.

I suggest that coaches use it as a checklist with their coachees, enabling them to know whether they are being effective. Over time it can be internalized and used implicitly to monitor interactions as they unfold.

TEN KEY QUESTIONS TO GUIDE YOUR WAY

It would be a mistake to think that there is an ultimate list of 'killer questions'. Coaching interactions always need to be appropriate to the individual in his or her unique position, and thus a coach who falls back on a predictable set of tried and trusted questions is likely to be mechanical and out of tune with the coachee. Having said this, the following list of questions (Alexander and Renshaw, 2005), based on thousands of hours of coaching, have a high probability of value to the coachee, particularly if couched in language that fits for both the coach and coachee.

1. What is your purpose in your life and your career?

This question helps coachees clarify their vision, mission and values. The outcome can be that coachees develop an effective and potent mission statement that captures their unique and enduring reason for being.

Typically I start by asking a coachee the purpose of his or her work and life. Given that many coachees have a variety of options for what he or she could be doing, the question helps to discover a person's drivers and motivations.

2. What would be the most valuable topic to focus on?

It's important at the outset of a coaching session to help coachees gain clarity about what they really want to focus on. In some cases gaining this insight plays a part in resolving it.

3. When you get up out of your chair, what outcome would be most valuable for you?

Having established the topic it is vital for a coachee to clarify what he or she really wants out of a coaching session and what would be the 'take-aways' at the end of the session.

4. What is the current situation?

It is vital for coachees to describe all aspects of their current reality in relation to the topic of the coaching session before moving on to resolution.

5. What could you do?

Having described current reality in rich detail, the coach then helps the coachee to identify options for moving forward in relation to the topic of the coaching session.

6. If you could do anything, what would you do?

On occasion it's appropriate for coachees to consider radical concepts that challenge their habitual frame of reference. The purpose of this type of questioning technique is to generate as many options (however unlikely, impractical or zany) as possible. This type of question facilitates a more 'outside the box' phase in the coaching process, and can be added to with the use of other creative thinking techniques.

7. If you could only take the one option that you believe would add the most value, what would it be?

Once the coachee has a comprehensive list of options the coach asks more open questions in order to pin down the best option.

8. What are the implications of taking this action?

The coachee arrives at one final option that he or she is ready to break down into specific action steps, but prior to this further probing is necessary.

9. What will you do, when?

Assuming the appropriateness of the option chosen, the coach now pins the coachee down to commit to action.

10. Is this an effective use of time?

A coach needs to check if a coaching session has moved too fast or too slowly. This type of question at the end of a session provides permission for feedback and space for a conversation on what is working and what is not working in the coaching relationship.

References

Alexander, G and Renshaw, B (2005) *SuperCoaching*, Random House Business Books, London

CIPD (2004) *Coaching and Buying Coaching Services*, Chartered Institute of Personnel and Development, London

Goleman, D (2002) *The New Leaders: Transforming the art of leadership into the science of results*, Little Brown, Boston, MA

Howell, W and Fleishman, E (eds) (1982) *Human Performance and Productivity. Vol. 2: Information processing and decision making*, Erlbaum, Hillsdale, NJ

5

Solution-focused coaching

Anthony M Grant

THE SOLUTION-FOCUSED COACHING MODEL EXPLAINED

Coaching is necessarily a solution-focused activity. Coaching focuses on where people want to go, how they are going to get there, and how they are going to achieve outstanding results. Rather than where they have been or what has happened to them in the past. Coaching can be defined as a collaborative, solution-focused, results-oriented and systematic process, in which the coach facilitates the enhancement of performance, life experience, self-directed learning and personal growth of individuals and organizations. Coaching is more about asking the right questions than telling coachees what to do. Coaches work with their coachee to help them identify and construct possible solutions, delineate a range of goals and options, and then facilitate the development and enactment of action plans to achieve those goals.

The solution-focused approach to coaching, like many coaching models, comes originally from the therapeutic world. Solution-focused approaches have their roots in Milton H Erickson's approach to strategic therapy. Brief solution-focused therapy was developed by therapists such as Insoo Kim Berg, and Steve de Shazer (de Shazer, 1988) at the Brief Family Therapy Centre in Milwaukee, which was founded in 1982 (see Berg and Szabo, 2005 for further information).

These therapists had become disenchanted with the diagnostic medical approach. Rather than trying to analyse problems, develop diagnoses, uncover root causes, and prescribe treatment plans based on an *a priori* theoretical model of the issue, they began to simply ask questions that focused their clients' attention on building solutions. They found that, in many cases, this could be a very effective methodology. Indeed, there is a body of research that shows that solution-focused therapy can be effective for a range of problems including couple counselling (Murray and Murray, 2004), child and adolescent counselling (Corcoran and Stephenson, 2000; Lethem, 2002) and depression (Dahl *et al*, 2000), and there is also research that supports the use of solution-focused coaching in both personal coaching (Green *et al*, 2006) and workplace coaching (Barrett, 2004).

CORE CHARACTERISTICS OF SOLUTION-FOCUSED COACHING

Coaching emerged during the mid-1990s as an important tool for personal and organizational change. Looking for fast and user-friendly ways to facilitate change, coaches began to use the techniques and principles of solution-focused therapy. Drawing on the work of O'Connell (1998), the following are central characteristics of solution-focused approaches, and the key principles underpinning the solution-focused approach to coaching:

▋ Use of a non-pathological framework: problems are not indications of pathology or dysfunctionality, rather they stem from a limited repertoire of behaviour.

▋ A focus on constructing solutions: the coach primarily facilitates the construction of solutions rather than trying to understand the aetiology of the problem.

▋ Coachee-based expertise: the idea is that the coachee is the expert in his or her own life rather than the coach.

▋ Learning from the coachee: each coaching session is an opportunity for the coach to learn more about coaching *from the coachee*. This is a useful attitude that helps prevent the solution-focused coach slipping into an 'I'm the expert' mindset. At the beginning of each session, ask yourself, 'What can I learn from this coachee?'

- Use of client resources: the coach helps the coachee recognize and utilize existing resources.

- Action-orientation: there is a fundamental expectation on the coach's part that positive change will occur, and the coach expects the coachee to do the work of change outside of the coaching session.

- Clear, specific goal setting: setting of stretching but attainable goals within a specific time frame.

- Assumption that change can happen in a short period of time: this stands in contrast to the assumption that change must be worked on over a long period of time.

- Strategic: coaching interventions are designed specifically for each coachee.

- Future-orientation: the emphasis is more on the future (what the coachee wants to have happen) than the present or the past.

- Attraction: the coaching process is designed and conducted in a way that is attractive and engaging for the coachee.

- Active and influential coaching: the coach is openly influential and challenges the coachee to think in a new way.

The emphasis on solution construction in preference to problem analysis, as well as the use of positive, non-pathological language is important in coaching. The use of pathological or medical terminology can be unhelpful (de Shazer, 1984) and may even create or maintain problem behaviours (Walter and Peller, 1996). This is not to say that a solution-focused approach ignores the existence of problems. As Insoo Kim Berg has said – just because we are solution-focused, it does not mean that we are problem-phobic! Many coachees want to talk about their problems, and stopping them from doing so can alienate them. Having the time and space to talk about problems can be cathartic. Indeed, in doing so coachees often develop significant clarity and insight, and such conversations can build rapport between coachee and coach.

The point here is that the solution-focused coach's skills lie in helping the coachee tell his or her problem story in a way that reframes the presenting problem as being solvable. The talk needs to move from a problem-focused discourse towards a discourse that emphasizes self directed learning, the coachee's resources and his or her own personal ability to define and then move toward a solution. The skilful coach can do this at quite a fast conversational pace while at the same time building a collaborative and motivating relationship.

Self-directed learning

Self-directed learning lies at the heart of the solution-focused approach. The principles of self-directed learning include a self-reliance on discovering solutions to problems, seeking and accepting feedback on progress and reflecting on such feedback, taking responsibility for creating change, the use of structured learning activities, and the integration of the learning experience into other aspects of one's life (Zachary, 2005). Self-directed learning and self-regulation go hand in hand in coaching.

Self-regulation is essentially about the ability to set and work towards goals. The cycle of self-regulation is an important part of the solution-focused approach. The cycle is a simple process of setting a goal, developing an action plan, acting, monitoring, evaluating, and then changing what does not work and doing more of what does (see Figure 5.1). The coach's role is to facilitate the coachee's journey through this cycle while holding the coachee's focus on his or her goal/s.

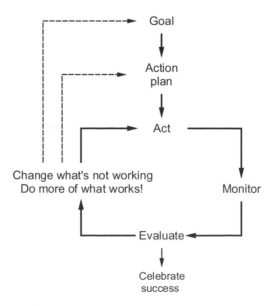

Figure 5.1   The cycle of self-regulation

Philosophical issues

There are some controversial philosophical issues related to the solution-focused approach that have important implications for both theory and coaching practice. It has been argued that solution-focused approaches are theory-free methodologies in which the coach does not need any expert knowledge about the coachee's problems, and only needs to ask the right questions in order to help the coachee develop appropriate solutions (eg, de Shazer, 1988).

However, this cannot truly be the case. For the coach to ask the right questions, the coach must have a theory about the issue, and a theory about what kind of question will best help the coachee articulate a solution. Furthermore, the coach needs to have solid well-developed skills in rapport building and process facilitation, and these involve the use of expert knowledge and the application of theory to practice. If the coach really had no expert knowledge or skills, or no theory about how best to help the coachee, then it is hard to understand why the coachee would employ the coach in the first place (see Held, 1996, for a detailed discussion of these issues).

Coaching is a process of facilitation in which the coach helps the coachee uncover solutions. This process requires a fine balance between asking questions that foster self-discovery and self-directed learning, and giving the coachee information or advice. The use of questions thus lie on a dimension, from being very non-directive, for example, asking 'What is the most useful thing you could do next?', to a more directive approach such as, 'Other people have found X and Y to be very helpful, because of Z. Which might work best for you?'

Asking the right questions and steering the coaching conversation towards solution-construction requires that the coach is constantly developing working hypotheses about what the presenting issues are and what the possible solutions could be. This kind of conceptualization is the theory that underpins any solution-focused coaching intervention. Although the coach is constantly developing ideas about the nature of the issue, and the factors that maintain the problem, in solution-focused coaching this information is not normally overtly brought into the conversation by the coach. Rather the emphasis is on what might work. Coaches needs to be able to draw on their knowledge of human change, and their understanding of the coachee's specific context in order to ask the right questions and move the conversation forward at just the right pace. Too fast and the coachee will be left fumbling in the dark reaching for answers that will not appear; too slow and the coachee will overly-focus on the problem.

Used well, the solution-focused approach enables people to access and use their own wealth of personal experience, skills, expertise and intuition to set goals and develop action plans. It allows coachees to find individualized and creative solutions to the issues and concerns that face them, and does so in a way that builds their skills, knowledge and well-being.

WHEN DOES THE SOLUTION-FOCUSED APPROACH WORK BEST?

What is needed for the solution-focused approach to be effective? Let's consider the coach's beliefs, feelings and behaviours.

First, the coach needs to *believe* in the solution-focused approach, to be engaged in a solution-focused mindset and be able to see the coachee as being resourceful, creative and able to construct possible solutions. Holding the coachee in such unconditional positive regard is not always easy, but it is vital because the quality of the working alliance significantly contributes to success (Horvath and Symonds, 1991). There will be many times when the coach will not know what to say, or how to handle a particular situation. Having the faith to fall back on basic solution-focused principles and techniques and apply these without knowing how the conversation will develop is challenging, particularly for coaches whose previous training has centred on the delivery of expert knowledge as therapists or business consultants.

Second, the coach needs to be able to generate the *feelings* that will best help coachees reach their goal. The coach works on multiple levels simultaneously with the coachee. As the conversation develops, the coach uses the basic communication skills of open or closed questioning, reflection, paraphrasing and summarizing to help raise the coachee's awareness of the *facts* of the issue, and in doing so, helps him or her articulate possible solutions. But the coach also needs to be working on an *emotional* level, recognizing emotions as they are expressed in the conversation, and then amplifying or moderating them through conversation in order to develop the coachee's levels of motivation and enthusiasm. This aspect of the coaching conversation is rarely discussed in the coaching literature, but it is a vital part of coaching. This is not about excessive emotional hyperbole; rather it is about judiciously recognizing when the coachee has a useful emotional response and then reflecting and amplifying that in order to enhance engagement and motivation.

Third, the coach needs a sophisticated set of *behavioural* skills: coaching is as much about *doing as being*. In addition to core communication skills, the coach needs the skills to work with a range of different coachees and issues and to be able to manage the coaching process. Such management skills include effectively structuring the individual coaching sessions and helping the coachee design action plans and action steps. In addition, skilful management of the processes and procedures involved in the coaching engagement is particularly important when providing external coaching for organizations, and many coaching engagements fail because the boundaries of the coaching engagement and its relationship to the sponsoring organization have not been skilfully defined (Jay, 2003).

The coachee's characteristics also impact on whether a solution-focused approach will be successful. Broadly speaking there are three factors. There needs to be *discontent with the present*. If there is no recognition that the situation could be better, then there is no motivation to change. The coach may need to work to amplify existing levels of discontent. Such discontent could come from a recognition of missed opportunities, unfulfilled dreams or some type of self-examination or from feedback from others.

The coachee also needs to have a *vision of the future*. This vision needs to incorporate both a vague 'fuzzy vision' of the distant future, and more specific immediately attainable goals. Clearly these need to be inspirational and motivational and be based on values and beliefs that are congruent with the coachee. Much of the solution-focused conversation will be about getting the coachee to articulate his or her preferred future vision and, in doing so, pathways to goal attainment will become clear.

Lastly, the coachee needs to have the *skills to do the work of change*. He or she needs the ability to form a plan of action, to enact the plan, to maintain action, and also to celebrate success. This process often involves developing an understanding of his or her personal responses to change and examining a range of assumptions about themselves and the world, and this can be personally quite challenging, particularly if the coachee is heavily problem-saturated.

Proud to be superficial?

The solution-focused approach avoids delving deeply into examinations of coachees' problems, their psychological profile, or in-depth explorations of other issues that may have been influential in the past. Is this a superficial, surface approach?

Solution-focused approaches have been criticized for being superficial (eg, Ellis, 1997), and it has been claimed that, for coaching to be truly effective, a 'deeper' approach is necessary (eg, Kilburg, 2004). Of course, there are times when the solution-focused approach is not appropriate, for example, when coachees have both longstanding problems and an entrenched need to explore aetiology, or the coachee comes to coaching with a strong commitment to a specific philosophical framework that is not congruent with the principles of solution-focused coaching. In these cases the coachees may already have embedded causal stories about how the problem arose, and such stories may well be an important and central part of their world view. For such coachees, the solution-focused approach may pose significant challenges, and here the solution-focused coach needs to make informed choices about whether to refer on, or work with the coachee. Indeed, to force a solution-focused perspective onto an unwilling coachee runs counter to the core principle of respecting the coachee's personal world view, although experience shows that giving coachees a solid rationale for the use of a solution-focused approach can significantly help foster a shift towards acceptance of such an approach.

It is interesting to note that the notion of any specific approach being 'surface' or 'deep' is really a subjective value judgement about the worth of different approaches, rather than an objective measurement of how much any specific approach strikes to the heart of an individual's sense of self. Further, it has been my experience when using solution-focused coaching approaches that if an issue is really important, it will become apparent in time, and then it can be addressed. There is no need to go looking for 'deeper' underlying issues. There is a real discipline in staying solution-focused, working with what is presented, working on the 'surface', and in this sense, solution-focused coaches should indeed be proud to be superficial!

TOOLS AND TECHNIQUES

A very useful tool to help coaches develop solution-focused skills is the ask-tell matrix (see Figure 5.2). The questions we ask as coaches lie on two intersecting dimensions: 'telling to asking', and 'why to how'. Observe yourself when you are coaching. Which quadrant are you in at any specific moment? Do you spend most of your time telling the coachee how to do things, or in asking how to? Or maybe you spend a lot of time telling them or asking them why? Of course, it is not wrong to ask coachees a 'why' question, or to give advice. The point is that a

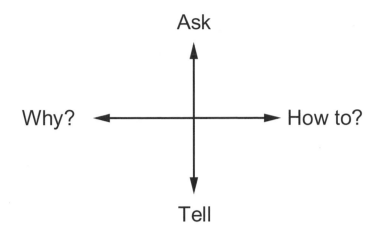

Figure 5.2 The ask-tell matrix

skilful solution-focused coach will emphasize asking 'how to questions' rather than 'telling or why'.

Change the viewing to change the doing!

There are two key factors involved in solution-focused work: 1) *changing the viewing* – that is, helping the coachee to see the situation anew, and 2) *changing the doing* – that is, helping the coachee to develop new behaviours.

Changing the viewing is about acknowledging the progress made so far; identifying exceptions to the problem; detailing the preferred outcome; amplifying existing resources; and building coachee self-efficacy.

Changing the doing is about recognizing possibilities by turning presenting problems into springboards for solution construction; asking 'how' questions instead of 'why' questions; generating coachee-centred multiple options; using small specific achievable action steps; and finding ways to leverage systems to facilitate individual change.

This is a non-exhaustive list of solution-focused tools and techniques to help change the viewing and the doing:

▌ A refusal to purchase the problem. In every conversation there is a buyer and a seller. One person 'sells' his or her explanatory story of the situation to the other, and the other person 'buys' it. Successful solution-focused coaches refuse to buy into problem stories. Rather, they keep listening until they hear the glimmer of a solution. Maintaining an attitude of intelligent curiosity, service and facilitation allows the coach to respectfully, but firmly, hold the conversation on solution construction.

∎ Compliments. Appropriately praising the coachee and paying them compliments builds self-confidence.

∎ Exceptions to the problem. Highlighting when the problem does not exist give clues as to what to do to make those exception times more frequent.

∎ Doing more of what works. Once you have uncovered when the problem does not exist, the coachee can plan to do more of whatever it is that is making the difference.

∎ Do less of what doesn't work. This sounds obvious, but we frequently keep trying to solve problems by using the same (failed) solutions. Insanity, as they say, is doing the same thing but expecting different results!

∎ Scaling. This is a versatile way of subjectively measuring experience, and can be used in many different ways, for example ask coachees to rate on a 1 to 10 scale how close to their goal they are, and then ask them what would take them to the next point on the scale.

∎ Small steps. Have coachees take small, easily achievable steps that build in time to overall stretching goals, rather than overwhelm them with large initial actions.

∎ Highlighting resources. Listen out for hidden and unacknowledged recourses. It is amazing how often a presenting problem holds unrecognized strengths and resources. It is a cliché but true, that every problem is the seed of its solution.

∎ Possibility language. This involves communicating with the coachee in a way that fosters discovery of potential solutions. A well-known technique is the 'magic question' in which the coach asks something like, 'Imagine that you went to bed tonight, and when you woke up the problem had somehow magically disappeared, and the solution was present . . . but you didn't know that the solution had arrived . . . what is the first thing that you'd notice that would tell you that the solution was present?' Sometimes this kind of language is not congruent with the coachee, and this kind of mismatch can make it quite difficult for the coachee to answer the question. A useful variation is the 'what if' question – 'If things were going a bit better, what would be different?'

∎ Reframing. Reframing is a vital tool. The coach needs to be able to reflect and reframe the coachee's statements in a way that creates new ways of viewing and doing.

Reframing draws on the tools and techniques above. Following are some examples of solution-focused reframing:

▋ Reframing that uses compliments. *Coachee:* 'It's far too expensive.' *Coach:* 'It's great that you are concerned about keeping on budget. How can we make it more affordable?'

▋ Reframing that highlights exceptions. *Coachee:* 'I really loath my work.' *Coach:* ' It sounds very unpleasant . . . tell me, which parts of your job are less unpleasant for you?'

▋ Reframing that acknowledges possibilities. *Coachee:* 'I just can't relate to those people.' *Coach:* 'So, up till now you haven't found a way to communicate with them. I wonder what might help to begin to develop good communication?'

▋ Reframing that clarifies goals. *Coachee:* 'I really want to improve my parenting skills.' *Coach:* 'So, what does good parenting mean to you?'

▋ Reframing that moves them forward and creates options. *Coachee:* 'I feel completely overwhelmed with this situation . . . I feel so lost.' *Coach:* 'So, you'd like to get back a sense of direction and control? What would give you that?'

▋ Reframing that rolls with resistance. *Coachee:* 'But I couldn't do all of that. . . .' *Coach:* 'So which bits could you do?'

▋ Reframing that fosters a shift to a systems perspective. *Coachee:* 'I really don't think I can handle this.' *Coach:* 'I wonder who would be most surprised to hear you say that?'

STRATEGIC OVERVIEW OF A SOLUTION-FOCUSED COACHING INTERVENTION

So, how are the ideas expressed so far actually applied in typical coaching engagement? The coaching process starts with the very first contact between the coachee and the coach. This is often a short phone call in which an appointment is made and a brief overview of the issues is normally presented by the coachee. Rather than wait for the first coaching session to begin, the solution-focused coach may ask the coachee to keep a lookout for any signs that things are getting better, and to be ready in the first coaching session to talk about any changes that he or she notices.

A useful initial task is for the coachee to keep a lookout for any 'nuggets' that might appear. Nuggets are those moments when things go really well, or events that are particularly good. It really is amazing how many nuggets there are in each day, yet oftentimes we simply are not on the lookout for them and we fail to notice the simple but great things that happen in our day-to-day lives. The coach should follow-up on the results of this experiment: any successes can form a useful beginning point for the coaching session.

The coaching agreement

The first coaching session would probably start with a brief explanation of what coaching is, and what it is not, and would explain that the coach's role is to ask questions that challenge coachees to find their own solutions rather than telling them what to do. This initial part of the coaching relationship is vital in setting expectations. Here the coach asks for permission to challenge and stretch the coachee. The coach might say something like, 'During our coaching, I will probably sometimes ask you questions that will be quite difficult or challenging. Is that ok with you?' Many professional coaches will have some kind of printed handout with such details. Experience shows that most of the problems in coaching can be circumvented by having a clear up-front coaching agreement.

The coach might then ask the coachee what he or she would like to get out of the coaching relationship, and also what he or she would like to get out of the present session. Sometimes coachees can clearly articulate exactly what they want to achieve. Sometimes coachees want to engage in problem talk, and explain the problem in great depth, but are much less clear about their goals.

The coach will try to shift from a problem-focused conversation to a solution-focused one as quickly as is possible without alienating the coachee. This shift can occur quite soon, within a few minutes. However, with some heavily problem-saturated coachees the coach will have to be patient. It is not unknown for coachees to take a number of sessions before they can start to adopt a solution-focused mindset.

Oscillating process

A typical process is for the coachee to start with problem talk, and then shift to solution talk, but then loop back again to problem talk, and then back to solution talk again. This kind of oscillation can be frustrating for the inexperienced coach. The tip here is for the coach to simply stay with the process: allow coachees to explore their thinking, and act as a facilitator rather than the expert who has to deliver a solution. Taking a 'not the expert consultant' position is one of the most powerful tools in the solution-focused coach's toolbox because it allows the coach to relax and enjoy the creative process of coaching without being fixated on delivering a specific outcome. It is the ability to sit with the uncertainty and ambiguity that marks creativity which differentiates the effective coach from the novice.

As the coaching conversation unfolds, the coach is working to build up a picture of the coachee's preferred future through reflection and reframing. Scaling can be used to help the coachee judge his or her progress in relation to specific goals. Scaling is nearly always an opportunity for the coach to give a compliment. Even if the coachees say that they are at a 3 on a 10-point scale, the coach can respond, 'Well done – one third of the way there already.' Although this comment is meant in all seriousness, this kind of technique clearly requires that the coach has a fairly robust and well-grounded sense of humour, while at the same time holding the coachee in genuine unconditional positive regard.

The miracle question

It might be useful during the above process to start asking direct possibility questions, such as the miracle question, once the coachee has shifted from a deliberative mindset to an implementational mindset (Gollwitzer, 1996; Heckhausen and Gollwitzer, 1987). The deliberative mindset is quite problem-focused, and is characterized by a careful weighing of the pros and cons of action (Carver and Scheier, 1998). The implementational mindset is more solution-focused and is engaged once the decision to act has been made. This mindset has a determined, focused quality, and is biased in favour of thinking about success rather than failure. To ask the miracle question before the coachee has moved into an implementational mindset can result in confusion, a lack of engagement, and even anger or resentment.

The timing of these questions is vital. To ask a big picture miracle question before the coachee has had a chance to move on from any problem talk about his or her current situation, will almost certainly not be effective, and could well result in the response from the coachee along the lines of, 'Well – that's what I'm paying you for . . . to tell me what to do. . . '. In such a case the coach has to make a choice. The coach could explain that, 'I understand . . . and as we discussed in the first session, sometimes my role is to ask difficult questions . . . this is one of those times . . . is that ok?' The coach could then either ask a more concrete variation of the magic question – such as the 'two videos' question. Here the coach asks the coachee to picture two videos in his or her mind's eye. One video shows the problem as it is, the other video shows the preferred outcome. The coachee's role is to simply describe the difference between the two. Most people can do this. Failing this the coach can ask, 'If you had a friend in the same situation, what would you advise them to do?' The point of these questions is to get coachees to take a meta-cognitive position, to stand outside of themselves and take a different perspective – to change the viewing to change the doing!

Such resistance from the coachee is often a sign that he or she has not spent enough time talking about the problem. So, when faced with resistance, the coach could just roll with it, move on, and change the topic by possibly revisiting some of the problem talk, and then come back to possibility talk later. When all fails, a useful question is to ask the coachee, 'What would be the most useful question I could ask you right now?' Such techniques can be very effective, but of course it is better to pace the session so that rapport is maintained.

One way to purposefully pace the coaching conversation is to give the session a clear structure. Structured sessions can be extremely powerful ways of holding the conversation on track, and depending on which models are used, can provide an invaluable road map of the coaching conversation. What is a structured coaching conversation? And why should the solution-focused coach use them?

Structuring the coaching session

A structured coaching session is one where there are clearly differentiated sections within a single coaching session, and each section has a particular function, for example, setting goals, uncovering barriers to change, or developing action plans, and within each section the coach tries to focus the conversation on those specific factors. This allows the conversation to be highly focused, and session structure has been shown to be positively related to outcomes (Howard *et al*, 1986). A skilful coach is able to track the coaching process and knows at any time which section they are in and where they are aiming to go next.

Coaching sessions are typically quite structured, although there should always be flexibility in the way structures are applied. Session structures tend to fall into one of two camps: those that have outcomes or goal setting as the very first activity in the session; and those that focus on the current situation, problem or issue before moving on to goal setting.

You can read elsewhere, such as in Chapter 4, ways in which you could structure the session. GROW offers a useful structure in which the solution-focused approach can work, moving the coachee from objective (goals) to action planning (way forward).

TEN KEY QUESTIONS TO GUIDE YOUR WAY

1. If our coaching sessions work out, what will be different for you?

This question could be asked at the beginning of the coaching relationship and would be asked to get the coachee to begin to articulate, from his or her *own personal perspective,* the key hallmarks of success. The coachee's ability (or inability) to give a coherent well-thought out response to this will give the coach useful insights about the extent to which the coachee is ready for change, what is important to him or her and how the coachee thinks about him or herself and the world. If the coachee has a lot of trouble answering this question, as many will, it may be best not to push for a specific response because that can make the coachee feel as if he or she has 'failed'. Instead, elicit a broad vague response and then try the next question.

2. How would other people be able to tell if our coaching had been successful?

The point of this question is to help the coachee look at the situation from other people's perspectives. This is a way of fostering a meta-cognitive viewpoint and can be very useful for coachees who are very bound up in their own personal experience, and who see themselves as being the total centre of the universe. Sometimes you will get a quite astonished reaction, almost as if the coachee had never thought about how other people might perceive them. This is a great question for exploring the system in which the coachee lives or works.

3. What do you want to take away from this session?

Use this question at the start of a session to set a goal for the session. Try to make the goal as specific as possible. Coachees will not always be able to articulate what they specifically want to get out of the session. If that is the case, then take time to visit and re-visit the goal over the course of the session. Beware of rushing to set the goal. Take your time. It will be important that the coachee is aware that each session will start with explicitly setting a goal, otherwise they may experience the goal-directed nature of these questions as invasive or intrusive.

4. What would you really like to do?

Emphasize the *really* and this question becomes a great tool for getting to the heart of what they *actually* want, as opposed to what they *think* they should want. You can use this question when you sense ambiguity or lack of commitment to a goal or action plan. The key to this question is to be comfortable with silence and uncertainty. Ask the question and then let it hang there.

5. Is it x or y that we need to focus on?

This question is a closed, double-bind question that encourages the coachee to make a decision. Use this question when both choices have been discussed and there is uncertainty in the coachee's mind, or the coaching conversation is going around in circles. Using this question at the wrong time, before adequate discussion has taken place, may result in increased resistance to making a choice.

6. What personal strengths do you bring to this?

This question can be asked once the goal has been articulated. This is a useful question when exploring options and action plans where the coachee seems to be hesitant in committing to action steps or seems to lack confidence. Used well this question can really build the coachees' self-efficacy through helping them to list all the resources they have. The coach may need to be very encouraging, as some people find it hard to list their personal strengths. Judicious (and genuine) use of compliments and praise may be useful here.

7. What are you committed to actually doing?

Asked well, this question cuts to the heart of the coachee's commitment to action. The coach will need to pace this question well, and emphasize the *actually doing*. This question gives the coachee permission to select some actions over others. Make sure that you ask this question from an attitude of facilitation, curiosity and service, rather than judgement. This can be quite a challenging, confrontational question so only ask it when there is good rapport with the coachee.

8. How confident are you, on a scale of 1 to 10, that you can do this?

This is a straightforward scaling question to help coachees self-assess their ability to actually do the action steps. The word 'confident' is important here as it is less threatening for many people than a word such as 'committed'. Unless they respond with '10' always ask, 'What would it take to take you to (the next point on the scale)?' This question should be asked at the end of all coaching sessions once action steps have been outlined. This question can act as a check to ensure that the action plans are truly congruent for the coachee. On occasion, despite apparent rapport and motivation during the session, a coachee will report quite low confidence. In that case spend some time to uncover what would make the difference. The coach should also learn from this how they could have improved his or her coaching technique.

9. How can you keep track of your successes?

This question should be asked in the wrap-up stage of the coaching session, during the action planning process. This question presupposes success and links the coaching action plans explicitly to the cycle of self-regulation: monitor, evaluate, change what's not working and do more of what works. The coachees need to be able to keep track of their successes in concrete measurable ways, and this will help keep the coaching grounded.

10. Tell me some more about that . . . ?

This is one of the most useful questions in the coach's toolbox and is an open question that invites the coachee to elaborate on previous comments. In addition to eliciting more detail from the coachee, this is also very useful for the times when the coach does not know what to say next!

SUMMARY

The solution-focused approach to coaching is about asking the right questions, about keeping coachees focused on what they want to achieve, not what has happened in the past. It is about stretching coachees so they can be the best they can be. Its primary focus on outcomes over analysis may seem simplistic to some, but the solution-focused approach takes pride in keeping it simple. Staying focused on solutions is the essence of great coaching.

References

Barrett, F (2004) Coaching for resilience, *Organization Development Journal*, **22** (1) pp 93–6

Berg, I K and Szabo, P (2005) *Brief Coaching for Lasting Solutions*, W W Norton, New York

Carver, C S and Scheier, M F (1998) *On the Self-regulation of Behaviour*, Cambridge University Press, Cambridge

Corcoran, J and Stephenson, M (2000) The effectiveness of solution-focused therapy with child behavior problems: A preliminary report, *Families in Society*, **81** (5) pp 468–74

Dahl, R, Bathel, D and Carreon, C (2000) The use of solution-focused therapy with an elderly population, *Journal of Systemic Therapies*, **19** (4) pp 45–55

de Shazer, S (1984) The imaginary pill technique, *Journal of Strategic & Systemic Therapies*, **3** (1) pp 30–34

de Shazer, S (1988) *Clues: Investigating solutions in brief therapy*, Norton and Co, New York

Ellis, A (1997) Response to Jeffrey T. Guterman's response to my critique of his article 'A social constructionist position for mental health counseling', *Journal of Mental Health Counseling*, **19** (1) pp 57–63

Gollwitzer, P M (1996) The volitional benefits of planning, in eds P M Gollwitzer and J A Bargh, *The Psychology of Action* (pp 287–312), Guilford, New York

Green, L S, Oades, L G and Grant, A M (2006) Cognitive-behavioural, solution-focused life coaching: Enhancing goal striving, well-being and hope, *Journal of Positive Psychology*, **1** (3) pp 142–49

Heckhausen, H and Gollwitzer, P M (1987) Thought contents and cognitive functioning in motivational versus volitional states of mind. *Motivation and Emotion*, **11**, 101–20

Held, B S (1996) Solution-focused therapy and the postmodern: A critical analysis, in (eds) S D Miller, M A Hubble and B L Duncan, *Handbook of Solution-focused Brief Therapy* (pp 27–43), Jossey-Bass, San Francisco, CA

Horvath, A O and Symonds, B (1991) Relation between working alliance and outcome in psychotherapy: A meta-analysis, *Journal of Counseling Psychology*, **38** (2) pp 139–49

Howard, K I, Kopta, S, Krause, M S and Orlinsky, D E (1986) The dose-effect relationship in psychotherapy, *American Psychologist*, **41** (2) pp 159–64

Jay, M (2003) Understanding how to leverage executive coaching, *Organization Development Journal*, **21** (2) pp 6–19

Kilburg, R R (2004) When shadows fall: using psychodynamic approaches in executive coaching, *Consulting Psychology Journal: Practice and Research*, **56** (4) pp 246–68

Lethem, J (2002) Brief solution-focused therapy, *Child and Adolescent Mental Health*, **7** (4) pp 189–92

Murray, C E and Murray, T L, Jr (2004) Solution-focused premarital counseling: Helping couples build a vision for their marriage, *Journal of Marital and Family Therapy*, **30** (3) pp 349–58

O'Connell, B (1998) *Solution-focused Therapy*, Sage, London

Walter, J L and Peller, J E (1996) Rethinking our assumptions: assuming anew in a postmodern world, in eds S C Miller, M A Hubble and B L Duncan, *Handbook of Solution-focused Brief Therapy* (pp 9–27), Jossey-Bass, San Francisco, CA

Zachary, L J (2005) Raising the bar in a mentoring culture, *Training & Development*, **59** (6) 26–27

6

Cognitive behavioural coaching

Michael Neenan

THE COGNITIVE BEHAVIOURAL COACHING MODEL EXPLAINED

Coaching helps individuals to get the best out of themselves in order to achieve their important work/life goals. While this may be an inspirational message for a coachee to hear, simply following a goal-oriented action plan is usually insufficient to bring about this end. What often blocks the way are the coachee's self-limiting/defeating thoughts and beliefs (eg, 'I'm not good enough'), counterproductive behaviours (eg, procrastination) and troublesome emotions (eg, prolonged anxiety). Cognitive behavioural coaching (CBC) helps coachees to identify, examine and change such thoughts and beliefs, develop productive behaviours and become more skilled at emotional management. The focus is on the coachee's current concerns. The ultimate goal of CBC is for the coachee to become his or her own coach.

CBC derives from the work of two leading cognitive behavioural theorists, researchers and therapists, Aaron Beck (1976) and Albert Ellis

(1962): Beck's model is known as cognitive therapy while Ellis's is called rational emotive behaviour therapy – the similarities and differences between the two models are beyond the scope of this chapter. The origins of cognitive behavioural therapy (CBT) can be traced back to the Stoic philosophers, Epictetus and Marcus Aurelius. Epictetus stated a profound truth that is at the heart of CBT: 'People are disturbed not by things, but by the views which they take of them.' In other words, the viewpoint we choose determines our reaction to 'things'. The idea of choosing a viewpoint can trigger a range of responses in coachees, from revelation and receptivity to resistance. With the first group, coachees are eager to discover new problem-solving perspectives; the second group are willing to engage with CBC and expect a successful outcome; the last group may insist that their views are determined, not chosen, by past or present events or other people, or are too ingrained to change but, reluctantly, give CBC the benefit of the doubt for a trial period.

By helping coachees to recognize their idiosyncratic styles of problem-perpetuating thinking and using reason and reality testing to modify them, they learn to think about their thinking (known as meta-cognition) in more helpful, balanced and adaptive ways. The philosopher Simon Blackburn describes self-reflection thus:

> Human beings are relentlessly capable of reflecting on themselves . . . We can habitually think things, and then reflect on what we are thinking. We can ask ourselves (or sometimes we get asked by other people) whether we know what we are talking about. To answer that we need to reflect on our own positions, our own understanding of what we are saying, our own sources of authority . . . We might start to wonder whether what we say is 'objectively' true, or merely the outcome of our own perspective, or our own 'take' on a situation. (Blackburn, 1999: 4)

CBT does *not* say that problems are created solely by one's thinking: adverse events do occur but how we think about these events can increase our difficulties in dealing with them (eg, accused of being the 'weak link' on a project, the person dwells on the unfairness of the accusation instead of dealing directly with it, falls behind with his work on the project thereby justifying the original accusation). CBT might suggest by its name that emotion is ignored, but this is untrue as it does explore upsetting feelings but not endlessly so, as this can actually strengthen these feelings and the beliefs underpinning them (Grieger and Boyd, 1980). The route to emotional change is through cognitive and behavioural change, as with a coachee who thinks her 'boss is a bully' and gets angry every time she sees or thinks about him; by developing an assertive outlook, the coachee is able to 'coach upwards' and moderate her boss's abrasive interpersonal style as well as her own anger.

CBT can sometimes be misconstrued as positive thinking: the therapist being a 'cheerleader' for always looking on the bright side of life (Leahy, 2003). Rather, CBT emphasizes realistic thinking, ie trying to ascertain how things actually are, free from distortions in our thinking (accepting that we live in a world of probability and chance rather than insisting on guarantees that our endeavours will never backfire). Positive thinking should not be confused with a positive attitude: the first outlook relies on mindless optimism while the second one seeks to find constructive ways of handling difficulty and distress with the expectation that things will eventually turn out well.

Beck and Ellis have been eager to move CBT out of the counsellor's office to reach a wider audience with their psychological problem-solving approaches. With this aim in mind, turning CBT into CBC has been growing apace in both personal and workplace coaching (Anderson, 2002; Grant and Greene, 2001; Kodish, 2002; Neenan and Dryden, 2002; Peltier, 2001; Reivich and Shatté, 2002).

Research

CBT, or more particularly Beck's cognitive therapy, has become the 'single most important and best validated psychotherapeutic approach. It is the psychological treatment of choice for a wide range of psychological problems' (Salkovskis, 1996: xiii). Moreover, 'there are indications that they [CBT approaches] may produce an enduring effect rarely shared by other approaches' (Hollon and Beck, 2004: 482). The current guidelines of the National Institute for Clinical Excellence (NICE, 2005) make CBT the first-line treatment for a range of clinical disorders.

Does the success of CBT in treating clinical problems translate into similar success in coaching with coachees who are striving for personal and professional satisfaction? Research into CBC is limited. Grant (2001) found that combined cognitive and behavioural approaches with trainee accountants, 'was associated with an increase in academic performance, deep and achieving approaches to learning, enhanced self-concepts related to academic performance, and a reduction in test anxiety'. Cognitive coaching, which is taught in educational and other settings, uses meta-cognition to enhance self-directed learning, improve decision-making skills and problem-solving capacities. Research in cognitive coaching has linked its implementation to increased student achievement, greater teacher efficacy and satisfaction, higher levels of conceptual thinking among teachers and more professional, collaborative cultures (Edwards, 2001).

Many coaching texts make great claims for the effectiveness of coaching but, presently, lack great empirical data to support such claims (though, of course, lack of adequate testing does not mean lack of effectiveness). However, as various authors observe, research into coaching is in its early stages but 'it is growing and the empirical foundations of the profession are strengthening' (Skiffington and Zeus, 2003: 5). Furnham (2004) states that to determine if coaching works it should be subjected to the 'gold standard' of scientific evaluation – randomized controlled trials (RCTs). These provide the highest grade of evidence for an intervention's effectiveness because it is the least likely to be contaminated by bias (Wessely, 2001).

CBC practice

The usual structure of each session is to discuss and clarify the coachee's issues, establish goals (clear, specific, measurable and within the coachee's control to achieve), develop action plans, confirm the coachee's responsibility for implementing these plans and, at the end of the session, gain feedback to determine what was helpful and unhelpful about the session in order to customize coaching to the coachee's preferences. At the next session, progress with the action plans is reviewed. This is the smooth-running view of coaching, which sometimes occurs.

More often than not, psychological difficulties intrude at the outset (eg, the coachee believes he or she has been 'sent' for coaching or is ambivalent about the benefits of change) and/or during its course (eg, the coachee becomes demoralized as the hard work of change kicks in). Cognitive behavioural coaching is therefore a twin-track approach to goal achievement: the psychological and the practical (Neenan and Dryden, 2002). The psychological track helps to remove the stumbling blocks to change such as procrastination, excessive self-doubt, indecisiveness, and self-deprecation, while the practical track assists coachees to develop an orderly sequence of goal-directed action steps (sometimes coachees articulate clear and exciting goals but are vague about the steps that are required to get them there). Cognitive behavioural coaches agree with Lee regarding the psychological dimension in coaching:

> This expansion in scope [of coaching] challenges coaches to be more sophisticated in their understanding of psychology. They need to develop skills and experience that enable them to move more freely between the psychological and practical. They need to understand a wider range of theoretical models and frameworks, and to be able to relate psychological insights to business performance. (Lee, 2003: 2)

However, the practical side of coaching can be neglected because, in my experience, some coaches, particularly from counselling backgrounds, are too eager to 'dig deep' into psychological issues or overly focus on them before there is evidence to warrant such an investigation or they have been given permission from the coachee to do so. Such behaviour is likely to lead to a poor coaching relationship punctuated by frequent ruptures. It is important to point out to these coaches that understanding and removing psychological blocks is necessary but not necessarily sufficient to bring about change: following an action plan leads to self-actualization and achieving the satisfactions that the coachee has been seeking. Therefore, dealing with the psychological and the practical is equally important.

The ABCDE model

A framework for understanding and dealing with psychological blocks in coaching is the ABCDE model (Dryden and Neenan, 2004; Ellis and MacLaren, 1998):

Situational A (activating event)

The coachee's objective description of the situation – giving a presentation to colleagues in two weeks' time.

Critical A (activating event)

The coachee's subjective account of the most troubling aspect of the situation – 'I might not be able to answer some of the questions.'

B = self-limiting/defeating beliefs

These are triggered by the critical A – 'I must be able to answer all the questions otherwise I'll be exposed as a phoney, derided as the so-called expert.'

C = consequences

Emotional	rising anxiety.
Behavioural	frantic over-preparation, sleep disturbance, reduced work performance.
Physical	continual tension, headaches.
Interpersonal	irritation with family and work colleagues.
Cognitive	catastrophic thoughts and images about the aftermath of being exposed as a 'phoney'.

D = disputing or examining these self-defeating beliefs

▎ Is this belief rigid or flexible: does it allow for outcomes other than the one demanded – answering all the questions?

▐ Is this belief extreme or non-extreme: is it immoderate for the person to call himself a 'phoney' because he may be unable to answer a question or two?

▐ Does this belief make sense: because he wants an outcome to occur (answering all the questions) does it follow logically that this outcome must occur?

▐ Is this belief realistic: where is the evidence that he must be able to answer all the questions rather than do the best that he can on the day? If he was a genuine phoney rather than an imagined one, would his boss have asked him to give the presentation?

▐ Is keeping this belief helpful: are the costs greater than the benefits?

E = new and effective outlook

(Adaptive, compassionate, balanced, and self- and performance-enhancing). 'I now realize that my standards are rigid and harsh. A true phoney would be attempting to deceive his audience, which I'm definitely not trying to do. On the other hand, an expert is very, not completely, knowledgeable. If I can't answer a question I will ask someone in the audience or find out myself. Gaps in my knowledge are to be filled, not condemned. I expect to give a competent performance with a strong preference for improvement over time. If one or two people do think I'm a phoney, then I can choose whether or not to agree with them.'

The coachee's new outlook is lengthy and elaborate because it takes a rounded view of the situation in stark contrast to the all-or-nothing quality of his original self-defeating belief. He is now able to view the forthcoming presentation with 'excited curiosity' instead of as a potential catastrophe. In order to internalize his new outlook, the coachee made regular presentations as a one-off presentation is unlikely to dislodge his old ideas.

When teaching the ABCDE model, the coach needs to emphasize that A (events – past, present or future) does not cause C (but contributes to it); B (beliefs) largely determines C (consequences). This is an empowering view of how change occurs because it allows us to develop different beliefs (D→E) about A and, consequently, modify our reactions at C; if A really did cause C it would be very difficult, if not impossible, to change our reactions at C.

WHEN DOES CBC WORK BEST?

CBC works best with coachees who are psychologically minded and are keen to detect, examine and change their maladaptive thinking because they see its adverse effects upon their performance. With coachees who are less psychologically adept at introspection, the presentation of the CBC model linked to examples of their current problematic behaviour can quickly help them to 'tune' into which aspects of their thinking need modifying which, in turn, can produce quickly observable performance improvements. Just as one swallow does not make a summer, initial gains from CBC need to be maintained over the longer term to demonstrate that substantial change has occurred. Maintenance of gains, including the ability to deal with setbacks by pinpointing the reactivation of former self-defeating thoughts and behaviours, shows that coachees have made optimal use of CBC.

CBC might not work well with people who find it difficult to engage in introspection, see it as an 'intimate' process they feel uncomfortable with, are not prepared to expend the effort to become aware of, examine and modify their problematic thinking, are worried about a stranger 'poking about in my head', or see action as the answer to their current concerns, not 'navel-gazing' (navel-gazing is self-absorption or profitless introspection whereas developing realistic thinking is goal-oriented). In my experience, the real problem is not usually outright rejection of the CBC model but how it is presented and implemented.

TOOLS AND TECHNIQUES

Tools and techniques are used to help coachees understand and implement the ABCDE model that is at the heart of CBC.

Teaching the cognitive model

This demonstrates how our thoughts are congruent with our mood and behaviour. For example, a coachee comes to coaching irritable and restless ('Coaching is just another bloody fad! All it's really about is how to get more work out of you'). The coach addresses the coachee's perceptions of coaching without dodging the issue of improved performance as an organizational goal; additionally, the coachee's personal needs are elicited ('I want to get these long hours under control'). By focusing on the organizational and personal, the coachee begins to feel hopeful and relaxed in the session ('Maybe there is something in it for me. I'm prepared to give it a go'). The coach then reviews the two different viewpoints that the coachee has expressed and their impact on her mood and behaviour, to demonstrate the cognitive model in action. The coach would also want to know if the coachee has any reservations about, objections to or criticisms of the model so that they can discuss them.

Other ways of teaching the model (and tweaking it for business purposes) would be to couple self-defeating beliefs to reductions in performance, productivity and profit such as a person believing that completing important paperwork is 'dull and boring', procrastinating over doing it and thereby missing deadlines and reducing sales.

Inference chaining

This involves asking your coachee a series of assumption-driven questions to tease out his or her personally significant inferences about a situation in order to pinpoint its most troubling aspect for her, called the critical A. In this example, a manager is anxious about confronting an employee about his poor performance and the coach follows the logical implications of each coachee thought:

Coach: What's anxiety-provoking in your mind about doing that?

Coachee: He probably won't like it.

Coach: And if he doesn't?

Coachee: He'll probably get angry.

Coach: And if he does respond like that?

Coachee: Then I'll be placed in an awkward position.

Coach: How so? (This is a clarifying question before resuming inference chaining.)

Coachee: I don't like dealing with angry people. I avoid it whenever I can.

Coach: And if you don't avoid it and have to deal with him?

Coachee: Then I'll become all tongue-tied, red-faced, my mind will go blank, and I'll probably crumble.

Coach: And if you do crumble?

Coachee: Then I'll have lost my credibility as a manager. It will be all round the office. Him smirking and strutting around like he's won.

Coach: So is losing your credibility as a manager the most troubling aspect of this situation?

Coachee: Losing my credibility. That's it. (The coachee's critical A has been located.)

The critical A triggered the coachee's rigid and unreasonable key belief: 'I must not lose my credibility as a manager in dealing with this man otherwise I will be seen as weak and pathetic.' Through discussion and cognitive restructuring (ie belief change), the coachee was able to see that he or she was taking one aspect of their role, dealing with interpersonal conflict, as the cornerstone of their credibility as a manager and forgetting or minimizing their managerial strengths (most of their staff respected him or her). By stepping back from this belief they were able to formulate a new one: 'The evidence shows I'm a competent manager but I do need to toughen-up in dealing with this man. I don't like confrontation and probably never will but it's something I want to try and get to grips with because it's likely to happen again.'

It is important that the coach does not push the coachee for radical restructuring of their beliefs ('learn to embrace confrontation') as this strategy is likely to be met with understandable resistance as they see their beliefs being undermined through forced, false and fast change. Coachees are more likely to modify their beliefs when change is gradual and stays within their value system (Dowd, 1996).

Common cognitive distortions (CCDs)

CCDs are also known as 'thinking traps', which result from coachees processing information in a consistently negative, biased way, thereby helping to maintain their troublesome feelings. Typical distortions include:

▮ All or nothing thinking – viewing events in either/or terms: 'Either you're for me or against me.'

▮ Overgeneralization – drawing sweeping conclusions on the basis of a single incident or insufficient evidence: 'As I wasn't given the lead on this project, I'll never lead another one.'

▮ Mental filter – only the negative aspects of a situation are noticed: 'Look at all the things that have gone wrong this week.'

▮ Catastrophizing – assuming the worst and, if it occurs, your inability to deal with it: 'It will be terrible if I don't get the promotion. I'll be stuck at this level for ever and vegetate.'

▮ Musts and shoulds – rigid rules that you impose on yourself and others: 'I must never show any weaknesses to my colleagues'; 'Everyone should work as long and as hard as I do.'

▮ Fallacy of fairness – believing in a just world: 'Bad things won't happen to you if you're a good, hard working, honest person.'

▮ Perfectionism – striving for standards that are beyond reach or reason (Burns, 1980): 'I must do everything perfectly or else I'm no good. A competent performance equals failure.'

Coachees can learn to identify the distortions in their thinking and determine the accuracy of them: 'There's that all or nothing thinking again about people being for or against me. Based on the evidence, people have a range of reactions to me, not simply for or against. I want to develop more balanced thinking about this issue and stop this extremist nonsense.'

Experiments

Thoughts are viewed as hypotheses, not facts (unless they can be verified). Carrying out experiments allows coachees to test the validity of their predictions. For example, a coachee thought that if she presented her ideas at a meeting they would be rejected or ridiculed. While her ideas were neither rejected nor ridiculed, they were considered to be 'insufficiently robust at the present time and need more work' (guidelines for improvement were suggested). While the coachee was not overly pleased with this outcome, at least it pointed the way to possible eventual acceptance of some of her ideas if she acted on the new information generated by the experiment.

Self-acceptance

This is a way of being, not a technique. Self-acceptance means rating aspects of oneself but never judging oneself on the basis of these aspects: 'My performance was poor in that situation based on the feedback. I want to learn from the feedback in order to improve my performance, but my performance can never define me.' A person is too complex to be given a global evaluation like 'useless' or 'worthless'; in other words, such evaluations are meaningless. Self-acceptance also involves looking at oneself in the round by acknowledging one's positive qualities and shortcomings and attempting to change the latter if desired, and frequently reminding oneself that human fallibility cannot be eradicated (so do not waste time trying!) but the incidence of fallible behaviour can be reduced by learning from one's mistakes, thereby making fewer of them.

Self-condemnation adds nothing of value or clarity to problem solving. If coachees doubt this, they can spend a week, for example, noting how much time they waste on self-condemnation and feeling frustrated when things go wrong instead of focusing on immediate problem solving. Self-acceptance can be difficult to learn but its practical effects can be seen and felt through higher levels of performance and motivation.

Task assignment record

This is filled in near the end of every session and helps to keep coachees focused on their goal-directed action steps:

▌ What is the task you are going to complete before the next session? ('Make three contacts as part of my marketing strategy to launch my coaching practice').

▌ What is the purpose of doing this? ('To stop procrastinating over setting myself up as a coach and to keep reminding myself that my confidence and competence as a coach develops over time, not straight away, so get on with it!').

▌ Any anticipated obstacles in completing the task and what solutions will you use to overcome them? ('I may start procrastinating again so I will make all three contacts in the next 48 hours rather than leaving them until the end of the week').

It is important that the tasks are reviewed at the beginning of every session to discover what the coachee did or did not do. Task review is based on *learning,* not success or failure. Whatever is learnt provides valuable information on progress towards goals and understanding and tackling impediments to achieving them.

Three key insights

These can act as an aide-memoire for present and future problem solving:

1. You largely feel the way you think ('largely' because you are influenced, but not controlled, by other factors). You can control your emotional destiny to an extent you may never have realized by paying attention to how you think when you get upset.

2. No matter how you acquired your unhelpful beliefs, you still choose to adhere to them today ('I didn't go to university so I have to keep proving I'm not stupid') and act in ways that strengthen these beliefs, such as trying to impress graduates you work with how smart you are.

3. The way to get rid of or weaken these beliefs is to continually and firmly think and act against them by adopting more helpful and realistic beliefs. 'I am an intelligent person because I now look at a wide range of factors connected to intelligence instead of the very narrow one of university or stupidity as in the past', and the person

stops trying to impress the graduates and lets them make up their own mind about him or her.

TEN KEY QUESTIONS TO GUIDE YOUR WAY

1. What thoughts are going through your mind in that situation?

This helps the coachee to become aware of and identify negative thoughts linked to unpleasant feelings, bodily sensations and counter-productive behaviours. A possible reply from the coachee is, 'I don't know.' This often results from the coach not helping the coachee to imagine the situation with video-like clarity. Once this is done, thoughts and feelings are usually forthcoming.

2. What stops you . . . (following a particular course of action)?

This is an assessment question to uncover blocks to change and discover what the maintaining factors are in holding back the coachee, such as low frustration tolerance ('It's too hard or boring') or perfectionism. The coachee might say, 'I'm not sure.' A way round this is to ask the coachee to imagine not being stuck and what would have changed in order for him or her to move on. Even if the blocks are practical ones like skills deficits or lack of knowledge, there is often a psychological block impeding reme-diation of these practical difficulties, so the same tactic can be used.

3. What are the short- and long-term costs and benefits of change?

Some coachees might reply, 'Lots of benefits', yet little change is occurring. This might be because these coachees are dwelling on the unarticulated costs of change ('I'm worried that it all could go wrong') while publicly espousing the benefits. What is 'hidden' needs to be uncovered and examined.

4. What is the clear and specific goal you want to achieve?

This is to clarify the coachee's thinking about goal selection and counter the vagueness of 'I want to be happier' or 'I want to be more confident'.

In what specific contexts does the coachee want to be more confident and what does more confident actually look like?

5. What's the problem with making mistakes or experiencing failure?

'Because I don't like it' comes the standard reply. On further investigation, coachees are often coupling their self-worth to performance failure, which therefore has a much deeper and unpleasant resonance than simply not liking it.

6. What advice would you give to someone else struggling with the same issue as yourself?

This encourages the coachee to step back from the issue to gain more objectivity in thinking about it. However, coachees often say, 'But I wouldn't follow my own advice.' This response reveals a double standard, which usually involves showing compassion and understanding to others ('If you miss a few performance targets it's not the end of the world'), but being harsh and unforgiving towards oneself ('Missing my targets shows how utterly incompetent I am. It does feel like the end of the world'), which would then require further examination.

7. What would be the first concrete steps towards reaching your goal?

Once the coachee's concerns have been clarified and goals agreed, specific action is now required rather than a general statement of intent: 'I'd better start getting into gear on this issue.'

8. How will you know you are making progress towards your goals?

A usual reply is, 'I'll feel better.' The coachee is informed that specific behavioural evidence is required to evaluate progress, not just subjective responses.

9. What are the most valuable ideas and techniques you have got from coaching?

If the coachee says, 'I got a lot from it', the coach needs to encourage him or her to be specific.

10. Acting as a self-coach, how will you maintain and strengthen your gains from coaching?

'Keep at it I suppose' might be the doubtful reply. Developing an idiosyncratic and detailed blueprint for the future reminds the coachee that self-coaching needs to become a way of life if his or her gains are not to decay.

SUMMARY

CBC is a powerful way to help coachees reach their potential by its focus on both the psychological and practical aspects of goal achievement. Coachees can learn that many obstacles to change are psychologically constructed rather than immutable facts, and thereby open up new perspectives that will help them to pursue a more fulfilling life.

References

Anderson, J P (2002) Executive coaching and REBT: Some comments from the field, *Journal of Rational-Emotive and Cognitive-Behavior Therapy*, **20** (3/4) pp 223–33

Beck, A T (1976) *Cognitive Therapy and the Emotional Disorders*, International Universities Press, New York

Blackburn, S (1999) *Think*, Oxford University Press, Oxford

Burns, D D (1980) The perfectionist's script for self-defeat, *Psychology Today*, November, pp 34–51

Dowd, E T (1996) Resistance and reactance in cognitive therapy, *International Cognitive Therapy Newsletter*, **10** (3) pp 3–5

Dryden, W and Neenan, M (2004) *Rational Emotive Behavioural Counselling in Action*, 3rd edn, Sage Publications, London

Edwards, J (2001) *Cognitive Coaching SM: A Synthesis of the Research*, Center for Cognitive Coaching, Highlands Ranch, CO

Ellis, A (1962) *Reason and Emotion in Psychotherapy*, Citadel, Secaucus, NJ (rev. edn Birch Lane Press, New York, 1994)

Ellis, A and MacLaren, C (1998) *Rational Emotive Behavior Therapy: A therapist's guide*, Impact Publishers, Atascadero, CA

Furnham, A (2004) *Management and Myths: Challenging business fads, fallacies and fashions*, Palgrave MacMillan: Basingstoke

Grant, A M (2001) Coaching for enhanced performance: comparing cognitive and behavioral approaches to coaching, Paper presented at the 3rd International Spearman Seminar: Extending Intelligence: Enhancement and New Constructs, Sydney

Grant, A M and Greene, J (2001) *It's Your Life – What are you going to do with it?*, Pearson Education, Harlow

Grieger, R and Boyd, J (1980) *Rational-Emotive Therapy: A skills-based approach*, Van Nostrand Reinhold, New York

Hollon, S D and Beck, A T (2004) Cognitive and cognitive behavioral therapies, in (ed) M J Lambert, *Bergin and Garfield's Handbook of Psychotherapy and Behavior Change* (pp 447–92), 5th edn, Wiley, New York

Kodish, S P (2002) Rational emotive behaviour coaching, *Journal of Rational-Emotive and Cognitive-Behavior Therapy,* **20** (3/4) pp 235–46

Leahy, R L (2003) *Cognitive Therapy Techniques: A Practitioner's Guide,* Guilford Press, New York

Lee, G (2003) *Leadership Coaching: From personal insight to organisational performance,* Chartered Institute of Personnel and Development, London

National Institute for Clinical Excellence (2005) *Clinical Guidelines for Treating Mental Health Problems,* National Institute for Clinical Excellence, London

Neenan, M and Dryden, W (2002) *Life Coaching: A cognitive-behavioural approach,* Brunner-Routledge, Hove

Peltier, B (2001) *The Psychology of Executive Coaching,* Brunner-Routledge, New York

Reivich, K and Shatté, A (2002) *The Resilience Factor: Seven essential skills for overcoming life's inevitable obstacles,* Broadway Books, New York

Salkovskis, P M (1996) Preface, in (ed) P M Salkovskis, *Frontiers of Cognitive Therapy,* Guilford Press, New York

Skiffington, S and Zeus, P (2003) *Behavioral Coaching: How to build sustainable personal and organizational strength,* McGraw-Hill, Sydney

Wessely, S (2001) Randomised controlled trials: the gold standard?, in (eds) C Mace, S Moorey and B Roberts, *Evidence in the Psychological Therapies: A critical guide for practitioners,* Brunner-Routledge, Hove

7

NLP coaching

Ian McDermott

THE NLP COACHING MODEL EXPLAINED

Originating in the USA in the mid-1970s, neuro-linguistic programming (NLP) has since spread around the world, primarily I suspect because it delivers practical tools that can greatly improve performance. But these are really just the fruits of a unique mindset that focuses on two things, the study and replication of excellence, and, the structure of subjective experience. Structure here refers not to the content of experience but to the way it is put together – not to the fact that a person feels overwhelmed but to exactly how that sensation and experience is put together internally. What we want to know are the building blocks of that experience.

The primary tool employed in NLP is modelling. A model is a simplified description of the key elements of a process. The value of any model is its usefulness. The title of the very first NLP book, *The Structure of Magic* (Bandler and Grinder, 1975), suggested that, though what certain therapists did seemed quite magical, there was in fact a structure to their way of working that could be discovered and organized into a working model. That model could then be taught to others.

In NLP the word 'model' is also used in another sense – one who is a model of excellence. NLP practitioners are interested in looking for models of excellence in just about any field of human endeavour and will be asking, 'How do they *do* that?' They seek to specify precisely what it is that makes this individual or organization outstanding. NLP has developed a range of tools and distinctions that aid this process. Another may be good but this one is outstanding. NLP is interested in what it is that makes the difference. Wouldn't you like to know just how an outstanding coach achieves such *consistent* excellence? Wouldn't you like to have the opportunity to achieve that level of excellence? That's what NLP aims to deliver.

In 1990 I proposed a four-fold typology of elements that represented the essence of an NLP approach. I called them the 'Four pillars of NLP' (O'Connor and McDermott, 1996). These have now been widely adopted. They are: the capacity to establish and maintain rapport, an outcome orientation, heightened sensory acuity and great behavioural flexibility.

Both NLP and coaching presuppose that most coachees have within them the ability to determine what they want and how they might go about achieving it. Both presuppose that it is possible for coachees to shape their destiny if they are able to access the resources they need. Both therefore presuppose a vast reservoir of potential that it's possible for the coachee to tap. NLP coaching offers a way of realizing these assumptions at a very practical level for both coach and coachee.

All coach training programmes say that it is important to listen to the coachee. NLP actually teaches people *how* to do this by giving them the linguistic tools to understand the structure of what is being said (eg, the meta model, page 111). Again, all training schools exhort their students to notice what's going on with the coachee. NLP empowers the coach to do this by teaching *how* to notice what's happening so students acquire a whole new level of sensory acuity.

Over the last few years I have been interested to see bona fide coaches applying to take our NLP practitioner training. When I've asked them why, they tell me the speed of NLP means they can be more effective in the limited time of a coaching session. However, as a trainer of coaches, what I've actually observed is that coaches who learn NLP work with a much greater degree of precision.

WHEN DOES NLP COACHING WORK BEST?

To answer this question accurately it's important to consider not only the coachee but also the coach. As regards coachees, NLP coaching works best when they are unclear either about what they want or how to achieve it.

As ever, a little motivation goes a long way, but an NLP approach is very well suited to working with ambivalence because it presupposes ambivalence to have a positive intention. (Specific techniques have been developed which allow all of the elements to be honoured.)

The tools developed make NLP coaching particularly valuable when coachees need to engage in belief change work, strategic thinking or learn the specific how-tos that are part of acquiring new capabilities. Whenever issues are multifactorial or require shifts in physiology NLP will have tools that make change easier.

The coaches most suited to an NLP approach are those who are naturally curious, ethical, willing to be flexible, able to address macro and micro issues, who don't need to know the answers and who are willing to work with issues at all logical levels (see page 109).

NLP coaching, however, is not for everybody. It is, of course, no substitute for therapy, not even NLP therapy (McDermott and Jago, 2001a). And it should be avoided when coachees are really seeking subject specialist input – eg financial planning. Because it is remarkably empowering NLP coaching makes it difficult to maintain the fiction that we are only on the receiving end of life: if you know how to change your internal experience you know how to change your life, and this may be more than some coachees are willing to take on. Similarly NLP coaching does not sit well with coaches who have a low tolerance for alternative maps of the world. Coaches who believe there is only one right way, who think they know what's best for the coachee, or who favour the relentless 'to do' list approach to coaching are unlikely to feel at ease with the NLP approach.

TOOLS AND TECHNIQUES

Over the last 30 years a remarkable array of NLP tools and techniques have been developed that offer specific intervention protocols that can be almost endlessly modified and enhanced to suit individual needs, requirements and circumstances. They provide a bridge between aspiration and realization by making new distinctions that can be operationalized and offer step-by-step how-to templates.

It is not possible here to do justice to such a range; a fuller account can be found in McDermott and Jago (2003). A book such as this is primarily a linguistic medium. I have therefore chosen to focus on linguistic tools as this medium can accommodate these most readily. Clearly this skews things. Even here, though, I want to start by highlighting the importance of states as they are central to NLP. Were this a DVD you'd be seeing a lot of this more limbic dimension of NLP as I'd probably be demonstrating how NLP works with physiology by showing you the remarkable changes that are possible.

States and physiology

Anyone who speaks more than one language fluently will know that the way you use your body is quite different depending on the language you are speaking. Each language has its own physiology. In the same way different activities – be they external behaviour or internal processing – have different physiologies. Arguably one of the most effective ways of increasing our choices is to extend the range of use of physiology that we are comfortable with. Getting into the right state can make all the difference. At one extreme it's the basis of 'fake it till you make it'; at the other it's what every world-class athlete does prior to the crucial event.

If coachees are to achieve the goals they aspire to they will need to be able to access the states that support what they're going for. But states are equally important for the coach. What's the optimal state for you to be in to coach at your best? Do you know how to access this at will? We owe it to our coachees to find out. NLP offers both coaches and coachees a range of specific techniques and protocols to establish and maintain an appropriate state – at will.

Logical levels

One of the primary ways we can achieve greater leverage in our lives is to make distinctions that clarify what kind of issues we are dealing with. Logical levels are a set of such distinctions which coaches and coachees find extraordinarily useful. They can both help identify what the 'real' issue is and the appropriate level at which to intervene.

Imagine that as a coach you hear the following six statements from six different coachees:

1. I wish I was doing a job that served some higher purpose.
2. I just don't feel I can be myself in this job.
3. I don't believe in this job.
4. I don't think I know how to do this job.
5. I don't know what to do in this job.
6. I don't think I can do this job in this kind of working environment.

Clearly these six coachees are talking about very different things:

1. When someone says they can't do the job in this kind of working environment, they're not saying they can't do the job. The implication

is that they could do the job if it were a different kind of working environment. So the issue is the *environment*.

2. If you don't know what to do that's different again. This is about what you actually do. It's a matter of *behaviour*.

3. Not knowing *how* to do something means you lack certain skills at least at this time. These would give you the *capability*.

4. When someone doesn't believe in something they are obviously telling you about their beliefs and this will probably take you into their values as well. So here we are addressing *beliefs and values*.

5. If you don't feel you can be yourself doing a certain job you're talking about your sense of yourself – *your identity*.

6. Finally, if you wish your job served a higher purpose you have now gone beyond your own identity; you may be envisaging some larger system, purpose or being. We might call this spiritual but I tend to use the more value-neutral phrase that in some way you have gone *beyond identity*.

We can represent these levels either as a series of concentric circles or a vertical hierarchy:

▮ beyond identity;
▮ identity;
▮ beliefs and values;
▮ capabilities;
▮ behaviour;
▮ environment.

None are more important than the others. But it is fascinating to note the biases that people – and not least coaches – betray. I often find trainee coaches are surprised to find that they prefer to work with issues at particular logical levels. From an NLP point of view I want them to be flexible enough to honour and work at any logical level. Often when I am training I will pause during a demonstration session with a coachee to ask students at what logical level the issue as just stated is. As they get used to thinking in this way their diagnostic skills – and the kind of interventions they deem appropriate – improve dramatically.

Many coachees find logical levels an invaluable strategic thinking tool. It sensitizes them to how frequently messages are sent from one level (eg, behaviour) but received at another (identity) – as in the annual review, a parent-child fracas or a lovers' quarrel. It also alerts them to incongruencies. Corporate clients, for instance, will often talk of the need to win hearts and minds. To achieve this they'll need to address the levels of beliefs and identity. Frequently, though, the proposed initiatives are at the behaviour level. Now they begin to understand why these are so ineffectual.

The value of the logical levels may also stem in part from how they seem to fit with idiomatic English where we sometimes make distinctions by referring to levels. As one of my coachees put it in a recent final review: 'On one level losing my major customer last year was a disaster, but on another it freed me up. It made me question whether I really wanted (beliefs and values) to keep doing (behaviour) the same kind of things. I had the skills (capabilities) to work in different corporate environments (environment). The question was, did I have the courage (beliefs and identity)? Over the past six months this coaching has given me faith in myself (identity), clarity about what to do next (behaviour) and why it really matters (beliefs and values) to *me* (identity).'

The meta model

The way we use language can be enormously informative for the coach. As ever, it ain't just what we say, it's the way that we say it. The linguistic distinctions that the meta model gives us enable us to examine the deeper structure of the language we use.

To make sense of our experience, NLP suggests we need to construct some kind of model of the world. The meta model postulates three primary processes we use to do this: deletion, generalization and distortion:

▌ *Deletion* – to avoid sensory overwhelm we ignore or don't notice a lot of information.

▌ *Generalization* – we devise rules that predict what is likely to happen and the way the world works.

▌ *Distortion* – we assign information – eg, other's behaviour – meaning often on minimal evidence.

In using the meta model the first step is to recognize the patterns that you or others are using. Are you deleting, generalizing or distorting and is that helping or hindering? Each process will be reflected in your use of language. At the absolute minimum we can identify a dozen different language patterns. Once you have identified the pattern you may choose to intervene and change the language used. So often when you change the language you change the experience. This, of course, has enormous implications for coaching.

In dealing with generalizations, for instance, the coach's outcome is to explore and sometimes challenge their accuracy and efficacy. By so doing they can expand the limits of the coachee's model of the world. 'I've never been any good at this.' 'Never? Never, ever. . . ? There has not been a single moment in your life when you have ever been any good at this at all?' Generalizations are extraordinarily vulnerable: it only takes one counter-example to require some qualification of the original claim. When that starts to happen new boundaries of reality are being delineated. 'Well, maybe there have been times when I've been able to.' 'And if you could do it once, what might be possible now. . . ?' These are the obvious kind of generalizations.

However, there is a more subtle form. Technically they are known as 'modal operators'. These articulate the coachee's beliefs about what is possible and necessary given their model of the world. An example: a coachee says, 'I can't speak to my boss.' If the coach asks, 'What stops you?' he will learn something of the coachee's model of the world as regards the perceived cause of his problem. Alternatively, if he inquires, 'What would happen if you did?' he will come to understand the presumed effects. Just two questions, therefore, could provide an insight into how this coachee has cause and effect structured in their understanding of this issue. Teasing this information into consciousness is itself a powerful intervention.

Meta programmes

Meta programmes are largely unconscious sorting patterns that we use to filter our experience and determine what to pay attention to. They help us clarify what is important for us and are the means by which we organize our experience. Many have been identified in NLP. I shall touch on just one which coaches have repeatedly told me has been especially valuable in their work. It's called 'Moving away from – moving toward'.

Suppose your coachee says, 'I want to stop spending so much time at work and I'm fed up with feeling tired.' Clearly, he or she wishes to move away from the current experience. At this moment the coach has no idea what he or she might wish to move towards. The NLP coach will seek to pace the coachee so that he or she can move from avoidance towards something he or she deems desirable. Learning to do this can make a profound difference for a coachee who is used to focusing on what he or she doesn't want.

Successful institutions and group leaders need to be able to recognize and accommodate both meta programmes. One dazzling example would be the Christian Church, which has appealed both towards and away from meta programmes for centuries by offering believers both the carrot of heaven and the stick of hell.

If you know your predominant meta programmes you can play to your strengths. For instance, you'll know how to motivate yourself, but people often presume that what works for them will surely work for others. Many times I have seen team leaders who have a strong towards meta programme provide wonderful towards incentives. But some members of their team just don't seem to respond. This is not surprising given that in any group you'll probably have a mix of towards and away froms. Motivating the away froms means making clear the unpleasant consequences of not following a proposed course of action. What's needed is the acuity to determine the predominant meta programme and the flexibility to respond appropriately in real time.

Each pattern is valuable, each has its strengths and weaknesses. Maybe an away from mindset seems a bit negative? But a coach needs to know that towards coachees who tell you what they want and what they like are often less adept at recognizing what should be avoided. They may tend to minimize negative consequences and at the extreme can be oblivious to what is going wrong. That's a different meta programme. NLP coaching can redress such imbalances, first interpersonally by providing a savvy coach, and second intra-psychically by helping the coachee internalize an additional way of thinking.

TEN KEY QUESTIONS TO GUIDE YOUR WAY

When I first read the brief from the editor for this chapter I was puzzled by this heading. When I am working with a coachee there most certainly is not a set of questions that I am working through. But as I thought about it more there certainly are considerations that I will probably address as I come to understand what it is that the coachee and I are focusing upon. They come from an orientation. In what follows I have coded this orientation in question format. A health warning: this list is neither comprehensive nor definitive.

1. What do you want?

This is one question that every NLP coach will ask explicitly of a coachee and often repeat over time. It presupposes that the coachee knows or can find out through exploration. Even in its simplest form it has extraordinary power. If you have been grappling with some problem this question will take you from the present state to the desired state. As you begin detailing what it is that you want, you make it more vivid. This has neurophysiological consequences. So often when coachees begin to focus on what they're really going for their state changes in palpably observable ways.

One of the more subtle effects of this basic question is the reorientation in time that it frequently achieves. It is not uncommon for it to move a coachee from the present to a hoped for future. However, it is not only a question for the coachee. A good coach will be asking this of him or herself in their own life as well as when working with a particular coachee.

2. How would you know if you got it?

'I just want to feel like I'm doing something worthwhile with my life.' But how will this coachee know when they are? This is a fundamental, epistemological question: how do we know what we know? And how will the coach know that this coachee has achieved his or her outcome? Both coach and coachee need to have some kind of evidence procedure. It could take many forms but to be most useful it will need to be sensory specific. So, what will you see, hear and feel (maybe even taste and smell) that will demonstrate to you that the outcome has been achieved? I find that paying attention to these specifics early on saves an awful lot of time later. In answering this inquiry coachees frequently get much clearer about what it is they do and don't want at the outset.

3. What is being presupposed here?

A coachee says, 'I wish I was more confident. Then I could meet somebody and settle down and be really happy.' Another, who has been referred by their manager for coaching says, 'But I'm really good at my job.' In both cases there's a lot that's being presupposed – for instance, more confidence will make new behaviour possible that could lead to romance, or that if you're good at your job you don't need a coach.

While it is important to understand how coachees' presuppositions are structuring their world it is just as important for the coach to be aware of their own. This is true moment by moment in any coaching session. Every question has built into it a number of presuppositions – not least that of all the questions one could ask, this particular question merits asking right now. These presuppositions frame our perception. So what will the coach be presupposing in the next question he or she asks? And will this be useful to the coachee?

4. What resources are needed?

One useful way of thinking about pretty much any issue that an individual or a corporate client might raise is that they come with a present state. We then determine what would be a desired state. The challenge is how to move from the former to the latter. In NLP coaching we will be looking for what resources are needed which, if applied, will make this transition possible. So many of the tools and techniques that have been developed in NLP are designed to provide the how-tos that make it possible to fully access these resources and incorporate them.

A resource can be almost anything. On occasion it may be some obvious external tangible asset, such as financial backing. More often though, the resources that can make all the difference are decidedly intangible: a change in attitude, an improved relationship sometimes with another, sometimes with oneself, a finding of purpose or the acquisition of a new skill set. We can formulate this way of thinking very simply:

Present State + Resources = Desired State.

5. How am I right now?

So often my own internal state is an invaluable barometer to what it is actually going on. There have been times when, after a good night's sleep, feeling refreshed and alert I am with a coachee and I notice a change in my own state. Maybe I have become suddenly uneasy, restless, tired or bored. On one occasion I found myself starting to feel bored and I couldn't think why. So I said to the coachee, 'You know it's a funny thing, up until a few minutes ago I was right with you but then my mind starting wandering, my energy's gone down and I now just feel a bit bored.' And the coachee's response? 'Me too . . . I think I was just trying to convince myself but it's a con really. I just don't believe what I was saying anymore.'

6. What is the structure of this subjective experience?

How we put our internal experience together can make our world heaven or hell. Our senses provide the building blocks of our experience. Our internal world is ultimately comprised of sensory data – ie what we see, hear, feel, taste and smell – which we represent to ourselves in endlessly varied ways. If you want to know just how powerful these representations can be, consider this. For anyone who has a phobia it is quite unnecessary to be physically in the presence of what they're phobic about for them to have a phobic response. Talk about it in enough detail and they'll start having that phobic response. From an NLP point of view this is very good news! You are generating the response so potentially it could come under your control. If you understand the *structure* of the subjective experience that you have created internally you can change it and produce an equally dramatic but beneficial change in your physiology.

All internal experience has a structure. When you know how something is put together you can effectively rearrange it if you choose. By exploring with coachees how they (usually unconsciously) manipulate images, sounds, feelings, tastes and smells to help or hinder their experience and aspirations, the NLP coach is often able to help a coachee design new ways of thinking, quite literally.

7. What is an appropriate state and physiology?

The state you are in at any given moment has an enormous impact on what you are capable of at that time. Imagine having to make most of your life's major decisions when in the state that goes with having flu! A person's physiology and internal state is critical. For the NLP coach a recurring question is going to be, what state is the coachee in and what state does he or she need to be in to achieve and sustain the changes he or she seeks?

While many elements can influence our state – for instance, the kind of thoughts we're having – one that is frequently focused on in NLP is our use of physiology. Just how we are standing, sitting and moving generally (or not) will have a profound impact on our state. Many times I have encouraged coachee to get up and walk around so that they may energize themselves and their thinking.

Suppose you needed to be at your best on a particular day because you were going to be making a presentation or going for an interview. How would you prepare? So often coachees attempt to resource themselves by acquiring information. But being able to be in the right state can make all the difference. NLP coaching can give coachees – and coaches – the tools to access at will the state they need to be in to give of their best.

8. What are the systemic implications?

Any proposed change has systemic implications (O'Connor and McDermott, 1997). After all, no man – or indeed woman – is an island. It's important to me to understand what the potential consequences of change could be for the larger system in which this individual operates. I think of that larger system as having three dimensions: the intra-psychic, the interpersonal, and the organizational. If we want the change to be real and sustainable we will need to take into account all three dimensions. The intra-psychic – if the coachee is at odds with himself this does not bode well: 'Well, part of me really wants to start a new life, but part of me says it's too late.' Clearly we have work to do. The interpersonal – you may have decided to become self-employed but how does your spouse feel about this? The organizational – even if you are the head of the organization you would be well advised to take into account the likely perceptions and implications of any change programme before you implement it.

9. What are the positive by-products of the present status quo?

In my experience coachees rarely seek coaching because everything is wonderful and they wish to make it even more so. Usually there is a strong desire to effect change that will, they believe, result in some kind of improvement. Sometimes this can produce an impatience and dissatisfaction with the way things are now. They want to get on, make the changes and be finished with the old.

However, in order that this can be achieved I often find myself in the somewhat paradoxical position, at least temporarily, of being an 'advocate' for the status quo. I'll be asking coachees, be they private individuals or employees, questions like, 'So, what do you get out of what you do now?' or, 'What might you be in danger of losing?' Many times I have asked someone who wanted to quit smoking what they get out of smoking. A Danish coachee who found smoking gave her 32 specific benefits holds the record. It was, for instance, the primary way she would 'give time to myself'. For her this was a revelation and finally explained why it had been so difficult to give up previously. We prioritized these benefits and looked at how she could find alternative ways of achieving them.

Too often when we seek change both individuals and organizations are in danger of throwing out the baby with the bath water. When we do so we make it hard to sustain the change because we are violating our own internal ecology. So often this could be avoided if someone had known and taken the trouble to ask: what do we get out of what we do now?

10. How do you do that?

Really this is a modelling question. The perseverance and attention to detail that modelling requires means you've really got to want to know! You need to be really curious. Curiosity is non-judgemental and can be applied not only to excellence but also to understanding how we mess up. It can be of enormous value in coaching.

Many times I have found that my own curiosity about just how clients manage to consistently achieve a result they do not want has been sufficient to enable them also, perhaps for the first time, to become genuinely curious about just how do they do that? Even as they pay closer attention than usual they actually step back and see things with a fresh eye. They can take a dispassionate interest in how they do what they do.

SUMMARY

I've sometimes been struck by how, when NLP coaches encounter coaches from different backgrounds, they are always curious about that alternative approach and want to know more. Equally striking, this curiosity is often not reciprocated. But such curiosity is invaluable not just for coachees but also for the coach's own development. If we want to be the best we can be more of the time, it's probably going to be useful to model our own best practice. So, when you've done a really good job you too might want to ask, 'Just how did I *do* that?'

References

Bandler, R and Grinder, J (1975) *The Structure of Magic*, Science and Behaviour Books, Palo Alto, CA

McDermott, I and Jago, W (2001a) *Brief NLP Therapy*, Sage, London

McDermott, I and Jago, W (2001b) *The NLP Coach*, Piatkus, London

McDermott, I and Jago, W (2003) *Your Inner Coach*, Piatkus, London

O'Connor, J and McDermott, I (1996) *Way of NLP*, Thorsons, London

O'Connor, J and McDermott, I (1997) *The Art of Systems Thinking*, Thorsons, London

8

Transpersonal coaching

John Whitmore and Hetty Einzig

THE TRANSPERSONAL COACHING MODEL EXPLAINED

Transpersonal coaching has its origins in the wider transpersonal psychological movement. Transpersonal means 'beyond the personal' though of course it includes the personal. For example, family therapy is beyond the personal because the child with psychological difficulties cannot be successfully treated in isolation. The therapist works with the whole family. The child is a part of a system. The transpersonal perspective is a systems approach: it recognizes the interconnectedness of individuals, families, communities and organizations and actively engages our deeper awareness of this (McBeath and Wynne, 1985). It also recognizes and works with the yearning, ingrained in the human psyche, for something *beyond the personal,* beyond the material and the everyday. This may be expressed in many different ways, through religious or ethical practice, through creativity within and outside the workplace, through volunteering, community work and other forms of service.

The most important distinguishing feature of transpersonal psychology is that it does not draw a line between personal and spiritual development but sees them as stages on a continuum. So what do we mean by spiritual? In the last several decades the word has more often than not aroused embarrassment in the West as religious practice declined rapidly with the rise of the consumer society. We equated spiritual with organized religion and rejected it along with rejection of the Church, preferring to keep our spiritual ideas or practices private. However, there has always been in the West a solid interest in Eastern spirituality and mysticism and many have turned to Buddhism or more esoteric religions for guidance and solace (The Dalai Lama and Cutler, 1998; Hardy, 1987). In recent years, and particularly with advances in physics and the neurosciences and the consequent revival of debates about mind and consciousness, the spiritual is slowly re-entering the agenda for debate, and in private and in public more people are quietly 'owning up' to the importance of the spiritual in their lives (Jaworski, 1998; Senge *et al*, 2004). Here is how one of the fathers of the transpersonal defines the spiritual:

> (the spiritual includes) not only the specific religious experience, but all the states of awareness, all the functions and activities which have as common denominator the possessing of values higher than the average, values such as the ethical, the aesthetic, the heroic, the humanitarian and the altruistic. (Assagioli, 1965)

It is this dimension that gives a uniquely human shape to our lives:

> that which gives . . . unique definition . . . to our humanity is our need to place our enterprises in a frame of wider meaning and purpose. The spiritual in human beings makes us ask why we are doing what we are going and makes us seek some fundamentally better way of doing it. It makes us want our lives . . . to make a difference. (Zohar and Marshall, 2004)

Just as the introduction of the concept of emotional intelligence – EQ (Goleman, 1995), moved us on from the IQ as the key measure of intelligence, so current reference to spiritual intelligence (SQ), is demanding a further shift in understanding (Zohar and Marshall, 2004). SQ requires us to access our sense of deeper purpose, a purpose aligned with one's own potential and also perhaps with wider, even global, needs – or as one coach put it, being willing to seek a win-win-win (wins for self, the organization and the planet). At its most basic level, fuelled by increased global competition and a highly fluid and insecure market, those who seek the edge of high performance in business are being challenged to identify what really matters to them, where their passion lies and how they can best serve the organization as a whole. This is the domain of the transpersonal work that is now being done in leadership training within the corporate sector.

Individuals express their spirituality in two principle ways: transcendent or immanent. 'Transcenders' are people who find the everyday world lacking and humdrum. They focus instead on big ideas and higher ideals and, if action-oriented, are often driven to change things. People who express their spirituality in an immanent way are more focused on 'right living', behaving ethically, with care and consideration, within everyday life. Most of us have both these orientations but a stronger tendency towards one or the other. Both expressions contain some element of service, of being more focused on the good of others rather than one's own gain.

The form of transpersonal psychology that lends itself extremely well to coaching is psychosynthesis. As well as supporting coaches in the underpinning spiritual approach they take to their work (as described above), psychosynthesis offers accessible maps and models that can be used creatively and flexibly in coaching interventions. We will explore some of these later in this chapter.

WHEN DOES TRANSPERSONAL COACHING WORK BEST?

Here is a sample list of the types of coaching issues coaches are often asked to address:

▌ solve a problem;

▌ perform a task better – well;

▌ learn a new skill;

▌ become a more effective manager;

▌ plan a career path;

▌ develop oneself personally;

▌ live a more balanced life;

▌ become more creative;

▌ address a crisis;

▌ find meaning and purpose in life;

▌ develop a career path of service.

The further down the list we go the more essential transpersonal coaching becomes. The last five issues can barely be addressed at all without recognition of the spiritual for they are largely spiritual issues; but what of the others?

Whereas good coaches will follow the agenda and the direction that the coachee takes in a session, they also, consciously or unconsciously, via their own attitudes and beliefs, prescribe the frame of the coaching sessions. So let us for a moment consider three ways in which a coach might perceive the coachee and thus set the frame:

1. If the coachee has a history of bringing problems to the table, it is understandable that the coach might no longer see a person coming through the door but, with sinking heart, feel, 'Here comes trouble! Yet another problem.'

2. An alternative view – and probably a healthier one for coachee and coach – is to see the coachee as 'a person who has a problem'.

3. A transpersonal coach is likely to have a very different frame for most situations, however great or small. It would be something like this: 'Here is a person who is full of potential and has all the skills and qualities needed to tackle his problems', or like this: 'Here is a soul who has challenges and obstacles to overcome on her journey through the university of life. This is another such learning opportunity.'

A coach adopting these transpersonal points of view will have far more compassion and positive regard for the coachee and for the coachee's problem. We suggest therefore that even if coaches are coaching coachees on more mundane issues most of the time, they and their coachees would gain much if the coaches were transpersonally-oriented.

Let us take another cut at what transpersonal coaching may be used for. The traditional or behavioural way to teach a new skill is to use demonstration, instruction and correction. The coaching approach is to facilitate the learner to discover 'how to do it' from the coachee's own experience with coaching enhanced awareness, possibly adding in a few hints and tips where discovery is not bearing fruit.

However, this too falls short of the coaching process. Gallwey (1974) identified this issue: 'you begin to play the Inner Game when you recognize that the opponent within your own head is more formidable that the one the other side of the net'. The object of the 'Inner Game' that Gallwey refers to is to eliminate the internal obstacles to learning, performance and enjoyment. Once those obstacles, of which fear of failure is the most common, are eliminated, a person is able to learn or to play at his or her best.

TOOLS AND TECHNIQUES

Psychosynthesis brings us many techniques and some maps and models, all highly applicable to coaching. We briefly outline the main ones here, however a word of caution. Transpersonal coaching is not a question of simply expanding the coach's toolkit with some clever new tricks. The techniques are deceptively simple in themselves since they are also powerful in opening doors not opened by more conventional cognitive methods. This may be daunting for the coach if he or she is not familiar with this deeper territory. As we said earlier on in this chapter, we advise anyone guiding someone on a journey to have been on or be currently travelling on their own journey of discovery.

The 'egg' model, devised by Assagioli (1974) – see Figure 8.1 – is a major contribution to psychological thinking in a number of ways. However, as all practitioners and writers on psychosynthesis always stress, it is a map, not the territory: it is not the truth. Discovery of the territory must be through each individual's journey. It is their personal experience that verifies the model, not the other way round.

Most important, the diagram gives equal weight to the super-conscious as to the lower unconscious. This means that focusing on our future and the development of our potential, on accessing more of our intuition and inspiration, and our higher feelings (eg, altruism, care, service) is every bit as important as examining our past or feelings and events we have repressed. While it is generally agreed that the realm of the lower unconscious belongs to those trained in counselling and psychotherapy, the super-conscious is very much the domain of transpersonal coaching.

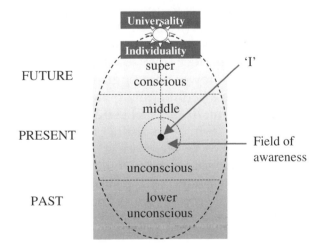

Figure 8.1 The 'egg' model

At the centre of our psyche is the 'I' or 'self'. This is linked to and reflects the higher Self. The Self (with a capital S) is half in and half out of the egg, which itself has a dotted line around it to indicate the permeable nature of the psyche, with energy flowing both ways.

Around the 'I' is the field of awareness instantly accessible to us at will, and beyond this are aspects of ourselves, others, our environment, of which we are more or less conscious. Most current coaching takes place in this realm, helping the coachee to become more aware of his or her current reality. As his or her awareness broadens, to include an understanding of the deeper organizational dynamics, of the marketplace, of the social and global context in which the company operates, the coachee and coach will draw increasingly on the field of the super-conscious.

Within the field of awareness will be what Ferrucci (1982) calls 'a disordered collection of clashing tendencies'. Perhaps the first aim of transpersonal coaching is to help the coachee meaningfully harmonize these around the centre, the 'I', to become effective and resilient. So what are these 'clashing tendencies'?

Sub-personalities

The concept that we are both unified and multiple – both one and many people within one skin – is not a new one: all philosophies, religions and psychologies have grappled with this paradox. It is a central feature of psychosynthesis and enables us to work with coachees in many different creative ways. Sub-personalities are parts of ourselves with distinct mini-personalities. They can form around our identification with stereotypical roles (father, worker, boss), with job titles (accountant, doctor), with personality characteristics (being clever, angry or always happy), with psychological formations (the winner, the victim), or with cultural, racial and social alliances. We each have a cast of characters within us (eg, the victim, nice guy, perfectionist, joker, stern father, fair manager, the charmer, control freak, tower of strength) each with its own beliefs and behaviours. Each has a certain quality, tone and triggers. The best analogy is with instruments in an orchestra: the French horn is very different to the violin and again quite distinct from the flute. But together they make up a whole: an orchestra.

The trouble is that we have a tendency to identify with whichever sub-personality is dominant, triggered by the situation. We forget that there are other perspectives on current reality, or that we have other skills and qualities that we might bring to bear on this situation. So the orchestra often sounds like it's tuning up – a cacophony of clashing voices and arguments as we bounce from one sub-personality to another.

The sub-personality principle is best used in coaching as an awareness-raising tool. When a coachee reveals a conflict between the desires of two sub-personalities, the coach might ask some of these questions: 'What part of you wants to do this and what part wants something else? What else does that part want? What need is that part of you seeking to meet? How else could you meet that need without an internal struggle? Let us imagine a negotiation between these two parts of you.' Most often the consequent understanding of the internal conflict is sufficient to dissolve it in the short term. As awareness of this sub-personality and its needs increases, its power to disrupt and undermine starts to dissipate.

During the coaching (individually or in a group) coachees can easily identify half a dozen different sub-personalities and the situations in which each comes to the fore. Of course, through these sub-personalities, we may play out our lives, but they are not who we really are. The coaching work may continue to focus largely on sub-personalities since the ideal is for the coachee to recognize, accept and harmonize them, as one would with a real team of different players or an orchestra – so that they can 'play music together'.

Dis-identification and the I

The transpersonal perspective asserts that we are all 'spiritual beings', that our core is pure spirit. We have a body, we have emotions, we have a mind and an intellect, but in essence we are a soul (or spirit, light, energy). This gives coaches a broader perspective of our coachees and allows us to help them gain a measure of distance from themselves and their problems. As coachees become more familiar with and accepting of their orchestra of sub-personalities, they start to see them more clearly, to be less driven by them, and they are able to feel less identified with them.

It may seem paradoxical but the process of dis-identifying gives us a stronger sense of self. Using a variety of techniques we can help the coachee to move closer to a sense of the essential I, to that sense of 'I am'. This is also described as one's core, one's centre, or essence. Identifying with one's 'I' is immensely freeing; it does not mean abandoning all the colour and interest of sub-personalities, but it does mean gaining a vantage point above the hurly burly and gaining some choice over one's actions. The 'I' is the conductor of the orchestra: it is the conductor who directs the various instruments in their playing and helps them create together a piece of music that is greater than the sum of the parts.

The 'I' is at the centre of the psyche, at the core of our being. It is difficult to describe because it is empty of content. The psychosynthesis definition sometimes used is: the place of pure consciousness and pure will. Here are the qualities we associate with the 'I':

∎ consciousness (awareness);
∎ will (responsibility);
∎ self-managing, self-directing, choice;
∎ free from distortion, restriction;
∎ individuality, identity;
∎ non-judgemental;
∎ stillness, constancy, continuity.

The will

In psychosynthesis the will is given a central part in the psyche paired with its counterpoint energy, love (expressed as awareness, consideration, empathy, care for others, tolerance, etc). Like yin and yang together they form the 'I'. Assagioli (1974) contributed this new understanding of will to counteract the Victorian notion of will-power, which smacked of duty and of 'pulling up your boot straps' and which was rejected fairly completely by the anti-authoritarian youth culture of the 1960s.

But will is essential if we are going to act in the world. It provides motive force, a sense of direction and energy to make things happen. It underpins our ability to live our lives with purpose. At a pragmatic level, will is expressed through responsibility – the choice to take ownership for one's actions; then through the purposeful life and, at the highest level, a sense of being a part of the purposeful universe. The roots of the core coaching concepts of awareness and responsibility (Whitmore, 2004) lie in the rich areas of love and will, which we find at the very heart of the human being.

Two dimensions of development

Our life can be seen as a journey. Figure 8.2 shows how, in our society, for the most part we develop along the lateral axis, maturing psychologically, gaining success in our careers and personal lives. However, many of us will at some point hit a crisis of meaning. This may be triggered by a dramatic event (a redundancy, a personal shock) or a creeping sense of meaninglessness, or by a sense of alienation from the values we once took for granted. This crisis was typically associated with mid-life, but we are now seeing it among many younger people too. It

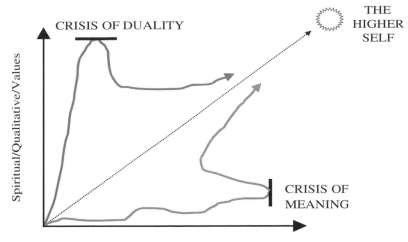

Figure 8.2 Developmental journey

can manifest in a myriad different ways: as depression, a sense of losing one's grip, fits of anger, uncontrollable stress, workaholism, dependency on escapist drugs and activities. The crisis may be sudden or last for years. Helping coachees realize the nature of this crisis, that they are not weak, useless or going mad, and that this is a stage in their life journey is a keynote of transpersonal coaching: it involves helping the coachee find a sense of purpose (Scouller, 2005; Whitmore, 2002). This crisis represents an opportunity for coachees to make a step change in their life, work and performance and we find that working with crises of this nature may precede the individual taking on significant leadership roles.

The vertical axis represents the spiritual development path. Again this may not look overtly 'spiritual' but may characterize those people who, for example, love the creative side of business but hate the compromises and sheer grind often needed to bring projects to fruition. You may recognize this orientation in those who are full of integrity, whose values are admirable, but who are unable to actualize, to pay the bills and keep their lives in a semblance of order; or the 'space cadets' full of marvellous plans but unwilling to get their hands dirty with everyday life. Those who are 'higher sidelining', as we sometimes call it, may at some point hit the crisis of duality. Essentially this is where the gap between the person's idealized vision of how the world should be and the 'crassness' of the world becomes so wide and so painful that a crisis ensues.

Apart from furthering the coach's understanding of the coachee's life journey, one application of this model is to simply present coachees with a paper on which is drawn the two axes and give them some time to draw their own journey to date as they see it. This awareness-raising process will throw up questions such as, 'What triggered this change in direction of your life line?', 'How did this change affect x?', 'What direction do you wish to go in now, and what would you have to do to achieve that?' It will soon become clear to the coachee that steering toward the middle path brings many benefits.

Emerging purpose: pain, crisis and failure

Coaching tends to be viewed in the business world as an action-oriented way of addressing problems. However, the traditional coaching focus on problem solving is based on a deficit model of work as a succession of problems to be dealt with. It presupposes an ideal that we are always trying, unsuccessfully, to reach – the glass is always half-empty. Furthermore it is a very limited model of the human being as destined to just fix what has gone wrong. This can become ultimately dispiriting and energy draining.

As a popular organizational development model, appreciative inquiry has done much to raise understanding that what we give attention, or oxygen, to will grow. Put simply, if we focus on problems, then we will get more of them. If we look for where the positive energy is, the vitality, the spirit, and explore and build on it then this is what will grow, within an individual or within a company.

Transpersonal coaching takes this deeper and proposes that every problem, crisis, moment of failure and pain harbours within it an emergent purpose: a clue to the next step on our journey. This is in no way to make light of the very real distress that people suffer, but on the contrary to experience and move through the situation with a sense of meaning and intention.

Usually when we hit a problem or crisis we react in the following ways: denial, anger, blaming, bargaining, self-pity, resistance, rebellion, paralysis or depression. As a coach we can help our coachees through their crisis by guiding a different process. The transpersonal coach asks the coachee to consider these questions:

∎ What does this mean for me, for us, for the organization?

∎ What needs to change here?

∎ What needs to happen?

∎ What is the next step?

∎ What is trying to emerge or unfold?

∎ What is the bigger picture?

All writers on the transpersonal, since the earliest times, talk about these moments of despair and crisis – at its most extreme, the 'dark night of the soul'. Leadership writer Warren Bennis sees what he terms 'crucible experiences' as the defining moments for stepping into leadership (Bennis and Thomas, 2002). It is the individual's ability to live through and be transformed by the crisis (from base metal to gold as in the alchemist's crucible) that differentiates the leader from the rest.

The key to coming through a time of crisis is how one chooses to perceive the situation: we cannot always change outer circumstances, but we can change our inner response. Acceptance is the point that needs to be reached before transformation can take place (Frankl, 1987; Kubler-Ross, 1969). This is not resignation but a true spiritual act of will, a choice to be in the present with no further striving to change it: eliminating the 'useless acts of rebellion' and 'collaborating with the inevitable', as Assagioli put it. Paradoxically, this is when real change can occur because we cease to be a victim. Energy is channelled, new insights are released and a sense of unity or wholeness is achieved. This imparts a new depth to the individual's character; perhaps a new gravitas, a stronger focus and sense of purpose resulting in a step-change rise in performance.

Guided imagery

Use of imagery is one of the main and most powerful techniques used in transpersonal coaching. More than a technique, it is central to transpersonal work since without imagination there is no empathy and no future: it is only our capacity to imagine the other and to imagine change that creates these. The Israeli novelist, Amos Oz went further in an article in *The Guardian* (3 September 2005). Reflecting on the need for understanding in the world today, he said 'imagining the other is a powerful antidote to fanaticism and hatred . . . It is also, in my view, a major moral imperative.'

Working with imagery directly reflects the language of the unconscious: this is non-rational, weaves stories and pictures, pays little heed to the rules of the 'real' world, relies strongly on intuition, instinct and insight, and experiences time completely differently to clock time. Using imagery, whether through guided visualizations, drawing, producing a symbol for a goal or idea, accesses and cultivates the skills and qualities of the unconscious and super-conscious, the myth-making, story-telling parts of ourselves, thereby developing EQ, SQ and general creativity (Whitmore, 2004).

The decision to use guided imagery must be based on the coach's assessment of the coachee's inner experience and behaviour. A contra-indication for using imagery work would be, for example, where the coachee appears ungrounded or 'flaky', talks in the abstract most of the time without giving specific examples, tends to 'higher sidelining', has an over-active imagination with little or no actualization or will to action. In effect this coachee has a shaky sense of identity and an underdeveloped 'I' (Whitmore, 2004).

There are two principal ways we work with imagery: *evocative* and *directive*. Evocative is the drawing out from the coachees' own uncon-scious an image or symbol to represent and deepen their understanding of a situation and themselves. Working with closed eyes to reduce dis-tractions and direct attention inwards, coachees might be asked to evoke the situation or problem they have just been talking about, see it clearly in detail again in their mind's eye and then at a certain point to allow an image or symbol to emerge for the problem, the other person or for what needs to happen to resolve the issue – whatever is most useful to move the coachee's awareness of the issue forwards.

In directive imagery work we draw on archetypal images to help cultivate a skill, quality or behaviour that the coachee most wants or needs to enhance at this point in his or her journey. Often this is done via a guided visualization.

Imagery always expands awareness; it creates new understanding and meaning. So if you use imagery you need to balance the coachee's new awareness with a focus on responsibility – the ability to respond: the coach will help the coachee integrate the new insights and ground them in action and in the coachee's life. This might look similar to the kind of coaching done in the will section of the GROW model.

TEN KEY QUESTIONS TO GUIDE YOUR WAY

1. What makes your heart sing? What are you passionate about outside work? What brings you joy?

We often use this type of question very early on in the coaching. It helps evoke the positive, enlivening energy of the client, which will feed into the work ahead by sparking the super-conscious. It also sets the tone for the style of coaching, letting coachees know that the coach is interested in their potential and the life-enhancing aspects of their inner world, not just their problems. The choice of out-of-ordinary words such as 'passion', 'joy', 'heart', 'sing' is deliberate and helps the client move out of the box of intellectual, workplace language.

2. What does this sub-personality want? What does he or she need? What benefits or 'gifts' do they bring?

This group of three questions, asked one by one, is always asked when working with sub-personalities. The first brings the most obvious and accessible drive of the sub-personality to awareness, the second asks the coachee to go deeper and understand what the underlying need might be, and the third encourages an appreciation of qualities and skills that this sub-personality gives to the coachee. This last question is especially important as we often identify our most troublesome and least likeable sub-personalities. The urge is to get rid of them, but they will keep sabotaging our best intentions until we understand and value their gifts.

3. How could these two parts of you come to an accommodation with or even cooperate with one another?

Usually a difficult sub-personality is clashing with another, equally insistent character – hence the circular conversations we have in our heads. This question is asked when the work indicated by question 2 has taken place, to encourage the coachee to harmonize and integrate the two within the overall personality. This, like all sub-personality work, is excellent for raising the coachee's awareness of, and skill in dealing with, conflict in his or her team and wider workplace.

4. What do you see when you step back and view the whole?

This encourages the coachee to adopt the observer position, perhaps after sub-personality work or talking through a complex situation involving others in the workplace. It provides fresh insight, and is the first step in dis-identification and towards the 'I'. The coachee will start to experience the stillness, compassion, non-judgemental quality of the 'I' as he or she becomes skilled at dis-identifying from his or her warring sub-personalities or the passions of workplace conflict.

5. What direction do you wish to go in now, and what would you have to do to achieve that?

As coachees begin to conceive of their life as a journey, they come to realize (through sub-personality and other coaching work) that they can make choices and take some control over steering their life course. This question galvanizes the coachees' will and stimulates their creativity in looking at different routes to achieve their choices.

6. What does this mean for me, for us, for the organization?

With transpersonal work we seek to look behind a problem for its meaning and wider implications, rather than dive into solutions. This question also fosters the coachee's ability to be aware of the interface and impacts across three key domains: the self, the immediate environment (team, department, function), and the wider environment (whole organization).

7. What needs to change here? What needs to happen? What is the next step?

Again these questions stimulate the coachees' will, their sense of responsibility, and their active creativity. This is key to moving coachees away from the victim position of, 'It's all their fault' or, 'They got us into this so they can sort it out.'

8. What is trying to emerge or unfold?

A quintessentially transpersonal question, this moves the coachee on from a solution-focused stance to understanding deeper patterns and meaning. The coachee is encouraged by this question to relate the current situation to his or her whole life journey, or to the organization's journey and growth.

9. What is an image or symbol for x?

Since the transpersonal works a great deal with the unconscious, this question aims to bring the insights hidden there to consciousness so they can enrich the coachee's understanding. Images have an essential force, they have power and they have extraordinary longevity. People can remember scenes and objects and people's faces from their earliest past quite vividly today – and the emotions associated with that time, place or person come flooding back just as sharply. It is the same with new images and symbols. These can provide the coachee with a kind of personal talisman that he or she can subsequently evoke at will when needed, and draw on the required feeling, energy, thoughts and physical sensations encapsulated by the symbol.

10. What is the bigger picture?

Finally, the transpersonal sees the individual as part of the whole, the micro within the macro, the interconnectedness of everything. This question encourages expanded thinking at all levels. It asks the coachee to imagine beyond his or her issue or problem to what this might reflect of the team, of the organization and the wider marketplace, both national and global and beyond. It encourages the coachee to tap into his or her higher self and thereby into the collective unconscious.

SUMMARY

From the egg diagram you will recognize by now that most regular coaching takes place in the middle unconscious realm, where the coach takes coachees deeper than their normal field of awareness into their partially unconscious mind, but generally using rational, cognitive methods.

You will also have recognized that a transpersonal perspective of the coachee and the issue might give better results even at this level of coaching. It is clear also that there is a whole new realm that the coachee can explore with the help of a transpersonal coach – the area known as the super-conscious where access to our higher qualities, creativity, aspiration, inspiration, peak experience and our meaning and purpose can be found.

When we are working transpersonally we are working with what the Greeks called 'entelechy': the dynamic propulsion to be all that we can be. Coaching in this wider context is highly rewarding for both parties and may give the coach a deep sense of fulfilment through assisting another person on their journey.

References

Assagioli, R (1974) *The Act of Will: A guide to self actualisation and self-realisation,* Turnstone Press, Wellingborough

Bennis, W and Thomas, R (2002) *Geeks and Geezers: How era, values and defining moments shape leaders,* Harvard Business School Press, Harvard

Dalai Lama, His Holiness the and Cutler, H (1998) *The Art of Happiness: A handbook for living,* Hodder and Stoughton, London

Ferrucci, P (1982) *What We May Be: The visions and techniques of psychosynthesis,* Turnstone Press, Wellingborough

Frankl, V (1987) *Man's Search for Meaning,* Hodder and Stoughton, London

Gallwey, T (1974) *The Inner Game of Tennis,* Random House, New York

Goleman, D (1995) *Emotional Intelligence,* Bloomsbury Press, London

Hardy, J (1987) *A Psychology with a Soul: Psychosynthesis in evolutionary context,* Routledge and Kegan Paul, London

Jaworski, J (1998) *Synchronicity: The inner path of leadership,* Berrett-Koehler, San Francisco, CA

Kubler-Ross, E (1969) *On Death and Dying,* Scribner, New York

McBeath, B and Wynne, D (1985) Integrating Systems in Psychosynthesis: Applications to Work with Families, Groups and Organisations, in (eds) J Weiser and T Yeomans, *Readings in Psychosynthesis: Theory, process and practice,* Department of Applied Psychology, The Ontario Institute for Studies in Education, Toronto

Scouller, J (2005) The Challenge of Coaching to Evoke a Sense of Purpose, MSc paper. MSc in Coaching and Development, Department of Business Studies, University of Portsmouth

Senge, P, Scharmer, C O, Jaworski, J and Flowers, B S (2004) *Presence: Human purpose and the field of the future,* SoL publishing, Cambridge, MA

Whitmore, D (2004) *Psychosynthesis Counselling in Action,* 3rd edn, Sage Publications, London

Whitmore, J (2002) *Coaching for Performance,* 3rd edn, Nicholas Brealey Publishing, London

Zohar, D and Marshall, I (2004) *Spiritual Capital: Wealth we can live by,* Bloomsbury, London

9

Integrative coaching

Jonathan Passmore

THE INTEGRATIVE COACHING MODEL EXPLAINED

Previous chapters in this book have offered frameworks based on single models. These models are often derived from psychological schools of thinking such as behaviourism (GROW) and cognitive psychology (cognitive behavioural coaching) or from theories of human behaviour and behavioural change (NLP and solution-focused). The integrative model seeks to depart from this approach. It offers a model that has been designed exclusively for executive coaching.

The integrative model consists of six streams that flow together to form an integrated model for use by the coach. The first two of the streams work collectively and are concerned with the formation and the maintenance of the relationship between the coach and coachee. The next four streams are the focus of the work between the coach and coachee. They are concerned with the coachees' behaviour, their conscious thought, their unconscious thoughts and environment. While working in each of these three streams, the coach maintains attention on the relationship and works

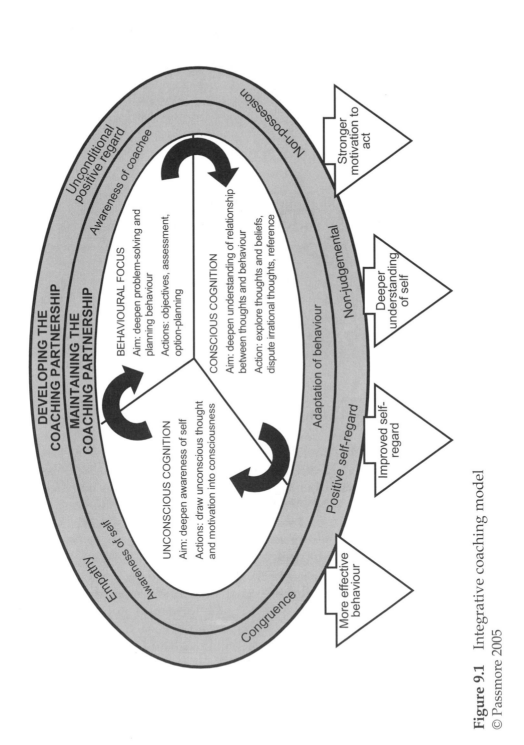

Figure 9.1 Integrative coaching model
© Passmore 2005

to sustain the relationship without which progress cannot be made. The final stream is systemic. An overview of the model is provided in Figure 9.1.

Streams 1 and 2. The coaching partnership

Before any coaching to enhance performance can begin the coach needs to build a working relationship with the coachee. It is this work that I have called stream 1 (developing the relationship). The potentially close and affirming relationship of coaching demands mutual respect and trust. To create these, the coach needs to invest in the relationship. However, once established this work on the relationship cannot stop, although less effort may be needed. It is at this point the coach moves into stream 2 (maintaining the relationship).

What makes the key ingredients to create an effective working relationship? This question has in part already been answered by writers within the counselling tradition, such as Carl Rogers (1961). Rogers suggested that a series of elements need to be in place for a successful 'therapeutic alliance' to be formed. These relationship elements are of importance to any work with individuals in the consulting world. However, the one-to-one nature of coaching demands a stronger investment in the relationship by the coach than training or consulting.

During the first and possibly the second coaching session the coachee is evaluating the coach: Do I trust them? Do I like them? Do I value what they are offering me? If the coachee reaches a conclusion that he or she does trust, like and value the coach, the real work can start. However, if coachees reach the conclusion that they do not trust or respect the coach, it is unlikely they will reveal much during coaching, even though coaching may continue, at least over an initially agreed set of sessions. If they don't like the coach, the relationship is most likely to come to an end.

Roger's six conditions provide an excellent starting point to help in the formation of a coaching partnership:

1. The first of these six elements Rogers called 'positive self-regard'. This is the coach's belief that he or she is able to work constructively in an adult relationship with another person. This may be typified by the 'I'm ok', part of the transactional analysis (TA) model (I'm ok, you're ok). A belief, that he or she, the coach, is a worthwhile and valuable person.

2. The second feature is 'unconditional positive regard' by the coach of the coachee. It is an acceptance of him or her as a whole person. This can be regarded as the 'you're ok' part of transactional analysis. It is

a belief that the coachee is a good person, even if the coach may disagree with or dislike aspects of the coachee's behaviour or values.

3. The third element is empathy. This is the ability of the coach to show understanding of the coachee's situation; 'to see their world, as if it was our own'.

4. The fourth element is the establishment and maintenance of a non-judgemental mind. This means the coach is slow to judge. If judgements are made these are restricted to behaviours outside of society's norms, such as murder. However, the person is never judged and categorized. An example of this is to challenge the behaviour of a murderer, but continue to value the person.

5. The fifth element is congruence. This is the idea that the coach should openly express what he or she feels. The coach, if angry, should appropriately express this anger with the coachee, in a way that is helpful to him or her, rather than pretend he or she is happy. The key aspect in this is to reveal material for the benefit of the coachee, rather than to satisfy the needs or desire of the coach.

6. The final element that supports the development of a coaching partnership is non-possessive warmth. This is the idea that the coach views the coachee as a capable person, who knows the solution to his or her own problem. The role of the coach is to act as a guide, helping them along a path until they discover this solution for themselves. This ability to maintain a non-possessive relationship means the coach can be free from responsibility for the executive's actions. The coach is neither a 'super-hero' if the coachee succeeds, nor a 'villain' if the coachee fails.

The result of these elements is the development of an appropriate, warm, trusting and open relationship, a relationship in which the coachee is able to share the full truth of his or her perception and feels accepted rather than judged. It is a relationship where coachees accept responsibility for their success. It is also a relationship in which the coach is able to gradually increase the level of personal challenge without devaluing the affirming nature of the relationship.

Once a relationship has been formed the role of the coach is to maintain this relationship. The maintenance of the relationship is the second stream, and flows on directly from the work of building the relationship.

To maintain the relationship an effective coach needs to pay attention to three further aspects: their own emotions and behaviours, the emotions and behaviours of the coachee, and to manage their emotions and adapt their behavioural responses appropriately to remain professionally detached while offering personal intimacy. These components make up the building blocks of emotional intelligence (Caruso and Salovey, 2004; Stein and Book, 2000).

In addition to emotional intelligence, the highly effective coach also needs to consider transference and counter-transference issues. These aspects are of particular importance in the executive boardroom where power and role modelling are key features. However, these aspects can be relevant to the close working relationship between any coach and coachee.

These two streams, building and maintaining the relationship, form a ring around the four remaining streams. Without this coaching partnership the coach is unable to begin to work in the three streams that will facilitate change.

Stream 3. Behavioural focus

The third and most popular stream in which the coach works is that of behavioural coaching. Whatever the coach's theoretical orientation, a focus on external behaviour and how this is developed is a central feature of almost all coaching relationships.

The popularity of behaviourism is rooted in the 1920s, with the work of Pavlov (1927). Pavlov uncovered the concept of conditioned reflex: a response to a situation that is an adaptation to environmental conditions. While human motivation is more complex and broader than that of other species, the use of appropriate rewards or punishments are still common features within the workplace.

This view informed much of subsequent management writing during the pre-and post-war period, with a belief that, with an appropriate stimulus, behavioural change could be brought about. Much of management writing has not acknowledged its behavioural basis, but in management today performance-related pay, performance management, goal setting and the use of competency frameworks all have links back to behavioural thinking.

In the 1970s, the work of Bandura (1969) took thinking into a new arena by adding social learning to the mix of stimulus-response models. Bandura argued that learning can take place not only in person, but also by observing others' successes and failures. The use of role models in organization, as well as mentoring schemes, provides further support of the extent of behaviourist thinking.

Perhaps the most interesting concept identified by Bandura was self-efficacy: a person's belief in their own abilities. The concept is based on a self-perception; how well the individual believes they perform a task. Bandura (1977) argued that people with high self-efficacy perform better, as they are able to persevere longer without corresponding increases in stress. Subsequent research (Gist and Mitchell, 1992; Locke and Latham, 1990) has shown a strong relationship between high self-efficacy and high work performance. Also key to performance is the use of goals as a focus for measuring behavioural output and for rewarding success.

The development of these behavioural concepts has contributed considerably to our thinking and practice in management, human learning and, more recently, executive coaching. The most popular example is the ubiquitous GROW model. The model initially developed by Alexander (Alexander and Renshaw, 2005) has been popularized by many coaching writers (Whitmore, 2002), and is used in many of the blue chip institutions as their own in-house coaching model.

GROW is a four-step coaching model, and has traditionally been viewed as a non-psychological model, suitable for coaches without psychological training. The coach adopts a Socratic learning style, using open questions to help the coachee move through the four steps. It aims to help coachees achieve enhanced performance or a stated goal.

The first of the steps is the identification of a goal. The second is a review of the current reality, the third a consideration of options, and the fourth a conclusion and the agreement on a way forward. There is considerable debate about the nature of goals, and is covered in more detail elsewhere (Passmore, 2003).

While rejected by some coaching psychologists as a non-psychological model, GROW is a simple and useful tool that can easily be taught to coachees during the coaching process. More sophisticated behavioural models have been developed that complement the essence of GROW (Passmore, 2005; Skeffington and Zeus, 2003). These add elements such as explicit statements about contracting; the ground rules of the coach-coachee relationship; and the more legal contractor aspects of times and fees; or have been developed for the coaching manager.

The behavioural approach is of greatest value at the start of a relationship. However, adopting a single methodology limits the coach's ability to facilitate change. Around half of coaching interventions stay in this stream, once a 'coaching partnership' has been established. As experience grows, either through participation in training events or through intuitive awareness, the more experienced coach broadens his or her approach.

Stream 4. Conscious cognition

The effective coach, having established the relationship and explored behaviours, is able to explore the cognitive patterns that sit behind the visible behaviours. In this stream the coach will typically draw upon cognitive behavioural techniques, initially developed by Beck (1991) and Ellis (1998) but refined by coaches (Neenan and Dryden, 2001; Peltier, 2001) to make them more suitable for the work of the coach than the counsellor.

Cognitive-based counselling interventions have grown significantly in popularity in the UK, and are now the most popular approach within government-funded counselling services. While this popularity has yet to extend to coaching, the growth in coaching training suggests that cognitive behavioural approaches will become the most popular approach used by experienced coaches.

In the integrative model, coaches would typically begin to explore thought patterns when they judged that the coachee was displaying or holding irrational thoughts that might inhibit successful performance, and they have already explored behavioural-based solutions. Such irrational thoughts might be harsh judgements about themselves as coachee or judgements of their current or future abilities. The key feature is that the judgement is irrational, that is, it is not substantiated by facts. One danger is that irrational is confused with 'negative'. So the coach seeks to help the coachee challenge all negative views or perspectives. This is not CBC. Such an approach, if always looking on the sunny side, is naïve and lacks any evidence of being an effective intervention.

Working in this stream shares many of the principles that are applied to the other five streams: a dynamic process where both the coach and the coachee are constantly changing, a collaborative process between the coach and coachee, a focus on solutions and particularly on an agreed goal, an emphasis on the present, and a desire to use the process to give the coachee the ability to act independently in the future. Each of these principles is important to maintaining the working relationship and using coaching in a way that builds the coachee's ability to become a self-sustaining learner rather than increases his or her dependence on the coach.

The central concept within this stream is encouraging coachees to identify the irrational beliefs and then help them to challenge these. This two-stage process is supported through the diverse range of cognitive behavioural and rational emotive behavioural techniques used within counselling. However, these need to be grounded within the appropriate context or focus of the coaching relationship. Michael Neenan provides some excellent examples of tools in his chapter, and a few of these are described below in 'Tools and techniques'. It is recognized that many of these techniques can be used equally successfully in the fourth stream.

Stream 5. Unconscious cognition

For some people the fifth stream has echoes of the psychodynamic tradition because of its explicit 'unconscious' label. This is deliberate, and reflects both a belief that unconscious thoughts influence our daily lives and behaviours, and that elements of the psychodynamic tradition can help the coach address these issues. However, this positive start also carries with it a warning. While many of the psychodynamic techniques may work well in the counselling room, they lack face validity for work with coachees, and are less appropriate for the short and more focused work of coaching.

A second technique that can be drawn upon is EMDR (Eye Movement Desensitization and Reprocessing), which can be a valuable intervention to explore unconscious thoughts, particularly involving traumatic stress (Passmore and Pena, 2005). EMDR has to date been primarily used in the treatment of post-traumatic stress disorder. (Further details of this approach are given in Chapter 11.) Given the limited space in this chapter, the focus is on exploring unconscious aspects of motivation, drawing on motivational interviewing (Miller and Rollnick, 2002).

Motivational interview (MI) is a technique that has been developed in addiction counselling to help address low motivation to change. The approach helps the counselling client bring into conscious awareness the consequences of his or her behaviours and thus stimulates a stronger motivation to act. For coaches, MI offers an additional tool that is particularly useful where the coachee is resistant to change, but is unclear why initial efforts to change stall before they take off.

As with humanistic, behavioural and cognitive streams within the integrative coaching model, MI has a track record of evidence-based application. This ranges from alcohol and substance abuse counselling (Burke *et al*, 2003; Miller and Moyers, 2002; Solomon and Fioritti, 2002) through management of chronic illness (Channon *et al*, 2003; Prochaska and Zinman, 2003) to working with teenage contraception counselling (Cowley *et al*, 2002). Despite this track record, the use of MI in the coaching sphere to date appears to be limited (Passmore and Tinwell, in press).

The MI approach requires the coach to recognize and understand ambivalence as a natural part of the change process (Miller and

Rollnick, 2002) and to move from using cognitive grounded questions to explore beliefs and thinking patterns. A starting point for the coach is identifying which stage the coachee is at in his or her personal change journey. To identify this, the coach could ask the coachee to rate his or her perceived readiness to change on a scale of 0 to 10, with 10 being that he or she has already made the change, and 0 being not at all interested in changing.

Change continuum

The coach then works with the coachee to help build arguments for change. Traditionally, in managing change the coach might offer counter-arguments that support change, effectively arguing against the coachee. MI takes a different perspective of change. It seeks to work alongside the person, to help him or her to more fully understand the consequences and benefits of his or her actions. In this sense it draws on aspects of rational thinking. One model for doing this, the balance sheet, is included below in 'Tools and techniques'.

As fits our overall integrative coaching model, there is a strongly collaborative approach, with the coach being an ally of the coachee, rather than being an expert into whose hands the coachee casts his or her troubles, or an authority issuing advice.

I would most typically step into the unconscious cognition stream where the coachee has been referred by others concerned about his or her work performance, or when the behaviours are having a significant impact on others and which the coachee feels pressure from others to address, although he or she may unconsciously be resistant to. Unlike the other streams, the coach working in this stream requires advanced skills and specialist training beyond what is offered on most coaching programmes.

0 Not interested in making a change	10 Changes already made

Figure 9.2 Change continuum

Stream 6. Systemic

The last and final stream that the coach works within is the environment and cultural context. This is the system that the individual coach and coachee work within. In some respects this stream captures and surrounds all of the preceding streams.

The coach may work simultaneously in this stream and in one of the three action streams of behavioural, conscious cognition or unconscious cognition. In this stream the task for the coach is to help coachees to understand the wider system within which they work, and how this system influences their behaviour and the behaviour of others they work with, including the coach. In this level the coach seeks to bring these individuals into the coaching room. These may be individuals who the coach works alongside, such as members of the team; it may be individuals from suppliers or customer organizations; it may include individuals and organizations from the wider environment that create legislation or influence the way work is conducted or people behave.

As well as helping the coachee to draw upon the influences of these individuals, the coach needs to make explicit their influence, as the coach too is part of this wider system.

WHEN DOES INTEGRATIVE COACHING WORK BEST?

It can be argued that the integrative model has almost universal application within the coaching environment. However, it is particularly suited to executive coaching and sports coaching. Its suitability for use in other areas of coaching such as health and life coaching is due largely to its use of a wide range of elements from other coaching traditions. The approach pays attention to the coachee's need to form a relationship. Without a relationship there is likely to be little progress in coaching.

Integrative coaching acknowledges that most people are, at least initially, drawn to coaching to be different. This difference may be being more successful at work or more successful in forming relationships. For some it may be about developing and refining a skill, or stopping a habit they have developed. In most cases this 'being different' involves behaving differently. The approach's use of behavioural elements enables it to contribute towards this behavioural goal.

Coachees, however, sometimes want something more. They recognize that their ineffective thinking or 'negative thoughts' get in the way of them succeeding. By addressing thinking styles, with a focus on developing more rational thinking, the model too can meet these needs.

For the most experienced coaches there is a recognition that addressing behaviour and thinking style is not always enough. To achieve the outcomes the coachee wants, the coach also needs to work at an unconscious level, sometimes with thinking styles, thoughts and beliefs that are outside of conscious awareness, and sometimes with motivation. In these cases the coach needs to help deepen self-awareness. The integrative model recognizes the role of the unconscious and seeks to integrate this into its pattern of working through drawing on elements from within the psychodynamic and motivational interviewing.

It may begin to feel as if integrative coaching is a magic bullet, a one-shot solution. The reality is that as an integrated approach it takes what works best for coaching from a series of previously evidenced-based approaches and blends them together. Arguably most experienced coaches probably do this already, and the model simply describes what they are doing.

The integrative model has its areas of weakness. These are inherent from its development within the executive coaching arena. The first of these weaknesses is that the model lacks a spiritual dimension. The desire to deepen one's spiritual self is a healthy and arguably central aspect to life. Where this is an explicit goal of the coachee, the coach is best to work with models such as the transpersonal model.

A second weakness of the model is that it assumes that behavioural change is what is being sought. Again, this is an outcome of its executive coaching focus. However, if the coachee is seeking a more general model to explore his or her experience of life and the future, a humanistic framework could arguable serve exclusively as a tool to achieve this objective.

TOOLS AND TECHNIQUES

The integrative model as described draws on tools and techniques from a range of approaches including behavioural, cognitive behavioural, psychodynamic and motivational interviewing approaches. In this section some suggestions are made for each stream: building and maintaining the partnership, engaging in behavioural change, developing performance enhancing thinking and deepening self-awareness.

In each case, the reader may wish to review the chapters such as GROW (behavioural), cognitive behavioural coaching and stress coaching where more detailed examples illustrate the techniques within these models. This section provides more of an overview for each area.

The first of these is the process of developing and maintaining the relationship. Here the coach is concerned with the relationship. A key tool at this stage is to set out the ground rules. In doing this the coach helps the coachee understand what is 'in' and what is 'outside' of the coaching relationship. It sets out the conditions for confidentiality: largely everything is confidential with the exception of risk of self-harm and illegal activities where the coach has a duty to protect others. The ground rules also provide an opportunity for the coach to set out his or her credentials, providing reassurance to the coachee that the coach is a competent and reliable person. A second technique to help build the relationship is to provide space for the coachee to talk at length during the early period of the first session. This opportunity for the coachee to tell his or her story is not primarily to gather information, but to listen and show the coach values what the coachee has to say. In listening, the coach may be summarizing and reflecting back to check understanding. Once the relationship has been built, the coach needs to continue to invest in it. However, the investment is contingent upon their coachee's needs. This draws the coach to deploy emotional intelligent responses.

The second set of techniques is within the behavioural focus stream. While there is a range of models, the GROW model offers a four-stage process. The coach encourages the coachee to set a clear SMART goal, which can be more difficult than first thought (Passmore, 2003). Once established, the coach works to help gather evidence on current performance. A useful technique for doing this would be to ask the coachee to bring or review behaviour evidence from colleagues and peers. A 360-degree competency questionnaire is an excellent tool for doing this. Outside of the workplace, the coach may ask the coachee to go and talk to others about how he or she is perceived, either generally or in relationship to the skills or behaviour and its impact on others. This development of a holistic picture provides the coachee with stronger evidence of his or her current reality than a personal perspective.

Another technique in the behavioural focus stream is to help the coachee to get specific on his or her action plan. Typically the coachee offers a vague action plan, with little regard to when, how or what gets in the way. The use of effective and robust challenge at this stage will help the coachee to make the goal real.

The third set of techniques is within the cognitive stream. Typical techniques in this stream include reframing, emersion, visualization and the use of homework tasks to support activities within the coaching process. In reframing, the coach engages in a process of moving the coachee from a view of the world that lacks rational evidence to one that is based on evidence. Questions might include: 'How would your boss, mentor or colleague view this situation?', 'How might Ghandi tackle this problem if you asked him?', 'What other possible outcomes are there?', 'How likely is each of the possible outcomes?'

A second approach is the use of emersion. This technique is used in counselling as a way to gradually overcome irrational fears. This is in contrast to flooding, which is a rapid and immediate process of encounter. To illustrate the contrast between the two, emersion is gradually getting into the pool from the shallow end, flooding is jumping in the deep end. While flooding is generally to be avoided, emersion can help the coachee to test his or her new behaviours or skills gradually.

Visualization is a technique that is commonly used in sports coaching. References to it are pervasive throughout sport, such as Daley Thompson's visualization for a quick start, leaving the starting blocks at the 'b' of the bang. These examples help the coach to improve the face validity of this technique for the coachee. One area in which visualization can be of real value for the coach is helping coachees visualize the task they have set themselves, and particularly to identify potential barriers, and them overcoming these barriers.

The last example of techniques from the cognitive stream is the use of homework. While in other streams I would encourage the coachees to reflect on the session, and maybe to practise new behaviours, in this stream the homework task is a useful component. This may be encouraging coachees to monitor their automatic thoughts. An alternative is to ask coachees to practise the skill or activity in a controlled way, so using emersion, and at the next session reviewing its impact or the feedback that they have received.

The final selection of techniques is from the unconscious cognitive stream. In this stream the coach may encourage the coachee to examine patterns. This may involve patterns of working over many jobs, and even patterns of behaviour back to childhood. The assumption is that such patterns may reveal unconscious processes about beliefs or thoughts.

A second way within the unconscious cognitive stream is to explore these patterns and their meaning. One technique is to use a metaphor for exploring the mind, such as the technique of the old house. In this technique the coach may ask the coachee to visualize an old house in which he or she lives, and like most of us, store stuff in the loft or cellar. In this house, however, there are a series of rooms in the loft. The idea is that the coach helps the coachee through the visualization to explore deeper into past events, stored in these rooms.

The third technique is drawn from motivational interviewing. This is the use of the balance sheet (see Figure 9.3). The balance sheet can help

Benefits of activity	Costs of activity	Benefits of change	Costs of change

Figure 9.3 Coaching for change balance sheet

coachees explore their motivation for change by listing the benefits and costs of the two options they are evaluating. One option may be to stay as they are; a second option would be for change. The aim of the coach is to help coachees to build up stronger benefits for change, where the current behaviour is destructive or damaging to them or others. The coachee, when evaluating the costs and benefits may only have identified the immediate benefits to him or her of the behaviour, and tends to ignore or minimize the impact of his or her behaviour on others. By bringing these elements into active consideration the coachee can begin to reflect consciously on a wider range of costs and benefits.

TEN KEY QUESTIONS TO GUIDE YOUR WAY

The first four questions are based within the behavioural focus stream, questions 5 to 7 are questions from the cognitive stream, and 8 to 10 from the unconscious cognitive stream.

1. What do you want to achieve?

This is a typical question for use within the behavioural GROW model. The aim of the question is to help the coachee to explicitly state his or her goal. Frequently less experienced coaches take at face value the first statement and move on, and thus need to return at a later stage to this. More experienced coaches recognize that time spent at this stage exploring the features of the goal, will save time later.

2. What is happening?

This question aims to help the coach and coachee gather evidence on what is the current situation. How close or far is the coachee from his or her goal? In gathering evidence, the less experienced coach can be tempted to accept at face value what the coachee provides as evidence. It is wise for the coach to challenge initial claims, and seek third-party evidence for these. A 360-degree questionnaire, psychometric questionnaire and appraisal feedback all provide such evidence, and help ensure that the coach and coachee are working with a rounded view, not a single perspective, whether this is the coachee's or their manager's.

3. What options do you think there are?

Exploring options is a valuable process in all coaching, if there is a belief that the coachee already has the answer to his or her own question. Reviewing options is a two-part process. The coachee needs to be clear what criteria he or she is evaluating the options against. As a result the coachee needs to generate the criteria first, before he or she can start a process of generating or evaluating options.

4. Can you summarize what you going to do and by when?

This question is concerned with action planning when working in the behavioural focus stream. The question encourages coachees to take responsibility for reviewing their process, summarizing what has been discussed and to formally state what they intend to do. This is a useful question to ask towards the end of a coaching session, even if the coach has been working with cognitive and unconscious cognitive aspects. The coach may then encourage the coachee to document this, and develop an action plan that includes a series of sub-goals or steps that take him or her to this goal over the coming week, month or year.

5. How would your boss, mentor or colleague see this situation?

This question encourages the coachee to begin to explore the issue or challenge that he or she faces from a number of different perspectives. Often an issue looks to be an insurmountable problem to us, but when considered from the perspective of another person, either solutions can be found or a deeper understanding of the issue gained. A parallel type question is asking the coachee to consider the challenge as if he or she were a famous person. For a management issue, the coach may ask the coachee to consider how Richard Branson would deal with the problem, followed by a question on how Ronald Reagan would deal with the challenge. For a relationship issue, the coach might select two different characters offering different perspectives: Marilyn Monroe and Nelson Mandela. Initially the coachee typically provides a short or flippant remark, but the coach needs to focus the coachee's response and ensure that he or she fully explores the issue and provides a what, where and when descriptive answer.

6. I would like you to close your eyes and describe to me what would happen if the event went perfectly

This visualization technique gets coachees to engage with a visualization and explore what they see and, with follow up questions, what they feel, smell and think. Evidence has shown in the sports psychology arena that visualization not only builds self-confidence but also creates physical changes in the brain structure that aid subsequent muscle movement and thus enhance performance.

7. Can you summarize for me the task that you will try out before we meet again?

The summarizing task that has already been discussed is applied in this context to focus the attention of the coachee on a homework task. The use of the task provides an opportunity for emersion: gradual exposure to the challenging behaviour. Follow up questions might be, 'What would stop you achieving this?', 'What could you do to overcome these barriers?' These questions enable the coachee to prepare for the real world of competing priorities and stakeholders who may need to be persuaded.

8. Tell me about a time when you have felt a similar feeling before

This may be a useful question to explore patterns. Preceding the question the coach will have encouraged coachees to talk about the current issue or problem, and in particular to draw out the feelings within their body which they experience. Using these bodily sensations the coach may then ask the pattern question that may help coachees to identify similar events, but to access these from bodily feelings rather than events.

9. How would others, such as your partner or family, be affected?

This question within motivational interviewing is drawn from work around the balance sheet. The coach may be exploring with coachees the costs and benefits of their behaviour. Coachees can underestimate the effect of their behaviour on others, and thus fail to include this in the calculation. The coach can focus the coachee's attention on this through the question and often build up the costs side of the equation for the coachee.

10. How ready do you feel you are to change on a scale of 1 to 10; where 10 is that you have already made the change, and 0 that you are not at all interested in changing?

This question refers to the motivational interviewing approach. This is a complex technique and suggests that the developing coach would benefit from training before making use of the technique. However, questions such as this provide clues to whether the coachee is likely to change, or if he or she needs more help to explore the benefits of changing. A low score of 1 to 7 would suggest that focusing on change tools would be a wasted effort; instead the coach needs to invest time exploring motivation and helping the coachee to develop the intrinsic motivation to change.

SUMMARY

Integrative coaching offers coaches a new model. It blends evidence-based practice from a range of disciplines to create a set of interventions. The coach's role is to select the intervention that best fits the challenges presented by the coachee.

References

Alexander, G and Renshaw, B (2005) *Supercoaching*, Random House, London

Bandura, A (1969) *Principles of Behaviour Modification*, Holt, Reinhart and Winston, New York

Bandura, A (1977) Self-efficacy: towards a unifying theory of behaviour change, *Psychological Review*, **84**, pp 191–215

Beck, A (1991) *Cognitive Therapy of Depression*, Guildford Press, New York

Burke, B L, Arkowitz, I I and Menchola, M (2003) The efficacy of motivational interviewing: a meta analysis of controlled clinical trials, *Journal of Consulting Clinical Psychology*, **71**, pp 843–61

Caruso, D and Salovey, P (2004) *The Emotionally Intelligent Manager: How to develop and use the four key emotional skills of leadership*, Jossey-Bass, San Francisco, CA

Channon, S, Smith, V J, and Gregory, J W (2003) A pilot study of motivational interviewing in adolescents with diabetes, *Archives of Disease in Childhood*, **88** (8), pp 680–83

Cowley, C B, Farley, T and Beamis, K (2002) 'Well, maybe I'll try the pill for just a few months'. . . . Brief motivational and narrative-based interventions to encourage contraceptive use among adolescents at high risk for early childbearing, *Families, Systems and Health*, **20**, pp 183

Ellis, A (1998) *The Practice of Rational Emotive Behavioural Therapy*, Free Association Books, London

Gist, M and Mitchell, T (1992) Self-efficacy: a theoretical analysis of its determinism and malleability, *Academy of Management Review*, **17**, (2), pp 183–211

Locke, E and Latham, G (1990) *A Theory of Goal Setting and Task Performance*, Prentice Hall, Englewood Cliffs, NJ

Miller, J H and Moyers, T (2002) Motivational interviewing in substance abuse: applications for occupational medicine, *Occupational Medicine*, **17** (1), pp 51–65

Miller, W R and Rollnick, S (2002) *Motivational Interviewing: Preparing people for change*, 2nd edn, Guilford Press, New York

Neenan, M and Dryden, W (2001) *Life Coaching: A cognitive behavioural approach*, Brunner-Routledge, London

Passmore, J (2003) Goal-focused coaching, *The Occupational Psychologist*, August

Passmore, J (2005) The heart of coaching, *The Coaching Psychologist*, Winter

Passmore, J and Pena, A (2005) How to manage trauma, *People Management*, 28 July pp 42–45

Passmore, J and Tinwell, C (in press) in (eds) S Palmer and A Whybrow, *The Handbook of Coaching Psychology*, Brunner-Routledge, London

Pavlov, I (1927) *Conditioned Reflexes*, Oxford University Press, Oxford

Peltier, B (2001) *The Psychology of Executive Coaching: Theory and application*, Brunner-Routledge, London

Prochaska, J O and Zinman, B (2003) Changes in diabetes self care behaviours make a difference in glycemic control: the Diabetes Stages of Change (DISC) study', *Diabetes Care*, **26**, pp 732–37

Rogers, C (1961) *On Becoming a Person*, Houghton Mifflin, Boston, MA

Skeffington, S and Zeus, P (2003) *Behavioural Coaching: How to build sustainable personal and organizational strength*, McGraw Hill, New York

Solomon, J and Fioritti, A (2002) Motivational intervention as applied to systems change: the case of dual diagnosis, *Substance Use and Misuse*, **37** (14), pp 1833–51

Stein, S and Book, H (2000) *The EQ edge: Emotional intelligence and your success*, MHS, Toronto

Whitmore, J (2002) '*Coaching for Performance: Growing people, performance and purpose*', Nicholas Brealey Publishing, London

10

Intercultural coaching

Philippe Rosinski and Geoffrey Abbott

INTEGRATING CULTURE INTO COACHING

We see culture as an important influence in all coaching relationships. Sometimes the influence is obvious, sometimes it is subtle – but it is always influential. By exploring the way culture might be influencing thoughts, feelings and behaviours in the different contexts of their coaches, coaches can utilize culture as a powerful force of change and development. We therefore see the consideration of culture as a virtual necessity in any high-impact coaching programme. Culture provides opportunity. We believe that coaching as a profession has not taken advantage of this opportunity. It is almost as though there is an underlying assumption that culture is an obstacle to be overcome, or that culture is not a factor.

Our experience is that a 'culture as opportunity' perspective can enhance the impact of any coaching intervention. We define coaching as the art of facilitating the unleashing of people's potential to reach meaningful, important objectives (Rosinski, 2003a). Intercultural coaching is the decision to recognize the possibilities of utilizing culture as a force of change to unleash coachee potential. Culture is always there as an influence; it is more a matter of how much attention we choose to give it. Intercultural coaching can bring to the surface issues and assumptions related to culture and harness them in unleashing coachee potential and facilitating positive change. This chapter highlights the benefits of leveraging differences that may be culturally based, rather than treating them as barriers, threats or irrelevancies.

Rosinski (2003a: 20) provides a working definition of culture as follows: 'A group's culture is the set of unique characteristics that distinguishes its members from another group.' Hall (1989: 17) describes culture as humankind's medium, and comments:

> there is not one aspect of human life that is not touched and altered by culture. This means personality, how people express themselves (including shows of emotion), the way they think, how they move, how problems are solved, how their cities are planned and laid out, how transportation systems function and are organized, as well as how economic and government systems are put together and function.

We underestimate the influence of culture at our peril.

Our work in intercultural coaching is based on extensive research that reveals differences between people due to culture, which result in people seeing the world from different perspectives. Much of this research has been done at the level of national culture (eg Hofstede, 1980; Schwartz, 1999; Trompenaars and Hampden-Turner, 1998). However, groups of all kinds have cultures. Groups originate from various categories, including geography, religion, profession, organization, social life, gender, sexual orientation, etc. Our individual *identities* can be viewed as a personal and dynamic synthesis of the cultures of the multiple groups to which we belong.

Caution is required when making generalizations about culture. It is very easy to fall into unhelpful or negative stereotyping. The inherent paradox is that knowledge of cultural preferences and dimensions can provide invaluable insights about a group, yet careless use of such knowledge can be misleading and destructive. Wars, natural disasters, globalization, etc have meant that many societies are multicultural and multiracial. Cultural diversity (of many kinds) within national boundaries means that there is often considerable variation in style among people from one country. Australia, for example, is a culturally diverse society with many people exhibiting cultural characteristics more typical of their homeland than of any statistical norm for the country. At the same time, it is useful to know that there are certain ways that many

Australian companies tend to do business. Generalization can provide insights, but we need to tread carefully. The same need for informed caution holds when considering work areas and organizational cultures where variation also occurs within groups as well as across them. There are individual personality differences that are based on genetic factors, and individuals are influenced by multiple cultural influences (such as when the parents are from different countries or religions).

Cultural influences are often subtle and operate beneath the surface, and people may have little awareness of the characteristics of various group cultures to which they are connected. They can therefore be oblivious of the influence culture may be having on their thoughts, behaviours and emotions. In organizations, often it is the outsider (such as the consultant, the coach, or the new employee) who can see the patterns and forces of culture at work. The people who are immersed in organizational culture, shape it, and are shaped by it may find it hard to define and virtually invisible. Trompenaars suggests that 'Culture is like gravity: you do not experience it until you jump six feet into the air' (Trompenaars and Hampden-Turner, 1998: 5).

To see how culture influences us, we need to create a little distance from our situation – to see ourselves 'in context' as others might see us. Similarly, to understand how others with whom we interact see the world, we need to make a mental shift out of our world and into theirs. This will provide rich material for leveraging cultural difference for personal, professional and societal growth. Intercultural coaching uses individual identity as the entry point to culture and provides an opportunity for people to work out into their worlds and to make use of the power of culture. Rosinski (2003a) has brought together diverse research on cultural difference into a cultural orientations framework (COF), which summarizes various orientations across which people differ. The COF is explained below, along with some ideas on how it might be used in coaching.

Traditional coaching has implicitly reflected particular norms, values and basic assumptions that reflect its originating culture – the USA. It is a well-researched fact that these do not necessarily hold true universally (see, for example, Nisbett, 2003). Intercultural coaching carries a Western assumption regarding our relationship to nature. We assume that our coachees have control over the direction of their lives, how they deploy their talents, and how they reach success. However, a wise coach also recognizes the relativity of the all-powerful control orientation. Simultaneously, we hold the assumption that many factors such as environment, genetic inheritance and luck can inhibit or enhance the degree of control we have at various times in our lives. The coach looks for balance and flow and understands the importance of timing. For the coachee, knowing your limits is not always obvious. But, humbly accepting them is paradoxically within your control. In the field of culture, contradictions and paradoxes are not uncommon and we encourage our coachees to roll with them and proceed on their journeys of positive change. We encourage coachees to consider the influence of culture through the process of reflective thought in the light of available evidence.

Intercultural coaching is a dynamic process that opens up possibilities for the client. Later in this chapter we describe a global coaching process (Rosinski, 2003a) that gives shape to the coaching approach. In the global coaching process, coaches and coachees connect their personal voyages with those of their families, friends, work colleagues, organizations, communities and society in general. Culture influences the direction of our individual journeys. If we travel with an attitude of curiosity and an eye for the potential of diversity, culture can enrich our experiences as we interact with others.

Intercultural coaching as we define it is a form of pragmatic humanism. It is pragmatic in that we draw on approaches and ideas that work in the context of the coachee. The measures of success are determined by the coachee. The approach is humanist in that we emphasize care of self and of others, quality of life and human growth. We will therefore work with coachees on approaches that are ethical and consistent with the humanist stance. Coaching from a cultural perspective is inconsistent, for example, with racial discrimination, or exploitative commercial practices.

Intercultural coaching – because it is pragmatic – makes sound business sense. The unleashing of individual potential and the leveraging of different approaches that are culturally based mean that companies receive sustainable benefits. Individuals become more productive, teams work better together, and solutions to issues become more creative and innovative. For example, joint venture companies (JVCs) across national boundaries are notoriously 'high risk'. A coaching approach that turns cultural differences into opportunities can increase the chances of JVC success.

EMBRACING DIVERSITY

Cultural difference is potential. We lead towards and embrace diversity. Intercultural coaching requires that we value and explore differences rather than automatically impose our norms, values and beliefs. Considering alternative belief systems and ways of operating, as they are represented in different cultures, can help coachees to broaden their perspectives. As they explore their own cultural assumptions and practices through the interaction with others they may see opportunities for change. Intercultural coaching can expand cultural repertoires and achieve sustainable change. The end result for coachees is that they deal with their individual challenges, and have a deeper understanding of their own contexts and those of others with whom they interact. From a pragmatic perspective, they will be better equipped to achieve their aims and objectives. We embrace the idea of canvassing many different sources to find approaches that work in the context of the coachee. Intercultural coaching requires an appreciation that there are different views of the world – and each potentially has something to offer every person as they undertake their unique journey.

Embracing diversity is easy at an intellectual level. However, intercultural coaching requires more. You need to become convinced in your heart and in your guts that a different truth or ideal is legitimate (though we do not of course propose that one should accept a cultural view that would promote intolerance, racism, xenophobia, or anti-Semitism). An emotional commitment is required. It is important that coaches learn as much as they can about the cultures that influence their clients. Books can help and there is an abundance of high-quality literature about culture. Experience informed by such knowledge is even better. Reflective interaction with the client is one way of experiencing his or her way of seeing the world. You can gain even more through extended onsite visits to a client's company, and talking to others there. Where national culture is a prominent influence, there are few better alternatives than travel.

People come to coaching with different approaches to dealing with cultural diversity. Interculturalist Milton Bennett (1993) describes six stages along a path towards enhanced cultural sensitivity. Coaches who operate with an awareness of these stages can assist their clients to follow their own journeys in productively exploring cultural diversity. In the early stages, Bennett describes approaches as 'ethnocentric pitfalls'. In stage 1, people ignore differences or deny they exist. In stage 2, there is recognition of differences but they are viewed negatively. Those who are different may be denigrated from a position of feeling superior. Stage 3 also sees recognition of differences, but they are trivialized. There is an assumption that regardless of small differences, we are all the same.

Beyond stage 3, there is a shift into what Bennett terms 'ethno relative approaches'. At stage 4, differences are recognized and acknowledged. At stage 5 there is a move out of the comfort zone. An empathetic perspective is possible where the person can take a temporary shift in perspective, but without adopting or assimilating that perspective. Bennett's stage 6 is one of integration. The person is able to hold different frames of reference and to analyse and evaluate situations from various cultural perspectives.

Intercultural coaching can assist coachees move through these stages, though the shifts are uneven and not easily measured. The coach encourages coachees to operate with ethno relative approaches. The coach supports coachees as they step outside their cultural comfort zones and accept alternate cultural views as valid. It requires a temporary suspension of one's own cultural viewpoint to genuinely take the view of another by imagining oneself to be the other person. This is a position of empathy, which is different from a position of sympathy where a person looks at another's view or situation still fixed in their own perspective. Bennett (1998) contrasts the golden rule of sympathy, 'Do unto others as you would have them do unto you' with the platinum rule of empathy, 'Do unto others as they themselves would have done unto them.' Bennett argues that the latter is more effective because people are different due to culture.

The common expression of seeking to put yourself into someone else's shoes illustrates the point. Getting into the shoes of someone very similar to ourselves is not much of an effort – same size, same style. However, it requires a leap of imagination to get into someone's shoes if that person is very different from you. The shift in thinking is to imagine yourself *as* the other person so that the shoes fit. The shift is temporary. Empathy does not mean permanently giving up your own cultural identity. The following case indicates the complexity:

A Canadian client was having difficulty adjusting to her new position as a manager of local staff in Peru. Ellen was confused because her Spanish was perfect and she knew a lot about the local culture, yet she felt resistance from her staff. We talked about her approach. It turned out that Ellen was almost trying to *be* Peruvian by changing her dress style and attempting to speak with a local accent. It seemed likely that her staff did not feel comfortable with her because they perceived she had abandoned her own identity.

Stage 6 in cultural sensitivity incorporates the capacity to hold various perspectives and to able to move from one to the other – but with a sure sense of self-identity to which you always return. Nevertheless, empathetic immersion in new cultures or perspectives is likely to add new dimensions to one's identity as a natural part of personal and professional growth.

Embracing diversity is a way of respecting the identity of others. It also makes good sense. Being able to switch cultural perspectives enables us to see issues and problems in different ways and to come up with new and powerful approaches and solutions. Creative integration of this kind has a cost. It requires a high level of self-questioning. We encourage coachees to question things that they previously held as a fixed reality. This is more difficult than living with certainties, but it brings rewards. Once coachees and coaches begin on this path, they are not passive observers of their cultural environments. Cultures shapes us, but we shape culture – albeit more slowly. It is not for the faint-hearted and there is a risk that we can become culturally disconnected and confused about our own values and identities. The coach can assist the coachee to remain grounded in reality, perhaps by recognizing a need for a client to withdraw a little back to the familiar and the comfortable before resuming the journey.

We believe there is potential for coachees to move beyond Bennett's stage 6 to another stage where they can leverage cultural differences. At this point coaches and coachees work together to strive for creative synergy. We look for gems in different cultures, to deal with paradox and contradiction, and to achieve unity through diversity.

LEVERAGING ALTERNATIVE CULTURAL PERSPECTIVES

The COF (see Table 10.1) is a useful tool for leveraging diversity. A common way of examining how values differ (or are similar) across cultures is to conceptualize them as to how people face universal challenges that confront them. Rosinski (2003a) has adapted the work of anthropologists, cross-cultural consultants and communications experts to identify challenges that are common across coaching situations. Different cultures choose different approaches in response to the challenges; these can be termed cultural orientations.

Our experience is that the COF is an effective tool when used with coaching. Use of the COF can help coachees to recognize cultural difference, thereby providing a potential for leveraging alternative perspectives. Clients are asked to identify their existing cultural orientations on the COF, and to examine other alternatives. Through experimentation and reflection, they then explore alternative orientations and work towards an approach that best suits their identities and contexts. This is an ongoing process of personal and professional growth and does not

Table 10.1 Cultural orientations framework

Categories	Dimensions	Description
Sense of power and responsibility	Control/harmony/humility	**Control**: people have a determinant power and responsibility to forge the life they want. **Harmony**: strive for balance and harmony with nature. **Humility**: accept inevitable natural limitations.
Time management approaches	Scarce/plentiful	**Scarce**: time is a scarce resource. Manage time carefully! **Plentiful**: time is abundant. Relax!
	Monochronic/polychronic	**Monochronic**: concentrate on one activity and/or relationship at a time. **Polychronic**: concentrate simultaneously on multiple tasks and/or people.
	Past/present/future	**Past**: learn from the past. The present is essentially a continuation or a repetition of past occurrences. **Present**: focus on the 'here and now' and short-term benefits. **Future**: have a bias towards long-term benefits. Promote a far-reaching vision.
Definitions of identity and purpose	Being/doing	**Being**: stress living itself and the development of talents and relationships. **Doing**: focus on accomplishments and visible achievements.
	Individualistic/collectivistic	**Individualistic**: emphasize individual attributes and projects. **Collectivistic**: emphasize affiliation with a group.
Organizational arrangements	Hierarchy/equality	**Hierarchy**: society and organizations must be socially stratified to function properly. **Equality**: people are equals who often happen to play different roles.
	Universalist/particularist	**Universalist**: all cases should be treated in the same universal manner. Adopt common processes for consistency and economies of scale.

	Stability/change	**Particularist**: emphasize particular circumstances. Favour decentralization and tailored solutions. **Stability**: value a static and orderly environment. Encourage efficiency through systematic and disciplined work. Minimize change and ambiguity, perceived as disruptive. **Change**: value a dynamic and flexible environment. Promote effectiveness through adaptability and innovation. Avoid routine, perceived as boring.
	Competitive/collaborative	**Competitive**: promote success and progress through competitive stimulation. **Collaborative**: promote success and progress through mutual support, sharing of best practices and solidarity.
Notions of territory and boundaries	Protective/sharing	**Protective**: protect oneself by keeping personal life and feelings private (mental boundaries), and by minimizing intrusions in one's physical space (physical boundaries). **Sharing**: build closer relationships by sharing one's psychological and physical domains.
Communication patterns	High-context/low-context	**High-context**: rely on implicit communication. Appreciate the meaning of gestures, postures, voice and context. **Low-context**: rely on explicit communication. Favour clear and detailed instructions.
	Direct/indirect	**Direct**: in a conflict or with a tough message to deliver, get your point across clearly at the risk of offending or hurting. **Indirect**: in a conflict or with a tough message to deliver, favour maintaining a cordial relationship at the risk of misunderstanding.
	Affective/neutral	**Affective**: display emotions and warmth when communicating. Establishing and maintaining personal and social connections is key. **Neutral**: stress conciseness, precision and detachment when communicating.

require letting go of original orientations, nor a surrendering of self. The approach is pragmatic in seeking to build on existing characteristics and strengths.

In using the COF the idea is not to select one approach or another, but to synthesize for maximum advantage. The approach is dialectical in working with the creative tension that exists between the different orientations. We look for contrast and for depth. New ideas, solutions and options emerge from the confrontation. The practice of deliberately accepting and building from apparently opposite approaches requires a certain comfort with paradox and complexity. One central paradox is that while major differences between people can provide a barrier to effective communication, differences can also be levers for positive change. Differences generally are seen as challenges and opportunities rather than problems or threats to be navigated.

As noted earlier, when working with the idea of cultural orientations and dimensions, there is a risk of stereotyping. The advantage of the COF is that it gives you and your coachee valuable information about the coachee's individual cultural orientations, which may be similar to or different from the coachee's national, community or organizational culture. Through the COF you may find, for example, that your coachee enjoys change and is an 'outlier' within his or her cultural environment, which favours stability. This situation offers opportunity for leveraging the differences. Your coachee may be an ideal candidate for leading change management processes in the company in the event of a merger or acquisition. It may also help your coachee to understand frustrations and tensions he or she has been experiencing at work.

THE GLOBAL COACHING PROCESS

The three-stage global coaching process (Rosinski, 2003a) provides a structure for embracing diversity in coaching. From the first meeting to the completion of the formal sessions, the coach encourages coachees to consider their lives in the broader context of their relationships and their society – always with a view to unleashing the coachee's potential.

Stage 1. Assessment

The assessment phase includes a systematic consideration of the self, as well as family and friends, organization, community and the world. Through exploration there comes a gradual emergence of objectives that separate the coachees from what others expect and turn them towards a future that is consistent with their individual desires, preferences and unique contexts. The coach may encourage coachees to assess approximately where they might be in relation to the stages of cultural sensitivity (outlined above) and to discuss their associated levels of effectiveness in cross-cultural adjustment and functioning. The COF may be used to assist the coachee in understanding his or her current orientations and those of others. It requires that the coach adopt an inherent bias of believing in coachee potential.

Stage 2. Setting targets

In the second stage, the global scorecard (see Figure 10.1) invites the coachee to devise measures of internal and external success across a broad variety of stakeholders, including self, family and friends, organization, community and the world. This process emphasizes the centrality of human relationships in personal and professional growth and extends the coaching outside of individual experiences and perceptions.

The categories help to incorporate the various cultural perspectives that influence the coachee's reality. There are various other indicators that are effectively used in individual coaching and in organizational development. What has been missing is a comprehensive framework for conceptualizing and tying together previous and disparate scorecards and extending the scope. The global scorecard seeks to fill this gap. By including the stakeholder category of 'Community and the world', the global scorecard focuses attention on an area that individual coaching sometimes neglects. Coaching relationships can enter the challenging and critical areas of business ethics, sustainable development, corporate citizenship, human rights, poverty and human creativity.

Stage 3. Making progress towards the target objectives

This is the action stage where coach and coachee focus on monitoring and making progress towards the targets. The objectives – like culture – are not static. Targets are revised as new experiences and new learning are integrated. The approach is pragmatic in focusing on what works in the context of the coachee.

The global coaching process is the vehicle for opening up possibilities through the overlay of a cultural perspective. It is a multilevel approach that acknowledges the influence of culture in our lives, while remaining consistent with the general principles and practice of high-quality coaching. Our view of how intercultural coaching fits within the broader profession of coaching is shaped by the very practice of intercultural

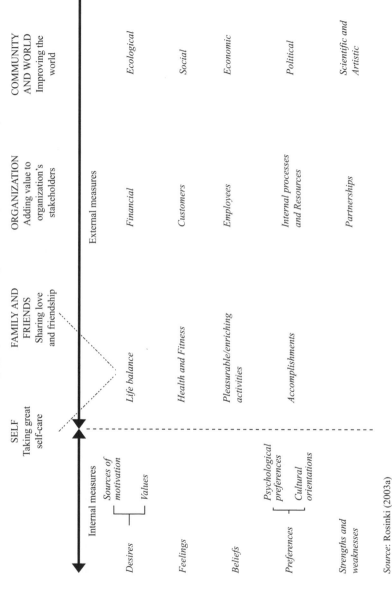

Figure 10.1 The global scorecard

The Global Scorecard

Devising appropriate measures of global success (drivers and outcomes)

	SELF Taking great self-care	FAMILY AND FRIENDS Sharing love and friendship	ORGANIZATION Adding value to organization's stakeholders	COMMUNITY AND WORLD Improving the world
			External measures	
	Life balance		Financial	Ecological
	Health and Fitness		Customers	Social
	Pleasurable/enriching activities		Employees	Economic
	Accomplishments		Internal processes and Resources	Political
			Partnerships	Scientific and Artistic

Internal measures

Sources of
motivation

Desires
Values

Feelings

Beliefs

Preferences
Psychological
preferences
Cultural
orientations

Strengths and
weaknesses

Source: Rosinski (2003a)

coaching. It is not an either/or choice. Culture is an 'and' in our profession. You lose nothing by including a cultural perspective. Instead you enhance the depth and the impact of whatever other approaches you favour.

CROSS-CULTURAL WORK IN PRACTICE

As a coach, it helps to keep in mind some of the following questions, particularly when the coaching relationship does not seem to be flowing:

▌ What are the cultural orientations of your coachee?

▌ What are your own cultural orientations?

▌ How might the interaction between your and the coachee's orientations be impacting on the coaching process?

▌ How might you leverage the different cultural orientations?

Below are two examples where the coach (in this case Geoffrey Abbott) was able to work with coachees to leverage differences. The cases are real but some details have been changed to protect confidentiality.

DIRECT vs INDIRECT COMMUNICATION STYLE

Julio felt stuck in his position as an expert problem-solver in the middle levels of a South African multinational company operating in his country in Latin America. Through the global coaching process, Julio clarified and explored the ambitions for himself, his family, his company, his community and his country. He wanted to move out of specialized project work into management, to give his children an opportunity to live and study overseas, to add value to his company, and demonstrate that local managers could make an impact in a multinational company. He also wanted to have an impact in promoting inclusive and empowering management practices in the company and his country.

Julio was receiving negative feedback about his communication and presentation skills, even though he rated himself highly on these. He had been a line manager in two large Latin American companies. He had given many presentations and training courses and had invariably received positive feedback.

In the first coaching session I noticed that Julio was expansive and rather indirect in the way he described his situation and how he responded to my questions. His language was also very formal, laced with technical terms and jargon. Julio confirmed a preference for an indirect and formal communication style (see Table 10.1). We discussed the cultural aspect of this style. I was familiar with the local business culture and was aware that Julio's style was quite typical in his country (though in other ways Julio was very atypical). We then discussed the dominant cultural orientation in the multinational company. Julio had been to South Africa for training. I had worked with several of the South African managers. It was obvious to both of us that the South Africans preferred a direct approach and were not interested in formality. The discussion quickly moved Julio to a realization that he needed to alter his communication style if he wanted to make a bigger impact in the company.

Through parts of the subsequent sessions I became more of a trainer than a coach in assisting Julio to be more direct. My Australian business background meant that I was comfortable and familiar with a style very similar to the South African approach. We worked with role-plays and practice presentations. Sometimes as we moved across discussions of some of Julio's other objectives I stopped the coaching session and invited Julio to reflect on how he was communicating (particularly if Julio was indirect in response to a direct question).

Julio's strength – and the reason why he was of such value to the company – was his grasp of detail and complexity. Our task therefore was to leverage difference, ie for Julio to keep control of the detail in a complex environment, but for him to succinctly present the ideas in an appropriate style. I used the metaphor of a back office full of organized files that were available from the front desk if requested. Within six months, Julio had successfully made representation to senior management to establish a new department in the company – the department in charge of the interface between complex financial data and operational systems. Julio had made short, high-impact presentations backed by detailed documentation. Also, Julio persuaded them to make him the departmental head and was able to put into practice his management philosophy and to open up a new future for himself and his family.

Perhaps coincidentally, Julio changed his diet, joined a gym, went from 215 pounds to 155 pounds, and became more active in playing with his children. At the traditional extended family barbeque each Sunday, Julio took his own lean meat and drank a glass or two of wine in place of beer. After some initial incredulity and resistance, some of Julio's friends and family members quietly asked him for the phone number of his nutritionist and began their own change processes.

AFFECTIVE vs NEUTRAL COMMUNICATION STYLE

Tracy was an African American information technology manager who was having some difficulty with her supervisor. In my introductory meeting, Tracy suggested that she perceived some racial issues in the attitude that her manager demonstrated towards her. I was conscious that I was of a similar demographic to her manager – ie white, male, Anglo background, 40s. We didn't meet again for some months. When we met outside my hotel, Tracy hugged me warmly. We then went to her office and began our coaching session.

The conversation moved slowly and I felt a tension similar to the one I experienced in our first meeting. There was no problem, but an underlying sense of separation and difference. I mentioned to Tracy that I had been slightly uncomfortable in receiving her warm hug when we met earlier in the day. She responded that she had noticed my reticence. I explained my Anglo heritage and how in my family and in my culture there was not the same spontaneity in the expression of emotions. While we had strong love for each other and our family was very close, we were the typical Anglo family in favouring a more neutral communication style (see Table 10.1). The conversation extended into a broader conversation about family and community connections in Tracy's life – in contrast to my rather mobile and sometimes self-contained life with my partner (see the COF individualistic and collectivist dimensions under definitions of identity and purpose). We started to understand each other much better and the tone moved to a kind of relaxed playfulness that for me was an indication that the coaching session was becoming a learning environment. The playful interaction around our differences was my way of helping the two of us to leverage cultural difference.

Later, these conversations proved very helpful for both of us in understanding other situations in Tracy's life, including her relationship with her manager.

When and how to raise such issues with a coachee are matters of professional judgement. However, the aim in intercultural coaching is to bring culture to the surface, so when in doubt it is probably better to raise the issue. How you raise the issue for maximum impact is best determined to some extent by the cultural orientation.

CONCLUSIONS

We are ambitious for the role of intercultural coaching in an expanding global economy. Intercultural coaching can unleash the potential of leaders and produce tangible benefits including empowerment, vision and creativity, and more effective cross-cultural communication (Rosinski, 2003b).

Intercultural coaching encourages the coaches to look deeply at themselves. The coach's own desires, strengths, weaknesses, contexts, and cultural and psychological preferences are directly relevant to the success of the coaching in unleashing coachee potential. We need to open ourselves to the possibility that our own cultural values, assumptions or backgrounds may potentially inhibit our effectiveness with a coachee. By being aware of ourselves and sensitive to our coachees we can be ready to develop authentic strategies to leverage contrasts we encounter.

The principles and practices of intercultural coaching we have described above can be applied when working with cultural diversity in many forms. Diversity can come through cultural difference based on nationality, sex, faith, sexual preference, disability, etc. The essence of intercultural coaching is to assume that the experience and perspective a client has gained by being part of a group opens up potential and possibility. When one has, for example, experienced extreme hardship through some form of discrimination and managed not only to survive but also to prosper, the perspectives gained can be utilized to create solutions to new problems and issues.

Intercultural coaching is challenging and goes to the essence of who we are. Hall (1989: 240) writes about the difficult journey beyond culture, 'because the greatest separation feat of all is when one manages to gradually free oneself from the grip of unconscious culture'. Coachees may initially be resistant to the idea that they are carrying assumptions and perspectives that are holding them back. Coaching can unleash potential by giving coachees greater understanding and choice about the way they are, the way they want to be, and the direction their lives will take.

Acknowledgement

Table 10.1 is reproduced with kind permission of Nicholas Brealey Publishing from *Coaching Across Cultures*, Philippe Rosinski.

References

Bennett, M J (1993) Towards ethno relativism: a developmental model of intercultural sensitivity, in R M Paige (ed), *Education for the Intercultural Experience*, (pp 21–71) Intercultural Press, Yarmouth

Bennett, M J (1998) Overcoming the golden rule: sympathy and empathy, in M J Bennett (ed), *Basic Concepts of Intercultural Communication: Selected readings*, (pp 191–214) Intercultural Press, Yarmouth

Hall, E T (1989) *Beyond Culture*, Anchor House, New York

Hofstede, G (1980) *Culture's consequences*, Sage, Beverly Hills

Nisbett, R E (2003) *The Geography of Thought: How Asians and Westerners think differently and why*, The Free Press, New York

Rosinski, P (2003a) *Coaching Across Cultures: New tools for leveraging national, corporate and professional differences*, Nicholas Brealey, London

Rosinski, P (2003b) The applications of coaching across cultures, *International Journal of Coaching in Organizations*, **1** (4), pp 4–16

Schwartz, S H (1999) A theory of cultural values and some implications for work, *Applied Psychology: An International Review*, **48** (1), pp 23–47

Trompenaars, F, and Hampden-Turner, C (1998) *Riding the Waves of Culture: Understanding cultural diversity in global business*, 2nd edn, McGraw Hill, New York

11

Coaching and stress

María Alicia Peña and Cary L Cooper

WHY FOCUS ON STRESS?

Today it is becoming more common to hear people talk about being stressed as a result of increasing demands in their lives. The gradual loss of energy and tiredness reduces physical health and well-being, which in turn has a negative effect on our ability to be productive at work.

The subject of stress has drawn the attention of professionals interested in promoting health and well-being at work. Stress has been identified as the second greatest factor in work-related health problems after musculoskeletal complaints, particularly in the non-manual worker population (Cooper *et al*, 2001). Cooper commented that in the early 1990s the National Institute of Occupational Safety and Health estimated that workplace stress (in relation to alcoholism) cost the USA $51 billion due to decreased productivity and $4 billion as a result of lost employment. Recent press releases on the American Psychological Association website (26 January 2006) reported that research had found that about 20 per cent of Americans are worried about the effects of stress on their health. It also mentioned that about

36 per cent of respondents commented that they coped by eating or drinking alcohol. Another article on the same website reported that a meta-analysis of 293 independent studies – between 1960 and 2001 – had found that long-term or chronic stress reduced the capacity of the immune system to protect the body from illness (Segerstrom and Miller, 2006).

From the research available it is evident that stress is a problem affecting individuals worldwide. Peterson (2005) argued from Australia that stress and stress-induced illnesses are the largest and most debilitating epidemics of the 21st century. In the UK, the Health and Safety Executive (2004) survey indicated that at least half a million in the UK population were experiencing work-related stress, and about one in five workers reported extreme symptoms of work-related stress (CIPD, 2004). A European research of work-related stress (Cox *et al*, 2000) found that 28 per cent of workers interviewed experienced stress; the research also found that in 1998 about 200 million days were lost due to sickness absence. A recent European Occupational Health Review indicated that mental ill-health was the biggest cause of long-term sickness absence. Stress and mental health problems were cited as main causes of long-term absence (CIPD, 2004). This report also indicated that three-quarters of executives mentioned that stress had a negative impact on their health as well as on their performance. Main factors mentioned as causes of stress were workload, tight deadlines, lack of support and feeling threatened at work (HSE, 2004/5).

This data provides clear indication of the scale and severity of the impact of stress on individuals. The interest in finding ways to support people's health has increased, and an indication of the importance of this topic is that stress at work has become a prominent area of research in occupational psychology both in the USA and Europe (Cox *et al*, 2000).

The cost of work-related stress to the UK economy has been estimated to be between £10 and £12 billion annually (HSE, 2004). The Health and Safety Executive encourages organizations to take preventative measures to reduce the impact of stress in the workplace, and it has developed management standards to achieve this aim. The management standards focus on six key areas:

1. demands (being able to manage the job);
2. control (having enough discretion over work that needs to be done);
3. support (good support from managers and peers);

4. roles (clarity of responsibilities);

5. relationships (good environment with no unacceptable behaviour);

6. change (awareness of, and participation in changes within the organization).

Given the incidence of stress, and its potential to lead to mental ill-health and long-term sickness, it is critical to take preventative action. The damaging effects of stress can be prevented by providing support to individuals and organizations to promote health and well-being at work. Coaching offers an effective intervention that can help individuals both manage work demands in the short term and develop new coping mechanisms that help over the long term.

What is stress?

The topic of stress has been discussed extensively. There is considerable debate on how to define it, and depending on the definition there are implications for research as well as for the design of interventions to manage stress (Cooper *et al*, 2001). The Health and Safety Executive (2004) defined stress as individuals' reaction to excessive pressure or demands, and this develops as individuals worry about their ability to cope. Selye (1976) first described stress in the 1950s as a non-specific response of the body to a demand, and defined it as a general adaptation syndrome. He identified a three-stage response: an alarm reaction (emergency) with an immediate psycho-physiological response to prepare the body to take action; an adaptation response (resistance) where energy is depleted over time; and exhaustion.

One way of viewing stress is to consider it from a relational perspective. This approach views stress as a result of transactions between the individual and the environment (Cox *et al*, 2000), and the intensity of the stress response would depend on the individual's perception of their ability to respond to the threat or challenge (Cooper *et al*, 2001; Lazarus, 1991). A work task could be perceived as demanding of resources that the individual might not have. Karasek and Theorell's (1990) demand-control model purports that the main sources of work-related stress are the psychological demands of the job, and job decision latitude. They expanded their model to include social processes as social relationships with co-workers influence productivity, and the level of support experienced influences behaviour as well as the perception of well-being.

How does it affect us?

When demands exceed our resources this challenges the natural tendency of the human body to maintain a stable internal state, and stress is the response to keep it balanced (Sapolsky, 1994). Stress puts strain on psychological and physical functioning, creating an imbalance that affects health (Cartwright and Cooper, 1997) and the effectiveness of the responses to stress will depend on the level of energy available to deal with it. A prolonged period of stress depletes energy, increasing the risk of developing anxiety or depression in addition to the potential risk of physical injury (if working with machinery, for example). This can lead to ill-health and to the need to be absent from work to restore health (Tehrani, 2004).

The depleted energy resources result in symptoms of stress. These are effectively raising the alarm that it is urgent to take action to prevent ill-health. Symptoms of stress include those listed in Table 11.1.

If no action is taken energy reserves are not restored and this can then result in exhaustion. If individuals do not have the opportunity to replenish their resources they may experience burnout – a state of mind accompanied by distress and low motivation that can result in disillusionment (van Dierendonck *et al*, 2005). Increased work demands and high expectations can lead to a negative attitude towards work as the individual gradually becomes exhausted (McMillan *et al*, 2003). Individuals who are strongly motivated to work and have a high sense of responsibility are more vulnerable to burnout. This is likely to happen because people do not pay attention to signs of stress and therefore extend their efforts beyond their capacity, exhausting their energy resources, which then may result in ill-health. Pearsall (2002) refers to striving to achieve as toxic success – when despite achieving, somehow individuals experience a sense of lack of meaning, disconnection from others and a sense of disappointment.

HOW CAN COACHING HELP TO MANAGE STRESS?

Most of us spend a significant amount of time working and interacting with others, and at times we can face stressful situations that reduce our sense of well-being. The number of self-help books giving guidance on how to improve our lives indicates that there is a growing interest in learning how to experience less dissatisfaction and more enjoyment. Events that are stressful can prevent us from achieving this aim.

We have already seen in Chapter 1 that the aim of coaching is to promote a positive approach to the improvement of performance and

Table 11.1 Symptoms of stress

Physical	Behavioural	Psychological	Work performance	Other behaviours
Sweating	Withdrawal	Easily upset	Reduced/inconsistent performance	Isolation
Tiredness	Lack of exercise	Lack of concentration	Loss of control	Sensitivity to feedback
Lethargy	Increased/decreased eating	Memory difficulties	Lack of motivation	Nervousness
Altered sleep	Impulsivity	Indecisiveness	Increased number of errors	Difficulty communicating
Restlessness	Out of character behaviour	Increased worry thoughts	Procrastination	Irritability
Tense	Increased alcohol/drugs/smoking	Fluctuating mood	Lack of planning	Aggression
Aches and pains	Unkempt appearance	Loss of meaning	Difficulty delegating	Bullying or harassment
Minor ailments		Feeling alone	Staying longer at work	Increased conflict
Weight gain/loss		Low mood	Absenteeism	
Headaches		Anxiety	Recklessness	
Burnout		Depression		
		Lack of confidence		

well-being. To support this aim coaching can benefit from positive psychology's study of positive emotions, optimal functioning and its focus on the understanding of human strengths (Linley and Harrington, 2005).

Over the past decade coaching has become an accepted strategy to manage stress as well as to improve performance. Through coaching individuals can identify stressors and work towards developing strategies to manage them and reduce the effects of stress. There is some evidence that those who have engaged in coaching practice have reported a reduction of stress and burnout as a result of the process (Gyllensten and Palmer, 2005).

Research indicates that work is good for us. If we are prevented from working when we would prefer to be doing so our self-perception and self-confidence can be affected. Understanding positive emotions can help us to develop these and increase our sense of well-being from engaging more authentically in our lives (Seligman, 2002). Having more optimal experiences can boost our sense of mastery and a feeling that we are more in control of our lives. This would lead then to experiencing flow – a state of mind of inner harmony that enhances motivation and a sense of contentment (Csikszentmihalyi, 1992). So, by learning to prevent the experience of stress – and to manage the symptoms when it occurs – we are likely to be able to remain at work, and also more likely to find meaning and satisfaction in what we do both at work and in our personal life.

MANAGING STRESS: A COMPREHENSIVE APPROACH

A comprehensive approach to the management of stress, both at an organizational and individual level, is essential to maximize the potential of reducing the effects of stressors and encourage a culture where people can work while maintaining their health (Cooper et al, 2001; Cox et al, 2000).

Employers can support the organizations' health by demonstrating that reducing stress is a priority. Making sure policies that support employees' well-being are in place, and monitoring that they are implemented is an essential first step. Designing policies that provide clear guidelines on how to deal with stress, bullying and harassment, and return to work can facilitate the reduction of the incidence of sickness absence, turnover, costly litigation and compensation cases (Nice and Thornton, 2004; Tehrani, 2004).

How can coaching help individuals?

Coaching provides individuals with the opportunity to develop strategies to maximize their potential to work effectively. The process allows them to identify their needs (eg, career development), and what they would like to achieve to enhance their performance while maintaining their sense of well-being. Identifying strengths, and using them regularly, can help to achieve this aim (Seligman, 2002).

A coaching process for well-being and performance

The effectiveness of coaching depends on designing a process suited to the individual, and adopting a flexible approach to be able to respond to his or her needs. It is recognized that it is essential to develop a trusting and collaborative relationship. It is also critical to assess the motivation of the coachee and readiness to engage in the coaching process. Establishing limits of confidentiality and having clearly defined aims for the process are also essential.

The expertise of the coach matters, particularly when dealing with health issues. Some coaches have a psychology degree, although this is not a requirement for coaching it does give an insight to human behaviour. Having training in counselling skills, experience in dealing with health issues and supervision (or consultation with an experienced colleague) are recommended. It is important that coaches are aware of when it is appropriate to refer to health professionals. Monitoring individual professional practice and reflecting on professional issues maintain and promote best practice.

Below are described some key components of a practical approach when coaching for well-being and performance.

1. Identifying areas to work on

The first aim is to identify the coachee's needs. Obtaining information about what is causing concern, and how the individual is feeling in general, allows the coach to identify the sources of stress. The coach needs to consider both work and personal factors, which are summarized in Table 11.2.

A discussion of these areas, and others considered relevant in agreement with coachees, helps to identify objectives and define what can realistically be achieved. This process is a useful intervention as it encourages coachees to reflect, away from external pressures, and allows them to clarify their thinking and feelings about what has been concerning them. Increasing understanding of the issues, and beginning to establish

Figure 11.1 Coaching flowchart

Flow (assessment):

Identify needs / Establish rapport → Identify symptoms of stress / Health status → Refer: YES → Contact HR, Occupational Health for specialist treatment

Refer: NO → Identify objectives → Identify performance issues / Development areas; Manage stressors; Work-life balance → Identify approach / Define boundaries

Raise awareness stress symptoms and impact on health, performance → Identify values / Priorities

Intervention areas:

Coping strategies to manage stress symptoms, develop health and increase performance	Communication skills	Increasing self-efficacy & resilience	Prevention
* Challenging negative thoughts * Relaxation * Exercise * Nutrition	* Managing conflict * Assertiveness * Problem solving * Decision making	* Identify strengths * Build confidence * Awareness of resources & support	* Become proactive * Monitor health * Monitor stressors * Regular meetings with line manager

Table 11.2 Stress factors

About work	About the individual
Job demands (tasks, relationships, skills)	Family/personal responsibilities
Level of job complexity	Interests, expectations (what is aiming for, would like)
Level of control/discretion	Perception of self (abilities, experience, strengths)
Roles and responsibilities (role clarity, objectives)	Health (stamina)
Relationship with manager/ peers/staff	Obstacles to achieving aims
Resources	Communication style (conflict)
	Support
	Motivation
	Meaning of work
	Values and priorities

positive action, raises confidence in their ability to self-manage and direct their own learning process.

At this stage it is essential to identify whether it is appropriate to work with the individual in a coaching process or whether he or she requires the support of health professionals.

When should the coach refer?

When the coach becomes aware that the individual's needs are beyond what can be dealt with in a coaching session, the best support he or she can provide is to make a timely referral for treatment with health professionals. This may be the person's GP and a health professional with clinical expertise. Some indicators of mental health problems are:

▌ high levels of distress;

▌ persisting low mood and negative thinking (negative outlook);

▌ high levels of anxiety;

▌ low self-esteem (high self-criticism);

▌ inability to find positive aspects;

▌ issues discussed are predominantly related to personal life;

▍ sense of hopelessness;

▍ sense of helplessness;

▍ poor physical health.

2. Identifying approach

Before starting to address issues it is essential to discuss with coachees how they prefer to work. In order to engage in the process some individuals prefer a very pragmatic and logical approach applied to the work environment only, whereas others prefer to engage in self-exploration and wish to discuss the wider picture including aspects of their personal life. Understanding different preferred styles (such as those described by Myers Briggs Type Indicator, learning styles), level of self-awareness, and the motivation for learning can provide information to identify which approach to adopt. The choice made will also depend on the individual's interests and the expertise of the coach.

3. Raising awareness of stress symptoms

It is likely that the individual will have been working under considerable pressure before engaging in coaching. As a result, he or she may have learnt to overlook signs of stress and might have developed a tolerance to them. Individuals who are very conscientious and take on responsibility too seriously are likely to be most at risk. Some may increase the time spent at work as a means of managing the increasing demands. The more senior the position (although not exclusively) the more likely that he or she may display this pattern, and feelings such as increased irritability can lead to conflict. The ability to manage conflict tends to be reduced due to the lack of energy and increased tension, and it affects individuals' ability to use their interpersonal skills effectively. Senior managers in particular, who have a responsibility for others, require their strength to make critical decisions (McMillan *et al*, 2003). Therefore, helping them to identify the symptoms, and giving them information on how they can cope more effectively is a positive intervention in itself.

Coaches can use a number of strategies to help their coachees develop awareness of the impact of stress. An initial interview where attention is directed to how the individual is functioning can trigger awareness and further exploration. Sometimes individuals say that stress is good for them; in this case it is important to explain the difference between pressure and stress. We all need an optimum level of pressure to summon our internal resources to keep us motivated and the stamina to function well. However, when we are effectively demanding our bodies to function without the resources to cope with the demand, we develop symptoms of stress. It is interesting to observe reactions when a similarity is drawn to the care we take of our car. When the flashing red light on the dashboard indicates that the car is running low on petrol, even if we are late for a very important and critical meeting, we are unlikely to say, 'I will continue to drive and I will fill up after the meeting.' We know we have to stop and go to a petrol station because the car will not go anywhere once it runs out of petrol. Symptoms of stress are like the red light warning us that we are running out of energy. We should do the same: stop and take time to restore energy so that we take good care of ourselves.

The Myers Briggs Type Indicator (MBTI) is a very useful tool to help individuals identify the areas that may be more demanding of their energy. We can make the most of our resources when we can work in our preferred style; when working in our non-preferred style we can experience more strain. Coachees generally express relief when they identify that the symptoms of stress may be due to working in a different style rather than necessarily an indication of a lack of ability. The areas of work that they find most difficult and demanding tend to be those tasks that require they use the opposite dimension from their preferred style. Quenk (1993) paid attention to the dynamics of types and suggested that job burnout symptoms could be the result of over-use of a particular dimension. Identifying strengths and areas that could be developed would help coachees increase their ability to manage tasks.

An effective technique to raise awareness is to use the initial illustration of signing as we normally do, and then with the opposite hand. For example, those who normally write with their right hand after the exercise tend to apologize for not writing well with their left hand (the same vice versa). If they are asked, 'How long have you been writing with your right (left) hand?', they are likely to say, 'Many years', or 'All my life.' Then asking, 'And how long have you been writing with your left (right) hand?', a common response is 'Rarely, never'. . . and a smile! This illustration helps to identify their expectations to perform well despite the lack of practice. They can be encouraged to keep the illustration in mind when they face a difficult task, or when they perceive they are not doing things as well as they would like. It is likely to be a task in which they are writing with their left (or right) hand! This tends to reduce the pressure they put themselves under, and encourages a positive attitude towards learning new ways to increase their competence in working with the opposite of their preferred style. For example, individuals who have a preference for intuition may find it difficult to present specific details; or a manager whose preferred style is introversion may find managing meetings very draining. Both can benefit from information about how they can develop strategies to manage work that demands more of other dimensions.

Coaches can draw attention to the need to complement the preferred style with developing the opposite dimensions. Some useful strategies are to take time to reflect on experiences so that coachees can practise skills and develop confidence in their abilities. Adapting expectations and applying strategies can reduce the pressure individuals experience when performing tasks that are more demanding. By building a sense of self-efficacy – increasing our belief in our ability to perform tasks – we can enhance our self-confidence (Bandura, 1997).

4. Identifying priorities

When stressed there is a tendency to pay more attention to symptoms and to what is going wrong, and as a result we can easily lose perspective. It is difficult to manage time when we are not clear about what is important and meaningful. In order to prioritize we first need to identify what is of value to us. Helping coachees to identify what their priorities are can allow them to channel their energy and direct their efforts to achieve their aims.

5. Communication style: managing conflict

We spend a significant amount of our time communicating with others, and even with the best of intentions at times we end up having difficult conversations. According to Tannen (1998) different interpretations of words and the different styles can lead to friction. Interpersonal relationships can produce great satisfaction and a sense of belonging. However, when arguments occur and differences cannot be reconciled, tensions prevail. Developing strategies to establish cooperation to achieve resolution can reduce tensions and increase self-confidence.

Difficulties in relationships at work can emerge for a variety of reasons – disagreement on how to approach a task, perception of not being liked or not being treated with respect. These difficulties can be managed by exploring communication style and attitude towards conflict. Dealing with difficult situations, such as a negative relationship with the line manager, can be very stressful and can seriously affect individuals' ability to cope at work. The Thomas-Kilmann (2002) conflict questionnaire can be a useful tool to explore attitudes and approaches to conflict. Again, the MBTI is a useful tool that can facilitate raising awareness of how we can manage conflict more constructively (Killen and Murphy, 2003).

Effective communication involves self-expression and listening. Communication skills can be strengthened by following a few steps: reflecting on the message to be communicated, expressing thoughts and feelings clearly, being direct and honest, addressing the issue not the individual, asking questions to check understanding of what the other said, and adopting an open attitude with the aim of creating understanding.

6. Developing coping strategies

The literature on counselling and clinical psychology provides information on various coping strategies that are effective in helping individuals restore their mental health. Using a solution-focused approach, where emphasis is on paying attention to the present, focusing on developing strengths, and enhancing the positive can provide tools to help individuals maximize their resources (O'Hanlon and Weiner-Davis, 1989). To help coachees develop resilience to be able to cope with stressors it is useful to draw attention to the mind-body connection. Integrating physical, mental and emotional dimensions can increase the potential to restore a sense of wellness. It has been suggested that it is also important to address the spiritual dimension as identifying what is of meaning to individuals will have an impact on their lives (van Dierendonck *et al*, 2005).

Challenging negative thinking

It is not the event that distresses us but how we perceive the situation. A negative perception can be distorted or magnified out of proportion resulting in considerable distress. A cognitive behavioural approach focuses on tackling the negative thinking that prevents us from being able to use our creativity to find solutions (Beck, 1979). These negative thoughts erode self-confidence and the belief in the capacity to manage complex and stressful situations. Meichenbaum (1977) developed a stress inoculation programme and used cognitive restructuring to help people manage stress. The aim is to help individuals modify their internal self-dialogue to build up positive thoughts. This process guides individuals to pay attention to the thoughts that run through their mind when dealing with stressful situations. Then, they are encouraged to challenge these thoughts and replace them with more realistic and constructive ones.

The approach used to deal with the situation will depend on how the situation is perceived, and what meaning it is given (threat or challenge). A problem-focused approach is where individuals make attempts to deal with the event, and an emotion-focused approach is where individuals try to deal with the emotional distress experienced as a result of the difficulties being faced (Lazarus, 1991). When using a problem-focused approach the first step is to examine the situation to understand what exactly is happening. Here the aim is to clarify whether the event presents a threat or a challenge, and questions such as, 'What is the difficulty? What information do I need? Do I need to respond now? What would I like as an outcome? Who else is affected? Who could provide support?' can help to explore and understand the situation better.

In order to find creative solutions it is essential to allow the imagination to freely explore ideas. Keeping the mind alert and being curious, looking for what is new or unusual can help free the mind from assumptions or negative thoughts. Asking oneself questions such as, 'What would be different if this was not a problem? What would be the ideal situation? What would happen if I did the opposite of what I normally do?' can help to identify options. Other techniques such as mind mapping (Buzan, 1994) and lateral thinking (de Bono, 1994) can help to develop our capacity for generating creative solutions. Next, identify the options available, choose the best one, take action and then observe what happens, learning from what works and what does not. This process of evaluation provides information to modify actions so that the outcome can be improved.

Developing resilience

Why do people react differently to stressors? The study of resiliency – the ability to bounce back from setbacks – suggests that those who cope with stress without developing ill-health are flexible and have a positive attitude. Siebert (2005) says that people who are resilient accept life's setbacks, and allow themselves to experience loss, grief and distress because they see it as a temporary situation. They do not develop a victim response. Individuals who have a high level of internal control can cope more effectively, whereas those who blame others or feel victimized tend to score high in external control and are likely to believe that they cannot make a difference to their situation. Those who are resilient expect to be able to recover after a setback and consciously decide to survive; by believing in their capacity to deal with the situation they reinforce their self-motivation and this allows them to thrive.

Resilience can be increased by developing self-awareness. Individuals who are resilient ask themselves, 'What can I learn from this? What would I do different next time?' Imagining an effective outcome helps to prepare for the next time. They do not undermine themselves with self-criticism and defeating thoughts that only reduce self-confidence and create a self-fulfilling prophecy. Maintaining a curious and playful spirit increases resilience because of the ongoing questions we may create, and these allow us to keep learning from our experiences.

Healthy eating and exercise

A prolonged period of stress will deplete our energy and will reduce the effectiveness of our immune system to protect us, increasing the risk of developing an illness (Sapolsky, 1994). Not only are we more likely to become ill, we are also less likely to be effective in what we do. In order to function properly our nervous system and muscles get energy from glucose as well as oxygen in our blood. We increase the use of energy when we engage in mental activity, so if our energy is low our body is less efficient and our ability to function as well as we would like is reduced (Dienstbier, 1989). Health professionals will encourage healthy eating to restore energy and maintain good health. Eating well and taking exercise stimulates the brain and promotes a positive attitude, increasing our potential to live and age well (Weil, 2005).

Studies on the effects of exercise show it promotes psychological well-being (Hayes, 1986). Exercise has a number of positive effects such as helping to release negative energy (aggression), and it can cultivate self-esteem and self-efficacy. For example, when engaging in exercise we can derive a sense of satisfaction because we know that we are doing something that is good for us. Another benefit is that exercise helps to reduce muscle tension and lifts our mood. As the body releases tension in addition to deriving a good feeling, it can also help to restore sleep as the mind and body are not overloaded as a result of stress (Dienstbier, 1989).

Exercise should be enjoyable so that we can maintain our efforts and make it a regular activity. By engaging in exercise – although not to excess – we can increase our sense of well-being and our resilience.

Relaxation

Coachees are encouraged to engage in activities that reduce tension. Engaging in relaxation helps to practise breathing and muscle relaxation to dissipate tension, restoring a sense of calm.

HOW CAN STRESS BE PREVENTED?

Organizations can be proactive and increase their efforts to provide their employees with a healthy work environment. Healthy employees have a better chance to develop their skills and abilities to increase their effectiveness at work. Acknowledging and actively working to manage stress can help to begin to dispel the stigma attached to mental health and turn it into an issue that is dealt with constructively. Raising awareness of stress and how to cope with it proactively is the first step. Through stress management training, information about the symptoms of stress and coping strategies can be shared with all employees. This approach can enhance the potential to change the organizational culture to one where the priority on health is encouraged. Increased information and coping strategies can encourage individuals to be proactive and seek solutions before their health is compromised.

Individuals who have experienced stress for a long time are likely to experience health problems and may need time off work to rehabilitate. It is important then to recommend that they seek professional support. The first port of call is their GP who could then refer them for psychological treatment, although waiting lists may be long. Alternatively, they could benefit from a private referral for psychological treatment. Some employers do offer medical advice through Occupational Health, and psychological support through their Employee Assistance Programmes, or have access to independent psychological treatment. The use of a case management approach where cooperation is established between various professionals can be an effective way to support individuals to restore their health.

When there is concern about an individual's health due to stress then the case manager can liaise with Occupational Health, HR and the line manager to coordinate the support to help the individual. Early intervention can prevent the development of chronic illness and the likely loss of confidence in the ability to return to work. If individuals are off work due to mental health issues they can be supported by providing a facilitated return to work process (Peña, in progress; Tehrani, 2004).

References

Bandura, A (1997) *Self-Efficacy: The exercise of control*, Freeman and Company, New York

Beck, A T (1979) *Cognitive Therapy of Depression*, Guildford Press, New York

Buzan, T (1994) *The Mind Map Book: How to use radiant thinking to utilize your brain's untapped potential*, E P Dutton, New York

Cartwright, S and Cooper, C (1997) *Managing Workplace Stress*, Sage, London

Chartered Institute of Personnel and Development (2004) *Employee Absence 2004: A survey of management policy and practice*, CIPD, London

Cooper, C L, Dewe, P J and O'Driscoll, M P (2001) *Organizational Stress: A Review and Critique of Theory, Research and Applications*, Sage, London

Cox, T, Griffiths, A and Rial-Gonzalez, E (2000) *Research on Work-related Stress*, European Agency for Safety and Health at Work, Brussels

Csikszentmihalyi, M (1992) *Flow: The Psychology of Happiness*, Rider Books, London

De Bono, F (1994) *Parallel Thinking: From Socratic to de Bono thinking*, Penguin Books, London

Dienstbier, R A (1989) Arousal and physiological toughness: implications for mental and physical health, *Psychological Review*, **96**, 1, pp 84−100

Gyllensten, K, and Palmer, S (2005) Can coaching reduce workplace stress?, *The Coaching Psychologist*, **1**, pp 15−17

Hayes, D (1986) Body and mind: The effect of exercise, overweight, and physical health on psychological well-being, *Journal of Health and Social Behaviour*, **27** (4), pp 387−400

Health and Safety Executive (2004) *Management Standards for Work-related Stress*, HSE, London, www.hse.gov.uk/stres/standards/indexhtm

Health and Safety Executive (2004/5) *Stress-related and Psychological Disorders*, Health and Safety Executive

Karasek, R A and Theorell, T (1990) *Healthy Work Stress, Productivity, and the Reconstruction of Working Life*, Basic Books, New York

Killen, D and Murphy, D (2003) *Introduction to Type and Conflict*, CPP, Palo Alto, CA

Lazarus, R S (1991) Psychological stress in the workplace, *Journal of Social Behaviour and Personality*, **6**, 1−13

Linley, A and Harrington, S (2005) Positive psychology and coaching psychology: perspectives on integration, *The Coaching Psychologist*, **1**, pp 13−14

McMillan, L H W, O'Driscoll, M P and Burke, R J (2003) Workaholism: A review of theory, research, and future directions, in (eds) CL Cooper and IT Robertson, *International Review of Industrial and Organizational Psychology*, **18**, pp 167−89

Meichenbaum, D H (1977) *Cognitive-Behaviour Modification*, Plenum Press, New York

Nice, K and Thornton, P (2004) *Job Retention and Rehabilitation Pilot: Employers' management of long-term sickness absence*, Department for Work and Pensions, Research Report N227

O'Hanlon, B and Weiner-Davis, M (1989) *In Search of Solutions: A new direction in psychotherapy*, WW Norton and Company, New York

Pearsall, P (2002) *Toxic Success: How to Stop Striving and Start Thriving*, Inner Ocean, Maui, HI

Peña, A (in progress) A Facilitated Return to Work Process: Identifying the factors that facilitate the reintegration to work after stress, anxiety and depression (working title) Professional Doctoral Research, Department of Occupational Psychology, University of East London

Peterson, C (2005) The Epidemic of Stress, in (eds) C Peterson and C Mayhew, *Occupational Health and Safety: International influences and the 'new' epidemics*, Baywood Publishing, USA

Quenk, N L (1993) *Beside Ourselves. Our hidden personality in everyday life*, Davies-Black, Palo Alto, CA

Sapolsky, R M (1994) *Why Zebras Don't Get Ulcers: An updated guide to stress, stress-related diseases, and coping*, WH Freeman and Company, New York

Segerstrom, S and Miller, G (2006) Stress affects immunity in ways related to stress type and duration, as shown by nearly 300 studies, American Psychological Association, press releases, www.apa.org/releases/stress_immunehtml

Seligman, M E P (2002) *Authentic Happiness: Using the new positive psychology to realize your potential for lasting fulfilment* Nicholas Brealey Publishing, London

Selye, H (1976) *Stress in Health and Disease,* Butterworths, London

Siebert, A (2005) *The Resilience Advantage: Master change, thrive under pressure, and bounce back from setbacks,* Berrett-Koehler Publishers, San Francisco, CA

Tannen, D (1998) *The Argument Culture: Changing the way we argue and debate,* Virago Press, London

Tehrani, N (2004) *Recovery, Rehabilitation and Retention: Maintaining a productive workforce. A guide,* Chartered Institute of Personnel and Development, London, www.cipd.co.uk/subjects/health/mentalhlth/recrehabretenthtm

Thomas, K W and Kilmann, R H (2002) *Thomas-Kilmann Conflict Mode Instrument,* Xicom, Incorporated (CPP, Palo Alto, CA)

Van Dierendonck, D, Garssen, B, and Visser, A (2005) Burnout prevention through personal growth, *Journal of Stress Management,* 1 February, **12,** 1

Weil, A (2005) *Healthy Aging: A lifelong guide to your physical and spiritual well-being,* Alfred A Knopf, New York

Part 3

Professional issues

12

Coaching ethics: integrity in the moment of choice

Allard de Jong

WHY ARE ETHICS IMPORTANT IN COACHING?

As I sit down to write this chapter on ethics, I'm utterly convinced that what we have here is one of the most important and stimulating topics in coaching today. I am not making this statement from the dark recesses of an inflated ego or as a deluded attempt to affirm my self-importance, but rather from the conviction that a) sound ethics are the essence and underpinning of good coaching, and that b) people acting as professional coaches must adhere to the highest standards of responsibility and accountability to protect the interests of the coachee.

The importance of getting training as a coach before practising the art of coaching should not be underestimated. One can understand that there are those who strongly favour different certification procedures in order to ensure a consistent quality of the coaching profession. But we must place ethics – in the Aristotelian sense of customs and character – above both training and professional accreditation. Why? Because it doesn't matter how well trained you are or how many stripes you have on your shirt, if you're not ethical you can potentially do harm to your coachee. If on the other hand, you act ethically and in accordance with the qualities of your spirit, you will make up for the training and/or certification that are not yet yours.

In contributing this chapter to this book, it is not my intention to convert you to accept my personal points of view on ethics or coaching. Nevertheless, I hope that you will share my passion for ethics and my wish for ethics to become a more conscious part of your coaching practice. There remains considerable debate about meanings and thus over the next few pages we will review several definitions and descriptions, simply to provide us with a common platform for reflection. As coaches I would invite you to question and challenge the ideas you come across in this chapter. As always, we all have something to learn and something to teach – but never is this truer than in the field of ethics.

So then, what is my intention? It is hoped that upon completing this chapter you'll approach the task of ethical decision making as a coach and a person with a deeper understanding of – and respect for – the difficulty and the complexity of the act of determining right from wrong and acting accordingly.

My goal in this chapter is to share my passion by investigating the links that exist between coaching, ethics and modern society at large, as represented by Figure 12.1.

More specifically, this chapter will attempt to provide answers to some of the questions that arise from the diagram:

▌ What is meant by 'ethics'?

▌ What is the place of ethics in today's society?

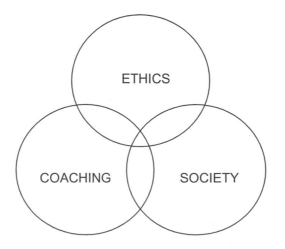

Figure 12.1 The links between coaching, ethics and modern society

▋ What is the role of coaching in society and how can coaches (or coaching) be a role model for moving towards a more ethical society?

▋ What are the main ethical considerations for our profession?

Before we get to these questions, allow me to rapidly clarify some of the terms that we'll use throughout this chapter in order to start this investigation from a common platform of understanding.

WHAT IS MEANT BY ETHICS?

Let's look, first of all, at the word 'ethics' itself. It's hard to believe the number of ways in which writers in the field have answered this seemingly easy question, 'What is ethics?' Often, ethics is concisely and simply described as the science of morality. Morality here is understood as a collection of relative judgements people make about what is right or wrong, good or bad, in the relations between people or groups of people. Others will define ethics as an intellectual practice that develops our perspectives of right and wrong. Merriam-Webster defines 'ethics' as: 1) the discipline dealing with what is good and bad and with moral duty and obligation and, 2) a set of moral principles or values, a theory or system of moral values, the principles of conduct governing an individual or a group and a guiding philosophy. One thing is for sure: as these definitions indicate, ethics is inseparably connected to the issue of morals or morality. The necessary relationship between ethics and morals is best summarized by reminding ourselves that ethics calls for moral practice. Indeed, the notion of ethics takes on its fullest sense when we translate theories into moral principles that can be used as drivers towards ideal ends.

It should also be noted that principles or values play an important part in all ethical decision making. Values are based upon our belief systems about what is desirable, rather than what is right and wrong. This means that ethics based on value systems is very relative, yet our values invariably come into play as we make ethical decisions. Principles make up our individual code of conduct and allow us to act with integrity. Principles are, therefore, based at least in part upon our values, and they may differ widely from one individual to another.

Last, but not least, this review of definitions would not be complete without taking into account the notion of professionalism. Professionalism is yet another term that is directly related to ethics and to ethical behaviour, given that high personal standards tend to bring about the emergence of both ethical and professional behaviour. Do note, however, that not all unprofessional behaviour is necessarily unethical. For example, while showing up late for a meeting with a coachee could be considered unprofessional, it is not deemed to be unethical.

As far as the rest of this chapter is concerned, ethics will be viewed as the way in which we determine what's right and wrong and being moral in doing the right thing. To be ethical means one is able to differentiate between acts that are good and those that are bad. What one does after that differentiation is made, is what determines whether or not we are moral persons. After all, distinguishing right from wrong is one thing – but to actually do what we believe to be right, and to refrain from doing what we believe to be wrong is quite another.

THE FOUNDATIONS OF ETHICAL THINKING

The meaning of 'ethics' and the definition of moral standards have changed throughout history. In early Greece, *ethos* meant character or customs. In early Latin, *mos* – from which we got our word morals – also referred to customs. The discussion of ethics in Aristotelian Athens referred not just to 'good versus bad', but also to such character traits as courage, justice or temperance. During the Middle Ages, much of ethics was replaced by religious or church-issued dogma and rules. Moral matters were no longer 'customs' or character qualifications but became matters of 'right' and 'wrong'.

Later still, ethics emerged as an intellectual pursuit, a discipline of philosophy. It is useful to quickly review the conclusions of theorists dealing with leading ethical theories as they attempt to define and defend a series of principles that we can use to reflect upon specific ethical actions and choose what we ought to do or what kind of persons we ought to become:

Results-based ethics

Sometimes called 'consequentialism', this theory states that moral goodness or badness is determined by the results or consequences of an act or rule. According to this theory, lying about our coaching experience is morally wrong because of the damage this lie will cause to the coach, the coachee and to an entire profession that depends on honest relationships. One model derived from this theory is called 'utilitarianism'. It was originated by Jeremy Bentham (*An Introduction to the Principles of Morals and Legislation*, 1789) who argued that the morally correct rule was the one that provided the greatest good to the greatest number of people.

Standards-based ethics

Also called the 'deontological' theory, standards-based ethics says we determine if an act or rule is morally right or wrong by investigating whether or not it meets a moral standard. One famous contributor to this theory was the German philosopher Immanuel Kant. He developed a 'universal test' to see if a rule could be a universal standard (*Groundwork of a Metaphysics of Morals*, 1785). For example, violating client confidentiality is morally wrong because you cannot make it a universal law that everyone can knowingly violate client confidentiality.

Ethical intuitionism

Ethical intuitionism was the dominant moral theory in Britain for much of the 18th, 19th and early 20th centuries, yet it is part of an older family of theories that ascribe to humanity a common moral faculty. Origins include the moral sentiment theories of Hume (*Of the Original Contract*, 1758). Under this view an act or rule is determined to be right or wrong by appeal to the common intuition of a person. This intuition is sometimes referred to as your 'conscience'. Any coach with a normal conscience will know that it is wrong to promise a client or a coachee something you know you can't deliver.

Virtue ethics

According to this ethical theory, ethics should develop character traits or virtues in a person so he or she will do what is morally right because he or she is a virtuous person. Aristotle was a famous exponent of this view and felt that virtue ethics was the way to attain true happiness.

ETHICAL PRINCIPLES THAT GUIDE COACHING PRACTICE

All codes of ethics and all ethical decision making should be guided by a set of underlying values or principles. In this section we'll quickly review the principles that have guided the fields of medicine, counselling and psychotherapy and how these have influenced ethics in coaching.

Biomedical ethics

The guiding principles of biomedical ethics, as outlined by Beauchamp and Childress (1979), represent a foundational piece in the field of medical ethics. The authors defend the four principles of respect for autonomy, non-malfeasance, beneficence and justice. Not only did these principles become very popular in writings about medical ethics, they also influenced ethics in the coaching field. In coaching decisions, our respect for the autonomy of the coachee would mean that the coachee has the capacity to act intentionally and that the coach's role is to foster that capacity and sense of responsible independence. Non-malfeasance requires that we do not intentionally create a needless harm or injury to the coachee. Beneficence refers to the coach's duty to be of a benefit to the coachee, and justice in coaching can be defined as a form of fairness. As we'll see next, the same principles also found their way into the fields of counselling and psychotherapy.

Ethics in counselling and psychotherapy

In the book, *Guide to Ethical Practice in Psychotherapy*, Thompson (1990) proposes a set of underlying tenants or virtues upon which all ethical decision making should be based. Kitchner (1988) describes similar foundational principles. The concepts that these authors put forward are offered to guide us towards a more ethical practice, and an understanding of these authors' work may help us demarcate the role of ethics in our practice of coaching:

▌ Beneficence is the virtue of helping others and providing services that are in the other individual's best interest; the virtue of doing good; a commitment to promoting the client's well-being.

▌ Non-malfeasance is the virtue of, and commitment to, not doing harm to the client; ensuring that our actions do not result in harm to anyone.

▌ Fidelity is the virtue of faithfulness; being true to our commitments and obligations to others. It's about honouring the trust placed in the practitioner, about being trustworthy. An important component of fidelity, veracity, implies we will be truthful and honest in all our endeavours.

▌ Promoting the autonomy of those one provides services to, is one of psychotherapy's overarching goals. This includes respect for the client's right and ability to be self-governing.

▌ Justice is the virtue of providing fair and impartial treatment to all clients and the provision of adequate services.

▌ The virtue of self-interest stresses the importance of adequate and appropriate attention to our own self-care so our competence and judgement do not become impaired. Self-interest, or self-respect, means fostering the practitioner's self-knowledge and that the practitioner appropriately applies all of the above principles to his or her own professional efforts, ie, they walk their talk.

As an example, the British Association for Counselling and Psychotherapy's list of ethical principles, which is shared by the large majority – if not all – of practitioners, is clearly based on the principles presented above, namely fidelity, autonomy, beneficence, non-malfeasance, justice and self-respect.

What the principles outlined above teach us is that in general, ethical decisions – in medicine, counselling and psychotherapy – that are strongly supported by one or more of these principles may be regarded as reasonably well founded. As such, they have been used as a platform for the establishment of ethical guidelines in the field of coaching that will be discussed later on in this chapter.

MODERN SOCIETY AND 'NEW ETHICS'

To what extent are the ethical principles outlined so far actually visible in today's society? What role do ethics play in today's world? It has been said – somewhat provokingly – on more than one occasion that we won't survive the 21st century with 20th-century ethics. There is strong evidence to support this affirmation. Indeed, a quick look at our planet today reveals a global situation that is characterized by the widening of at least three important gaps:

▌ between the 'haves' and the 'have nots';

▌ between rhetoric and reality;

▌ between those that heed the well-being of others and those that ignore it.

These gaps are indicators of eroding ethics. In spite of the loftiest ethical intentions, we can't seem to translate our ideals into action and collectively work towards bridging these gaps in an organized and sustainable manner. The Dalai Lama convincingly argues (2001) that much of today's troubles are due to a fundamental neglect of our inner dimension and that, until we address this underlying neglect, we will not solve our problems. Others such as Blanchard writing from a Christian perspective have echoed this call in his writing on leadership (Blanchard *et al*, 2003)). He calls for a reawakening of certain qualities of the human spirit and concludes this idea by pointing out that the common denominator among these qualities is a concern for others' well-being and an ethical restraint through which we 'curb our own harmful impulses and desires'. In essence, and if one agrees with this point of view, what is required is a form of inner bonding, if you wish, with our spirit.

At the same time, modern society is characterized by high levels of uncertainty regarding questions of right and wrong and people are unsure as to who or what to turn to for answers and direction. Zohar and Marshall (1999) have argued that 'unlike IQ, which orients itself with respect to rules, and EQ, which is guided by the situation in which it finds itself SQ [spiritual intelligence] lights our way to what mystics have called the "eye of the heart".' As such, they too recommend reconnecting with our source, our ground of being, our spirit, in order to recapture a feeling of certainty, guidance and ultimately ethics.

One way to respond to this erosion of ethics in modern society may well be to turn to within ourselves, rather than established or emerging external sources. For practical purposes, we could refer to this emerging alternative as 'new ethics'.

What exactly is meant by 'new ethics'? New ethics takes on the view that our ethical viewpoints, decisions and actions are determined to be right or wrong by using our spiritual intelligence to access and bond with our human 'beingness', a shared inner source of knowing. New ethics hold that all forms of externally imposed ethics are, in the long run, unsustainable due to lack of ownership and subjective morality – and ultimately a degrading form of alienation and estrangement of people from themselves. New ethics trusts people to know for themselves how to act with integrity and treat other people well. As such, new ethics suggest that people are able to develop their own 'vows' in a manner that is harmonious with others and in due course positive for mankind as a whole. Though most probably not an exact definition quite yet, I will refer to this description throughout the remainder of this chapter.

There exists a huge role for coaching in bringing about ethical practice in society. Why? Because a new ethics-based society cannot be implemented by an outside authority. People will need to be encouraged to develop their spiritual qualities from within, to reconnect with their source of inner wisdom. This is a central way in which ethics can become a conscious, attractive and creative part of our daily lives as coaches and as citizens. While sharing the opinion of those that claim that coaching is a powerful force for making the world 'a better place', one might underline that the responsibility lies with 'coaching' and not 'coaches'. What is meant by this is that as coaches, we are change agents, stimulating and supporting change at the individual level. One of the motives that attracts many of us to this work is the possibility of doing good and making the world a better and more ethical place. This thrusts upon us the responsibility of placing integrity at the centre of our work. The word integrity comes from the Latin *integritas*, meaning integer or entire, and has connotations of incorruptibility, soundness, completeness, honesty, sincerity, fairness and straightforwardness of conduct.

How can we, as coaches and role models for tomorrow's society, continue to develop our ethics? What is required of us to advance in our quest to resolve the specific ethical questions that arise in our work as coaching professionals? We know from observing the world around us that it does not always follow that a person who distinguishes between right and wrong automatically does the right thing, and refrains from doing wrong; there is work to be done. Furthering the cause of ethics in ourselves, our work and our world will only be achieved through the informed and conscientious practice of new ethics and by observing specific codes to guide our decisions.

So in answer to the question, 'Can we actually be ethical?', one reply could be that we indeed have the necessary capacity, knowledge and tools to be so and that the power of choosing right and wrong, good and evil, is within the reach of all. But the question begs another: 'Can we be moral?' This is a lot more difficult to answer than the previous one. In spite of all the books, codes and guidelines we have been handed over the years, the answer remains elusive to say the least. By definition, and in truth, the only way to be moral is by putting the qualities of our spirit, of our heart, into action.

What better way to tap into ourselves and into the self of others than coaching? New ethics and coaching are intrinsically linked. Action taken from our deepest sense of self, the core of what makes us human beings, can be stimulated by stirring our own and our clients' connection with what Moore (2001) called our 'original self'.

New ethics, in coaching and in life, must come from that place of personal and intrinsic power – and again, isn't that what coaching is all about? At the end of the day, only you can ensure your integrity in your moments of choice.

ETHICAL STANDARDS FOR COACHING

To help us walk a path of ethical practice, organizations such as the Association for Coaching in the UK offers, in one way or another, a code of ethics and good practice. The code sets out the essential elements of sound ethical practice and are called into life to ensure that members operate in accordance with ethical, competent and effective guidelines. The code of conduct can indeed be very useful, as coaches can expect to run into a series of ethical questions arising from such issues as maintaining confidentiality and objectivity, managing conflicts of interest, being clear about what they can or cannot deliver, or correctly representing the coaching process to existing and potential clients. Yet any code of conduct should be seen as a collective position and a transitory phase as we move towards the development of new ethics.

What about situations that are not specified in the current standards? No ethical code can provide coaches with guidance on how to act in all situations or how best to respond to all possible ethical dilemmas. Merely following these guidelines, therefore, will not be sufficient for responding to the myriad of ethical dilemmas by which coaches are regularly confronted. So it bears repeating that what is needed is a deeper connection to one's own sense of new ethics.

ETHICAL THEMES AND SCENARIOS FROM COACHING

So far we have made the case for ethics to be used by coaches to bring about ethical change. However, what about the responsibility that coaches have in their relationships with their coachees? Maybe this issue is best explored by imagining a series of not so improbable scenarios and seeing how some of the main guidelines set forth by the Association for Coaching's code of ethics and good practice apply.

Scenario 1

Suppose that a romantic attraction develops between your coachee and yourself. Having reviewed the Association for Coaching's code, you know that coaches must act in a manner that does not bring the profession of coaching into disrepute and that coaches are required to respect the coachee's right to terminate coaching at any point during the coaching process. Coaches need to be aware of this danger, one that results in the largest number of complaints to the BACP (British Association for Counselling and Psychotherapy). Therefore, as soon as you become aware of the budding reciprocal passion, you could suggest to your coachee that the two of you come to a mutual agreement to terminate the formal coaching relationship and that you set a period aside, maybe four to eight weeks, as a cooling-off period. This allows space and time between the old professional coaching relationship and a new personal relationship. It also recognizes that attraction may be generated from transference within the intimate space of the coaching relationship, and that this interest may wane when the coaching relationship is terminated.

Scenario 2

As a seasoned executive coach, you are approached by a former coachee who wants to find a romantic partner and wants to hire you with that objective in mind. You explain that, as someone specializing in business issues, you are not an expert in that area. After exploring the coachee's objectives in some more depth, you suggest that he might want to consider a dating service. He informs you that he has been down that road but to no avail and that he just knows that working with you is the right thing for him to do at this time. Coaches are required to recognize both personal and professional limitations. As per the code of ethics, you would indeed want to assess whether or not your experience is appropriate to meet the coachee's requirements. Should this not be the case, the coachee should be referred to other appropriate services, such as more experienced coaches, counsellors, psychotherapists or other specialist services.

Scenario 3

Imagine a coachee who complains of constant tiredness, wants to stay in bed, is irritable, cannot sleep and expresses feelings of hopelessness about his condition, thinking he will never get better. The coachee denies being depressed and instead simply expresses frustration at a host of circumstantial factors. As a coach, you are required to be sensitive to the possibility that some coachees will require more psychological support than most coaches are trained to offer. In these cases, referral should be made to an appropriate source of care. This might be the person's GP, a counsellor or coaching psychologist.

Scenario 4

A professional acquaintance has just referred a close friend to you. She is very enthusiastic about beginning the coaching straight away, based on your acquaintance's flattering introduction. Even though she does not have a clear idea of what coaching really is, she tells you money is not an issue and that it won't be necessary to prepare a coaching contract. Coaches are responsible for ensuring that coachees are fully informed of the coaching contract, terms and conditions, prior to or at the initial session. These matters include confidentiality and the cost and frequency of sessions. It is your responsibility to generate a frank discussion around what this potential coachee may or may not expect and respond to her requests for information about the methods, techniques and ways in which the coaching process will be conducted. This should be done both prior to contract agreement and during the full term of the contract.

Scenario 5

Suppose that during a coaching session a coachee discloses a desire to do himself harm. He has just lost his job, feels ashamed about the situation and can see no way forward. All information obtained in the course of coaching relationship is confidential, but on occasions there can be a compelling reason for this rule to be broken. The coach should include this as part of the contracting discussion. Such occasions would be where there is genuine concern that coachees would do harm to themselves or others, or where a serious criminal offence has been committed, and a failure to disclose would itself be a criminal offence.

Scenario 6

You are working with a coachee and it's just not going well; both she and you are frustrated with the pace and the lack of results. Rather than simply terminating the coaching by telling the coachee she is not coachable, you might want to look into the value of the coaching you provide and the dynamic of the relationship between you. Coaches are required to monitor the quality of their work and to seek feedback, for example at the end of each session. If things are not working in a relationship, this may be due to the coach and his or her ability to adapt, but may also be a product of the relationship. Talk frankly about this and identify a suitable alternative, such as a referral for the coachee.

References

Beauchamp and Childress (1979) *Principles of Biomedical Ethics*, Oxford University Press, Oxford

Blanchard, K, Hodges, P, Ross, L and Willis, A (2003) *Lead like Jesus: Beginning the journey*, Thomas Nelson Books, Nashville, TN

Dali Lama (2001) *Ancient Wisdom, Modern World: Ethics for the new millennium*, Abacus, London

Kitchner, J (1988) Dual role relationships: What makes them so problematic?, *Journal of Counselling and Development*, **67**, pp 222–26

Moore, T (2001) *Original Self: Living with paradox and originality*, Harper Perennial, London

Thompson, A (1990) *Guide to Ethical Practice in Psychotherapy*, Wiley, New York

Zohar, D and Marshall, I (1999) *Spiritual Intelligence: The ultimate intelligence*, Bloomsbury, London

13

Coaching supervision

Peter Hawkins

WHAT IS SUPERVISION?

Coaching, mentoring and organizational consultancy have all been areas of enormous growth in the last ten years. Berglas (2002) writing in the *Harvard Business Review*, estimated that there were at least 10,000 professional coaches working for businesses in the USA and predicted that the figure would exceed 50,000 in 2007. In response, many of the professional bodies are developing professional standards requiring coaches to have some form of supervision, but developing clear models of practice for coaching supervision and quality training programmes for coaching supervisors has lagged behind. There has been a danger of coaching supervision being much promoted yet very little practised. In this chapter I set out to define supervision, and its main functions, and provide some models for its practice, before going on to explore what is needed for supervisor training.

In the field of coaching supervision there are a number of emerging definitions. Bluckert (2005) writes:

> Supervision sessions are a place for the coach to reflect on the work they are undertaking, with another more experienced coach. It has the dual

purpose of supporting the continued learning and development of the coach, as well as giving a degree of protection to the person being coached.

Bachkirova *et al* (2005) write:

> Coaching supervision is a formal process of professional support, which ensures continuing development of the coach and effectiveness of his/her coaching practice through interactive reflection, interpretative evaluation and the sharing of expertise.

Our own definition is:

> The process by which a Coach with the help of a Supervisor, can attend to understanding better both the Client system and themselves as part of the Client-Coach system, and by so doing transform their work and develop their craft. (Hawkins and Smith, 2006)

We believe that coaching supervision has three elements:

1. Coaching the coach on his or her coaching.
2. Mentoring the coach on his or her development in the profession.
3. Providing an external perspective to ensure quality of practice.

This three-function model parallels the three functions that Kadushin (1992) put forward for social work supervision and Proctor (1997) espoused for counselling supervision. Kadushin talked of the 'managerial, educative and supportive' aspects of supervision and Proctor of supervision being 'normative, formative and restorative'.

Having worked with these two models for many years we have found both to be rather confined to their own field, Kadushin in social work and Proctor in counselling, and so have developed our own model that defines the three main functions as developmental, resourcing and qualitative (see Table 13.1). Kadushin focuses on the role of the supervisor, Proctor on the supervisee benefit, and our new distinctions on the process that both supervisor and supervisee are engaged in.

Table 13.1 Three main functions of supervision

Hawkins	Proctor	Kadushin
Developmental	Formative	Educational
Resourcing	Restorative	Supportive
Qualitative	Normative	Managerial

In Hawkins and Shohet (1989, 2000) I outlined a number of the primary foci of supervision and we have now linked these to the new categories (see Figure 13.1).

ROLE AND PURPOSE OF SUPERVISION

I believe that the role and purpose of supervision of executive coaches builds strongly on the work done on supervision of those in the helping professions, but needs to make some important changes in order to really support the executive coaching agenda.

Supervision is a key element in both the training process for coaches and lifetime continuing professional development (CPD). In training it is the process of rigorous supervision that helps the trainee link the theory and skills they learn on courses to the real-time experience of working live with coachees. In workshops you can learn models and develop competencies, but these do not by themselves produce an excellent coach. Supervision provides the reflective container for the trainee to turn his or her competencies into capabilities and to develop his or her personal and coaching capacities.

Main categories of focus	Function Category
To provide a regular space for the supervisees to reflect upon the *content and process* of their work	Developmental
To develop understanding and skills within the work	Developmental
To receive information and another perspective concerning one's work	Developmental/resourcing
To receive both content and process feedback	Developmental/resourcing supportive
To be validated and supported both as a person and as a worker	Resourcing
To ensure that as a person and as a worker one is not left to carry, unnecessarily, difficulties, problems and projections alone	Resourcing
To have space to explore and express personal distress, restimulation, transference or counter-transference that may be brought up by the work	Qualitative/resourcing
To plan and utilize their *personal and professional* resources better	Qualitative/resourcing
To be pro-active rather than re-active	Qualitative/resourcing
To ensure quality of work	Qualitative

Figure 13.1 Primary foci of supervision

Why is coaching supervision so widely promoted and yet so little practiced?

At the core of CPD is continual *personal* development, where our own development is weaved through every aspect of our practice, where every coachee is a teacher, every piece of feedback an opportunity for new learning, and we have practices that support the balanced cycle of action, reflection, new understanding and new practice. In Hawkins and Smith (2006) we have shown why we believe that having supervision is a fundamental aspect of continuing personal and professional development for coaches, mentors and consultants, providing a protected and disciplined space in which coaches can reflect on particular coachee situations and relationships, the reactivity and patterns they invoke for them and by transforming these live in supervision, can profoundly benefit the coachee.

O'Neill (2000) does not use the term 'supervision', but talks of the importance of coaching for the coach. She writes:

> Everyone need help to stay on track in the powerful interactional fields of organizations . . . One of the best ways that coaches can stay effective in their role is to receive coaching themselves . . . I used to think that that my need for a coach would diminish once I had worked with numerous clients and had many years under my belt. Twenty years and over a hundred clients later, my effectiveness has dramatically increased, but my desire to use a coach myself has remained high. I no longer see using a coach as a sign of incompetence but a smart investment.

For too long the themes of continuing development and supervision of coaches and mentors has been neglected. Flaherty (1999) writing in the USA about the area of coaches' continuing development says:

> I haven't found this aspect of coaching in any other text on the topic, but self-development seems to be a self-evident component of coaching . . . Psychiatrists, physicians, teachers and lawyers all confer with peers and mentors in difficult cases. Coaches are, it seems to me, no exception to this practice.

Downey (2003) writing in the UK, says: 'Very few coaches have any supervision, but it is a vital ingredient in effective coaching.'

So what is the lack of practice due to? In talking to a wide range of coaches and mentors we have been offered a number of different explanations.

∎ Lack of clarity about what supervision involves.
∎ Lack of quality trained supervisors.

▌ Lack of commitment to personal development as it makes us vulnerable.

▌ Lack of discipline among coaches.

▌ Addiction to being in the role of the person enabling others, rather than receiving.

Probably, all of these have some degree of truth and a full answer needs to include these and other factors. In the absence of a body of good theories, training and practitioners, many coaches have turned to counsellors, psychologists and psychotherapists for supervision or supervisory models. While there is much we can learn from these and other 'people professions' that have been practising quality supervision for longer than coaching, there are also dangers, as I outline below.

SIMILARITIES AND DIFFERENCES TO COUNSELLING AND PSYCHOTHERAPY SUPERVISION

Whether we call the process supervision, or coaching on one's coaching, the need to have another attend to one's practice is increasingly being recognized as essential. It is important to remember that supervision in counselling and psychotherapy was only developed in the 1980s and when we and others in this field were developing our theories and methods we drew on the experience of counselling psychology and social work, which had developed their approaches in the 1970s (see Hawkins and Shohet, 1989, 2000).

There is much each of the helping professions can learn from each other, but it is also important to recognize the difference between the fundamental work of each professional group, and hence the dangers of over-applying the theories and models of one group to the work of another. One of the dangers of a coach going for supervision to a counsellor or counselling psychologist is that the supervisor's professional focus will tend towards understanding the psychology of the coachee. Depending on their orientation the supervisor might also focus on the relationship of coach and coachee and may have a tendency to focus more on pathology than on health! The biggest danger is when a fundamental orientation that is more interested in individuals than organizations, tips over into an unrecognized tendency to see individuals as victims of 'bad' or 'unfeeling' organizations. At worst this can create a classic drama triangle of 'organization as persecutor; coachee as victim and coach as rescuer'.

THE STAGES IN A SUPERVISION SESSION

The earliest model we developed for supervision in the 1980s was to apply our five-stage coaching model CLEAR (Contract, Listen, Explore, Action, Review) to the stages of supervision or coaching the coach.

In this model the supervisor starts by *contracting* with the supervisee on both the boundaries and focus of the work. Then the supervisor *listens* to the issues that the coach wishes to bring, listening not only to the content, but also to the feelings and the ways of framing the story that the coach is using. Before moving on, it is important that the supervisor lets the coach know that he or she has not only heard the story, but has got what it feels like to be in the coach's situation. Only then is it useful to move on to the next stage to *explore* with the coach what is happening in the dynamics of both the coaching relationship and the live supervisory relationship, before facilitating the coach to explore new *action*. Finally, *review* the process and what has been agreed about next steps. In this short chapter I will just write about the contracting phase, which is the foundation for all that follows.

Contracting for supervision

All forms of supervision relationship need to begin with a clear contract, which is created and formed by both parties, and also reflects the expectations of the organizations and professions involved.

We propose that in contracting there are five key areas that should be covered:

1. practicalities;
2. boundaries;
3. working alliance;
4. the session format;
5. the organizational and professional context.

1. Practicalities

In forming the contract it is necessary to be clear about the practical arrangements such as the times, frequency, place, what might be allowed to interrupt or postpone the session, and any payment that is involved.

2. Boundaries

A boundary that often worries both coachees and new coaches is the one between coaching and counselling or therapy.

The basic boundary in this area is that coaching should always start from exploring issues from work and should end with looking at where the coachee goes next with the work that has been explored. Personal material should only come into the session if it is directly affecting, or being affected by, the work discussed; or if it is affecting the coaching or supervision relationships. If such an exploration uncovered more material than could be appropriately dealt with in the supervision, the supervisor may suggest that the worker might want to get counselling or other forms of support in exploring these personal issues.

A supervision contract should also include clear boundaries concerning confidentiality. Confidentiality is an old chestnut that is of concern to many new coaches and new supervisors. So many supervisors fall into the trap of saying or implying to the supervisee that everything that is shared in the supervision is confidential, only to find that some unexpected situation arises where it is necessary to share material from the supervision beyond the boundaries of the session.

Thus, in contracting the appropriate confidentiality boundary for any form of supervision, it is inappropriate either to say everything is confidential that is shared here, or to say nothing here is confidential. The supervisor should instead be clear what sort of information either would need to take over the boundary of the relationship; in what circumstances; how they would do this; and to whom they would take the information. Clearly every possible situation cannot be anticipated, but such a general exploration can diminish the possibility of what may be experienced as sudden betrayal.

We also give our supervisees the undertaking that we will treat everything they share with us in a professional manner and not gossip about their situation.

3. Working alliance

Forming the working alliance starts from sharing mutual expectations: what style of coaching the supervisee most wants, and on which of the possible foci do they wish the supervision to concentrate. The supervisor also needs to state clearly what his or her preferred mode of supervision is, and any expectations he or she has of the supervisee. We find it useful at the contracting phase to not only share conscious expectations but also hopes and fears. It can be useful to complete sentences such as: 'My image of successful supervision is . . .'; 'What I fear happening in supervision is . . .'.

A good working alliance is not built on a list of agreements or rules, but on growing trust, respect and goodwill between both parties. The contract provides a holding frame in which the relationship can develop, and any lapses in fulfilling the contract need to be seen as opportunities for reflection, learning and relationship building, not judgement and defence.

4. The session format

As well as sharing hopes, fears and expectations, it is useful to ground the discussions in an exploration of what a typical session format might be like. Will all the time be spent on one situation? Does the supervisor expect the supervisee to bring written-up notes?

5. The organizational and professional context

In most supervision situations there are other critical stakeholders in the supervision contract besides the direct parties. There is the expectation of the organization or organizations in which the work is being carried out. The organization may have its own explicit supervision policy where the expectations of supervision are clarified. Where a clear policy does not exist, it is still essential that the implicit expectations of the organizations are discussed. This could include what responsibility the organization might expect the supervisor to take in ensuring quality work and what report it requires on the supervision. Likewise, it is important to clarify the professional and ethical codes of conduct that both may be party to.

Most professional associations have codes of conduct and statements of ethics that stipulate the boundaries of appropriate behaviour between a coach and a coachee, and also provide the right of appeal for the coachee against any possible inappropriate behaviour by the coach. Many professions are not as clear about their code of practice for supervision. We do not want to prescribe what we think are appropriate ethical standards for supervision, because this must invariably vary from one setting to another. However, we do consider it imperative that all new supervisors check whether there are ethics statements covering coaching within their profession and/or organization. If no such statement exists, we suggest that you review the ethical standards for work with coachees and become clear yourself, which of them you feel apply to the supervision context. It is important that all supervisors are clear about the ethical boundaries of their supervision practice and are able to articulate these to their supervisees.

THE SEVEN-EYED COACHING SUPERVISION MODEL

In the late 1980s we developed a more in-depth model of super-vision (Hawkins and Shohet, 1989), which later became known as the 'seven-eyed supervision model', and has been used across many different people professions in many countries. Its purpose is the exploration of the various different influences on supervisory activity in the room. It is based on a systems understanding of the ways things connect, interrelate and drive activity. This model also integrates insights and aspects of psychotherapy and the internal life of individuals. I will set out in more detail these seven areas of potential focus to supervisor and supervisee in reviewing their practice.

1. The coachee's system

Here the focus is on the content of what happened with the coachee's system, the problem the coachee system wants help with and how they are presenting the issues.

Mode 1 skill

The supervisor's skill in this mode is to help coaches accurately return to what actually happened with the coachee; what they saw, what they heard and what they felt, and to try and separate this actual data from their preconceptions, assumptions and interpretations. It is also useful for coaches to be helped to attend to what happened at the boundaries of their time with the coachee, their arrival and exit, for it is often at the boundaries that the richest unconscious material is most active.

2. The coach's interventions

This looks at what interventions the coach made and alternative choices that might have been used. It might also focus on a situation that the coach is about to intervene in and explore the possible options and the likely impact of each.

Mode 2 skill

Often coaches will ask for help with an impasse they have arrived at in facilitating the change process. They will often present this impasse in the form of an 'either-or' such as: 'Should I collude with this situation or confront the issue?' The skill of the supervisor is to avoid the trap of debating the either/or options, and instead to enable coaches to realize how they are limiting their choice to two polarized possibilities and facilitate a shared brainstorming that frees up the energy and creates new options. Then the benefits and difficulties of these options can be explored and some possible interventions can be tried out in role-play.

3. The relationship between the coach and the coachee

Here the focus is neither solely on the coachee and his or her system or the coach, but the relationship that they are creating together.

Mode 3 skill

The supervisor has to facilitate the coach to stand outside of the relationship that he or she is part of and see it afresh, from a new angle. The Chinese have a proverb, that the last one to know about the sea is the fish, because they are constantly immersed in it. In this mode the supervisor is helping the coach to be a flying fish, so he or she can see the water in which he or she is normally swimming.

4. The coach

The focus is on coaches beginning to look at themselves, both what is being re-stimulated in them by the coachee's material, and also themselves as an instrument for registering what is happening beneath the surface of the coaching system.

Mode 4 skill

In this mode the supervisor helps coaches to work through any re-stimulation of their own feelings that has been triggered by the work with

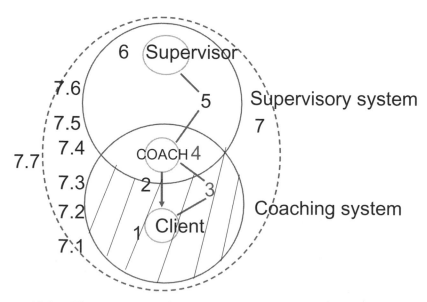

Figure 13.2   The seven-eyed model of coaching supervision

this client. Having done this, the coaches can also be helped to explore how their own feelings may be very useful data for understanding what the coachee and their system is experiencing but unable to articulate directly. The coaches also explore how their own blocks may be preventing them from facilitating the coachee and their system to change.

5. The parallel process

Here the focus is on what the coach has absorbed unconsciously from the coachee system and how it may be being played out in the relationship to the supervisor. The coach can, unaware, treat the supervisor the way his or her coachee treated them.

Mode 5 skill

Here the supervisor needs to be able to attend not only to what he or she is being told about the coaching system, but also what is happening in the relationship in the room. Having acquired this skill, the supervisor can then at times offer tentative reflections on the impact of the presented material on the coaching relationship to illuminate the coaching dynamic. When done skilfully this process can help the coaches bridge the gap between their conscious understanding of the coaching relationship and the emotional impact it has had upon them.

6. The supervisor self-reflection

The focus for mode 6 is the supervisor's 'here and now' experience while with the coach and what can be learnt about the coach/coachee relationship from the supervisor's response to the coach and the material he or she presents.

Mode 6 skill

In this mode the supervisor has to attend not only to presented material and its impact on the 'here and now' relationship, but also his or her own internal process. The supervisor can also discover the presence of unconscious material related to the coaching relationship by attending to his or her own feelings, thoughts and fantasies while listening to the presentation of the coaching situation. These can tentatively be commented on and made available as possible indicators of what lies buried in the relationship with the coachee. The additional skill is to have a means of sharing this with the coach in a non-judgemental and speculative way.

7. The wider context

The focus of mode 7 is on the organizational, social, cultural, ethical and contractual context in which the coaching is taking place. This includes being aware of the wider group of stakeholders in the process that is being focused on; these may be the client organization and its stakeholders, the coach's organization and its stakeholders, and the organization or professional network of the supervisor.

Mode 7 skill

The supervisor has to be able to bring a whole-systems perspective to understand how the systemic context of what is being presented is affecting not only the behaviour, mindsets, emotional ground and motivations of the coach and coachee, but also themselves. The skill is to appropriately attend to the needs of the critical stakeholders in the wider systems, and also to understand how the culture of the systemic context might be creating illusions, delusions and collusions in the coach and oneself. To attend to mode 7 also requires a high level of transcultural competence (see Hawkins and Shohet, 2000, Chapter 7).

Using all seven modes

In talking with both supervisors and coaches who have gone to others in search of help in exploring coaching situations, we have discovered that often different supervisors are stuck in the groove of predominantly using one of the seven modes of working. Some focus entirely on the situation out there with the coachee and adopt a pose of pseudo objectivity (mode 1). Others see their job as coming up with better interventions than the coach managed to produce (mode 2). This can often leave the coach feeling inadequate or determined to show that these suggested interventions are as useless as the ones he or she had previously tried. Other coaches have reported taking a problem with a coachee and having left supervision feeling that the problem was entirely their pathology (mode 4).

'Single-eyed vision', which focuses only on one aspect of the process, will always lead to partial and limited perspectives. This model suggests a way of engaging in an exploration that looks at the same situation from many different perspectives and can thus create a critical subjectivity, where subjective awareness from one perspective is tested against other subjective data.

Each mode of supervision can be done in a skilful and elegant manner, or ineffectively, but no matter how skilful one is in one mode, it will prove inadequate without the skill to move from mode to mode. We have devised a training method for helping the supervisor use each of the modes with skill and precision and to explore the timing and appropriateness for moving from one mode to another.

The most common order for moving through the modes is to start with mode 1, talking about specific coaching situations, then to move into modes 3 and 4 to explore what is happening both in the coaching relationship and for the coach/supervisee. This may well explore the here and now relationship in the room between the coach and the supervisor (modes 5 and 6), and/or bringing into awareness the wider context (mode 7). Finally, having gained new insight and created a shift in the supervisory matrix, the attention may turn back to mode 2, to explore what different interventions the coach might use in the next session to create the needed shift in the coaching matrix. The coach might even try-out some of these interventions in what we term a 'fast-forward rehearsal'. From our experience we have learnt that if the change starts to happen live in the supervision, it is far more likely to happen back in the coaching.

The model has also been used as a way of empowering the coach, who is the customer receiving the supervision, to be able to give feedback on the help they are being given and request a change in focus. It can be used as a framework for a joint review of the supervision process by the coach and supervisor.

TRAINING AS A COACHING SUPERVISOR

In 2002 the debate about the need for supervision in coaching began to change. The professional coaching bodies, such as the Association for Coaching and the European Mentoring and Coaching Council, started to argue that all coaches should receive supervision from trained and qualified supervisors. In response, the Bath Consultancy Group led the way in the development of a certified training programme in the supervision of coaches and mentors. Our starting belief was that these professions had much in common with other helping professions when it came to supervision, but were also significantly different. The difference was particularly in the fact that as a counsellor, psychotherapist, psychologist, nurse, etc the work was focused primarily on the individual client, where as coaches, mentors and organizational consultants always have a minimum of three clients:

1. the coachee or mentee;
2. the organization they work in and for;
3. the relationship between them and the organization.

This led us to design a training programme that had a foundation module and final advanced supervision module just for people who were experienced executive coaches, mentors and consultants, but required the participants to choose two further modules that they would undertake alongside other helping professionals.

Our second assumption is that learning to be a supervisor is best undertaken through cycles of action learning, not by sitting in a classroom. Thus the training involves a great deal of supervision practice in threes, comprising a supervisor, supervisee and shadow supervisor, who gives feedback to the supervisor, sometimes at the end of the practice session, and sometimes in the middle, in structured 'time-outs'. The trainee supervisors, as well as undertaking the modules, receive 10 hours of supervision on their supervision, from an experienced supervisor, as well as two tutorials to help them maximize their individual learning programme.

We constantly learn more from each cohort of new trainees about the fascinating craft of supervising coaches and the lifelong journey to develop this craft. Increasingly we are reminded that at the heart of being a good coach or a good coaching supervisor is not academic knowledge, a collection of theories and models, or an armoury of tools and techniques, but a constant dedication to developing one's human capacity to be fully present for another, acting with what we term 'ruthless compassion'. For it is the ruthless compassion we can bring, not only for our coachee but also the work they do in the world and for our craft, that ultimately allows the fear and anxiety that pervades so many work situations to be overcome, and for our coachees to find new strength to act courageously.

References

Bachkirova, T, Stevens, P and Willis, P (2005) Oxford Brookes Coaching and Mentoring Society, www.brookes.ac.uk

Berglas, B (2002) The very real dangers of executive coaching, *Harvard Business Review*, June, pp 86–92

Downey, M (2003) *Effective Coaching: Lessons from the coaches' couch*, Texere/Thomson, New York

Flaherty, J (1999) *Coaching: Evoking Excellence in Others*, Butterworth-Heinemann, Woburn, MA

Hawkins, P and Shohet, R (1989, 2000) *Supervision in the Helping Profession*, Open University Press, Milton Keynes

Hawkins, P and Smith N (2006) *Coaches, Mentors and Organisational Consults: Their supervision and development*, Open University Press, Milton Keynes

Kadushin, A (1992) *Supervision in Social Work*, 3rd edn, Columbia University Press, New York

O'Neill, M B (2000) *Coaching with Backbone and Heart: A systems approach to engaging leaders with their challenges*, Jossey-Bass, San Francisco, CA

Proctor, B (1997) Contracting in supervision, in (ed) C Sills, *Contracts in Counselling*. Sage, London

Index

NB *italics* indicate a table or figure